Cookbook
from a
Melting Pot

Cookbook from a Melting Pot

BY

ELIZABETH PAULUCCI

An E. Paulucci Book

Distributed by

Grosset & Dunlap, Inc. New York, New York

Printed in the United States of America

Distributed by Grosset & Dunlap, Inc., 51 Madison Avenue New York, New York 10010

ISBN: 0-448-16860-X

Illustrations by Amy Yammer

CONTENTS

COOKBOOK FROM A MELTING POT   9
HOME, HOME ON THE (IRON) RANGE   13
AMERICAN INDIAN   19
ENGLISH   29
IRISH   51
GERMAN   59
SCANDINAVIAN   69
FRENCH   81
FINNISH   141
ITALIAN   147
EASTERN EUROPEAN   199
GREEK   207
JEWISH   215
LATIN AMERICAN   221
FAR EASTERN   229
U.S. — US   245
INDEX   281

*Dedicated to my Mother Michelina
and to my Brother Jeno Paulucci.*

*With many thanks to my husband Norman,
my friends and family
who inspired and taste-tested my efforts.*

A special thanks to Jane Moore Ramsey for all her secretarial help.

COOKBOOK FROM A MELTING POT

This book, like its author, was born in a melting pot called the Mesabi Iron Range. What other kind of book could it be than a cookbook!

My melting pot is in uppermost northern Minnesota, U.S.A. Almost every nationality in the world lived there, including my own group, the Italians. But when I was growing up there, I had no idea there was anything unusual about it.

To me, it was only natural to live in one of a string of small towns which together had a population of only about 50,000 but which included families of Bulgarians, Chinese, Japanese, Croatians, Cornish English, Canadian French, Germans, Greeks, Irish, Jews, Montenegrins, Norwegians, Finnish, Slovenians, Swedes, and us Italians. And a lot more.

It was simply a fact of life that almost all my friends had one language they spoke at home, and another language, spoken at school, at church, and at work in the afternoons after school—English. And, *that* language was also a special kind of English. The Iron Range dialect took something from each nationality, a little of this and a little of that, much like a great recipe from a great family cook. Some of the more colorful examples of the Iron Range dialect are being lovingly collected, before they disappear entirely, by a local historian named Mike Kalibabky. His volumes of "Iron Rayncher" speech include such words as "ahminah," as in, "If I find out dat you drank da las beer, ahminah kill you."

Well, I don't know if we talked like that. And at this date, people on the Iron Range, homogenized by television and other mass communication, talk pretty much like all other Americans. The national groups are also less recognizable today, all blending into general American.

That's okay. What else is a melting pot for?

But what an interesting polyglot past we had!

Why did so many different nationalities immigrate to this semiwilderness in the frigid north? They came to mine "red gold," the rich iron deposits discovered in the north country of Minnesota and Michigan. Our Minnesota ore was shipped out through the port of Duluth across Lake Superior and on to the blast furnaces of the world. The rich deposits are gone now, but the industry lives on in the form of taconite processing, which is the kind of deposit that's left after the red gold is gone.

Actually, the Iron Range of Minnesota is composed of three separate ranges, the largest, and the one where I lived, is called the Mesabi (an Indian word meaning "height of the land"). It's a crescent-shaped ridge of rolling hills that cut through the deep evergreen forests, dotted with the clear and cold lakes of Minnesota, known in legend as the footsteps of Paul Bunyan.

The iron deposits discovered here in the late 1800s were a magnet that drew people from all over the world, mostly from places where they had learned the skills of mining. My father and mother, for instance, came from the town of Bellisio Solfare ("beautiful sulfur") in the sulfur-mining province of Pesaro, Italy.

Michelina Buratti was eighteen years old when she left her home in Bellisio Solfare to come to the United States. Along with her sister Francesca, and Francesca's three children, she took a slow boat that reached Ellis Island, the American immigration center in New York harbor, in fifteen days. There they were shuttled through and "stamped" with approval to enter the United States—final destination, Hibbing, Minnesota, then the iron ore capital of the world.

In Hibbing, Michelina married Ettore Paulucci, her betrothed, who had come to America a year earlier. And in Hibbing, they raised their children—a daughter, Elizabeth (that's me) and a son, Luigino (now known all over the country as the one and only Jeno, founder of Jeno's Italian Foods and earlier of Chun King Chinese Foods).

Michelina and Ettore had a hard life for many years. The pay of an immigrant miner ran to $4.20 a day. Mother took in boarders, made their meals, packed their lunches, and washed and scrubbed, getting water from the town pump.

The country was beautiful. It still is. But even to miners from the north of Italy, the climate was a bit challenging in the winter, dropping to 30 below and counting, for weeks or even months.

But it was a happy life, by and large, and I had the wonderful good fortune to grow up with an understanding, or at least a working knowledge, of the customs and beliefs—and the recipes—of an incredibly large segment of international life.

How large? Below is a breakdown of the population of the town of Hibbing and twelve other communities of the Mesabi around 1910, as reported by the U.S. Immigration Commission:

American (white)	12,000
American (black)	27
Belgian	50
Bohemian	315
Bulgarian	460
Chinese	100
Croatian	3,410
Dalmatian	30
Danish	240
Dutch (Hollanders)	70
English	2,115
Finnish	7,250
French	130
Canadian French	875
German	850
Greek	218
Hebrew	1,140
Irish	2,225
Italian, North	1,070
Italian, South	3,270
Magyar	285
Montenegrin	2,650
Norwegian	1,300
Polish	755
Russian	241
Scotch	435
Serbian	515
Slovak	845
Slovenian	3,600
Swedish	3,580
Syrian	110
Welsh	30
Total	50,191

And that didn't even include the Chippewas and Ojibwas and other American Indians who'd been harvesting wild rice and fishing on the lakes for generations.

What an opportunity to learn about people! And what an opportunity to learn about that most basic of human customs—the way people prepare the food that was placed within their reach. The 50,000 people of my iron range between them had forgotten more about cooking than most entire nations ever learn.

I didn't realize how magnificent the variety of cooking was until years later, when I became a serious student of cuisine and attended a Cordon Bleu school in French cooking taught by George Vogelbacher in Orlando, Florida. It was then that I understood that the most sophisticated French cooking has something in common with the homely, solid cooking of the many nationalities of my home. And that something is an understanding that the possibilities of variety are endless.

There is no *one* way to cook anything. Trying all the many ways is what adds spice to your cooking, and your life.

In my travels as an adult, throughout America, Europe, Latin America, and elsewhere, I've never lost an interest in what people eat, how they prepare it, and how their cooking customs compare with those of my own home melting pot. The result of it all: what I hope you will find to be a truly international cookbook, one that encourages you to broaden your cooking horizons, to try new methods and new techniques, and to open the windows of your kitchen to the world.

HOME, HOME
ON THE (IRON) RANGE

Although our family lived at the poverty level, it wasn't a bad life—not at all.

For one thing, there was the country itself. I am writing this in the springtime in Sanford, Florida, where I've lived for a number of years, and it's beautiful here in the South. But there's nothing in the world like the Mesabi Iron Range of Minnesota bursting into bloom with sweetpeas, peonies, hollyhocks, and the tiger lily, with its stamen bearing pollen the color of iron ore. And the lilacs! We used to raid the neighborhood for these fragrant blossoms, and take them to school.

We mining people lived in modest little houses, but nearly every home had its flower garden of dahlias, marigolds, zinnias, tuberoses, and chrysanthemums. We considered the flower garden just as necessary for our well-being as the vegetable garden next to it.

In the woods and fields, we used to look for chokeberry and pincherry trees. We picked wild pussy willows and cattails and violets. We picked wild blueberries, too, and mushrooms. To test the mushrooms, we'd boil them with a silver dollar. If the dollar blackened, the mushrooms were poisonous. I guess we were lucky; our silver dollar always gleamed.

Amid the fields and woods were the mines. Unlike the iron mines of Michigan, with their tiny shafts leading to great underground caverns the size of a small town, our mines were stripped off the land—huge, open, man-made canyons in the ground. The greatest of all was known as the Mahoning Hull Rust Open Pit mine, which is more than four miles long, mostly a mile wide, and 350 feet deep. The entire city of

Hibbing, population 15,000 in 1918, was once on this very site. When engineers reported that the main body of iron ore extended under the city, the town packed up and moved a mile south over a period of three years, as the great crater grew even larger.

Calvin Coolidge stood on the rim of the Hibbing pit in 1928 and remarked with his characteristic understatement: "That's a pretty big hole."

The pit is still worked today, for the residual taconite. You can stand on the rim as Coolidge did and gaze down on what appear to be toy steam shovels, each one picking up thirteen tons of ore at a scoop. During the day, the terraces of iron are crimson in the Minnesota sun.

Stewart H. Holbrook, in a book called *Iron Brew*, wrote in 1939 what's still true today:

The crimson deepens as the day wears on, and when the Mesabi's brief twilight falls over the range, the reds dissolve into rich browns and blues and brooding purples. To stand on the rim and look as night comes down is to know a mood akin to that cast by the sea. A man who says he has seen America but has never gazed on the Hibbing pit is deluding himself.

We lived in North Hibbing before the big move south, on McKinley Street, and then on Lincoln Street. This was at the other end of town from the original part of Cedar, Center and Pine Streets, where I was born.

We went to Washington and Jefferson Schools through the sixth grade. Then on to Lincoln Junior High School. In home economics class, each student had a miniature kitchen, complete with cupboards stocked with ingredients, and an individual little stove.

The Carnegie Library was a beautiful building of brick and marble. It brings back memories of spending many an hour looking at slides with a stereoscope or reading books such as *Little Women, Dandelion Cottage*, and the *Dr. Doolittle* series, with my favorite character, "Push-Me-Pull."

These buildings all had a short existence as did the Blessed Sacrament Church, Hy Bloom's Clothing Store, Kleffman's Candy Shop. Other buildings were loaded onto heavy trailers and moved to the new site. The Rood Hospital was moved successfully to South (new) Hibbing and later became the YWCA.

The new Hibbing, moved to accommodate the mines, had a lot going for it. Because of the income from mine taxes, the village could afford to spend a considerable amount for good schools and other civic services. All the streets were paved, even the alleys. Central heat from the Power & Light Company heated our homes. In those days, Hibbing spent as much tax money a year as the city of Minneapolis.

The new Hibbing High School cost $6 million to build, which in those days (1920) was really *money*. I went to school there.

And it was a thrilling event to join thousands of graduates in the year 1976 to celebrate the Hibbing High School All-Class Reunion, 1903–1976. Even one of the two graduates of the first graduating class of 1903 was there.

What nostalgia and pride to climb the granite steps to this "medieval castle" with its twin turrets, standing on an elevated plat of lush green lawns. It was built of brick and limestone, with tapestried walls, staircases of marble, and cork hallway floors. It still boasts an auditorium not excelled to this day, with decor in gold and velvet, and with crystal chandeliers the size of round dining room tables.

The Home Economics Department dining room was furnished with the best of sterling silver, beautiful linens, and bone china. The cafeteria served the finest of lunches at cost. Even though many of us were limited in our amount of lunch money, we did quite well with one scoop of mashed potatoes (5¢), one scoop of vanilla ice cream (5¢), and all the free crackers we wanted.

The teaching staff and equipment in the entire school system were of the highest quality. Pens, books, note pads—all school supplies were distributed free to the students.

It was possible in those days to go from kindergarten through two years of junior college all under one roof.

We had cultural opportunities. Maestro Luigi Lombardi and his wife Ida created a Conservatory of Music on Howard Street in Hibbing. Maestro organized the Range Symphony Orchestra. He could sing the score of a symphony in solfeggio for each instrument. His wife Ida taught piano and voice. An illustrious pupil was Rosa Tentoni from Buhl, who became an opera star at the Metropolitan Opera in New York City.

We had other notables from the Iron Range: Judy Garland came from Grand Rapids. One of my classmates and a good friend was Beatrice Stone. Her son is known as Bob Dylan. There was "Bus Andy," who pioneered a transit idea and turned it into the Greyhound Bus Lines. There was U.S. Congressman John Blatnik, Governor Rudy Perpich, and, of course, Jeno.

The Iron Range used to draw great name bands. We danced to the music of Ozzie and Harriet, Ina Ray Hutton, Ben Bernie, Tommy Dorsey, Kay Kaiser, Frankie Yankovic. A favorite story that circulated every now and then was that Wayne King came from Eveleth and that his real name was Waino Kakkela!

But there were labor problems in the mines. The myriad of nationalities who had come from the four corners of the world to dig in the earth of Minnesota weren't dumb. They realized that although the town was rich, they were dirt poor. Some joined the International Workers of the World, the IWW. Since strikes meant the temporary ceasing of work by the union members, we kids called it the "I Won't Work."

At the same time, my mother had opened a neighborhood grocery store. It was mostly cash on the barrel, but we had a few special customers whom we would carry on the cuff when there were labor problems in the mines. These people were very unhappy about being laid off or having to go on strike. Puzzled, I asked a Mr. Ericson, one of the unhappy strikers, why they voted to strike if they didn't really want to strike.

He said, "They call a meeting. And they ask us, 'Do you want more pay?' And of course we say yes. So the next day we're on strike."

That's the way it was in that bubbling, boiling, melting pot called the Iron Range.

We kids learned smart-aleck sayings. If someone asked us, "Where do you live?" we'd say, "Upstairs of an empty lot." I think that came about because as Calvin Coolidge observed, our former town had become "a pretty big hole."

We teased each other about our nationalities, but we exchanged ideas and thoughts and customs and recipes—and even dances. We learned the Highland Fling, the Fox Trot, *La Tarantella*, the Jig, the Two Step, the Waltz, the Clog. We danced the Frankie Yankovic Polkas and Mazurkas, the Chisholm Hop, and the Charleston.

My home and family group, of course, were the Wops or Dagos. And we were a nationality of many dialects. Each *provincia* in Italy had its own. There were the marchigiano, siciliano, piemontese, calabrese, bolognese, milanese, genovese, abbruzzese, and many more, each with its distinct accent.

"*Non va fuori che ti meno piu forte,*" was an admonishment to a child—"don't you go outdoors or I'll hit you harder." In one dialect, it would sound like, "*Nohn vah fwoh ree kay tee maynoh pew fohr tay;*" in another, "*Nohn hee hohr kay tee haynoh who hort.*"

The Italians were somewhat clannish and had their Sons of Italy and Daughters of Italy halls for their social and club activities. However, to me, there seemed to be a lot of jealousy and envy among themselves. To me, the Italian husband and father from the Old Country seemed chauvinistic. I vowed I would never marry an Italian when I grew up.

Italians have been noted for their love of music. "O Sole Mio," "Santa Lucia," "L'Espagnuola si va Cosi" were popular songs. I remember hearing them sung at a naturalization program when Mother became an American citizen. Each nationality group sang songs from its native country.

Our family was very proud. During the flu epidemic of 1918, boarders in other homes were dying like flies. But no one got sick in Mother's house. She used plenty of Lysol, and everyone had to keep raw garlic cloves in their mouths to ward off infection!

My mother was and is something else. We used to make wine, quite illegally, to supplement my father's pay from the mines. One time Mother decided to feed the grape mash (known as *vinaccia*) to our cow. Poor Bossy. She got so drunk, she didn't get up for three days.

Determined to become a good English-speaking citizen, Mama Michelina (mee keh lee nah) started by having the storekeeper name each item whenever she went out shopping. She was never tolerant of those who made no effort to learn English.

Mother's cooking is a legend. She catered her *culinaria* long before we knew what catering was. When customers would come into our store for a loaf of bread, the aroma drifting from the kitchen was so inviting that they ended up in the kitchen sampling her antipasto or *pesce piquante* (spicy fish delight). To this day, she is the consultant in the test kitchens of Jeno's, Inc.

That's my mother.

And speaking of Jeno's, let me tell you about another great power in the world of food. My brother Jeno has become a world figure, honored with awards from all over the country and abroad, not only for his success in the food business but also for his efforts in the community and the humanities. In case you haven't kept up with his career, he is the poor Italian from the Iron Range who built a company called Chun King into a national name, sold it for $63 million, and then built another empire called Jeno's. He is probably one of the ten or fifteen best-known businessmen in the United States.

I remember his first arrival. I was swinging on the garden gate when the nurse and the doctor with his little black satchel came to deliver my brother Jeno. That's my brother.

As for me, I began to have an interest in food at an early age, ever since my mother would command me to "go stir the pot before it sticks." I was the envy of my classmates with my clothes that Mother designed and sewed for me. We kept the treadle sewing machine in our large kitchen and there, as she pedaled away, she would direct and supervise me in the step-by-step preparation of Italian dishes.

We couldn't afford a piano, so I learned to play a twenty-five dollar violin. Years later, I played with the Duluth Symphony and the Range Symphony Orchestra.

I was graduated from the University of Minnesota; taught high school French, English, and American history; and at age twenty directed a forty-piece school orchestra. I was a Navy WAVE from 1944 to 1946, and later served as executive secretary and treasurer of The Chun King Corporation.

Then I came to Florida—to Sanford, the celery capital of the world, to buy celery for the Oriental foods operation. I've lived here ever since, though I do travel a great deal of the time. I'm thankful to have had the opportunity and the time to keep on expanding my own cooking horizons—from the delicacies of classic French cuisine to the soul food of the great cooks of the American South.

That's me.

THE IRON RANGES

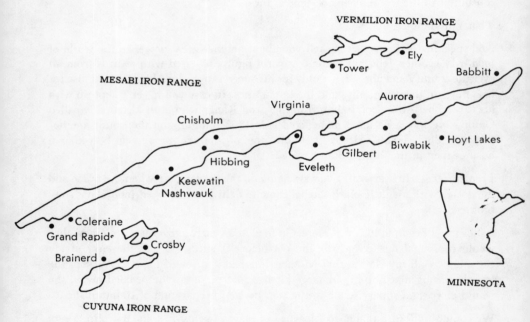

AMERICAN INDIAN

Thousands of years ago, from Esconawbaw (Upper Peninsula Michigan) to Gitche Gumee (Lake Superior) to the mighty Mississippi roamed the Chippewas, Ojibiways, Sioux, Crees, and Dacotahs. There in the forests of pine and fir trees, in the land of bear, reindeer, otter, lynx, and ermine—where nested the wild goose Wawa, the blue heron Shuh shuh Gah, the robin Opechee, and the bluebird Owaissa—dwelled the Indians in their wigwams of deer hide. In the meadows Muskoday, covered with wildflowers, the squirrels chattered and scolded, and at night, in the light of the flitting, twinkling fireflies, one could hear the hooting of the owls.

There the women with names of Nokomis, Wenonah, and Minnehaha planted and harvested corn, dressed deerskins to make clothes and moccasins, and harvested the wild rice. They gathered blueberries Meenahaga, strawberries Odahmin, and gooseberries Shahbomin. The men provided food by hunting with their bows (of ash) and arrows which were tipped with flint and winged with feathers. In canoes of birch and cedar, they fished for sturgeon Nahma, perch Sahwa, and pike Maskenozha.

They were the warriors of painted face, with belts of wampum (small beads made of white or black shells, and their symbol of power), and bedecked with eagle feathers. Through the smoke Pukwana of the calumet (peace pipe made of red quarry stone and reeds), they would listen to legends such as of Mudjekeewis, Wabun, Kabibonokka, Shawondasee—the winds of the heavens. And they depicted the stories of war, hunting, and love by painting symbols: picture writing in different colors on birch bark and deerskin.

They honored their dead by burying them with their furs, wampum, even their pots and kettles. Food was left for them and fires were lighted on their graves for four nights so the dead could find their way to the Hereafter, Islands of the Blessed.

Indian names were symbolic and many names remain with us: Dacotahs (Dakota), Calumet, Omawhas (Omaha), Bemidji, Wenonah (Winona), Esconawbaw (Escanoba), Mahnomonee (Menomonie), and Minnehaha, meaning "laughing waters," a park in Minneapolis. Keewatin meant "north wind" in Cree.

But times changed, and from the East and from the big sea waters, in wooden boats with paddles, came a new breed—white faces and bearded—the Paleface. The first to arrive were the Priests of Prayer, the missionaries. Then came the lumbermen, the miners and merchants, speaking many languages. The Indians began to disperse, to weaken, and to war among themselves.

On the Mesabi Range the Chippewas edged out the other tribal nations and in 1853 they sold their rights to this land to the U.S. Government. The Indians, even after the first iron ore miners arrived, had ignored the thick, rich deposits of red ore—except to make colorful paint!

Corn or "maize" was the "friend of man"—grain from the Great Spirit, Mondamin. The Indian wife deemed it her prerogative to do the corn planting and cultivating. And, in order to insure a prolific crop, the myth goes that once the maize was planted, a ritual was performed. In the dark of night, completely disrobed, she would secretly slip out of the wigwam and walk silently around the cornfields, drawing a circle around them with her footprints. Or, she would drag a garment, her matchecota, all around the fields. The belief was that it would prevent insects and worms from creeping over this magic line. But it was the warrior who protected the crop from devastation from crows and blackbirds by snaring them and hanging them aloft on poles as scarecrows!

In Autumn, all the women joined in the corn gathering. Children and the old men in the household would also help with the harvesting and husking. And if a young maiden found a red ear in the cornhusking, everyone would shout, "Nushka, look, you shall have a sweetheart." But, if the ear was crooked, no matter what color, it meant there was a crooked old man in the cornfield!

Hominy was made from parched corn. The dry kernels were boiled in a lye (ash) solution to remove the hull and germ. The hominy was then boiled with venison stock. Also, after drying, the hominy was pounded into a coarsely ground meal for baking corncakes or for puddings.

In Europe, corn was considered animal fodder. But when the Indians introduced corn as a delicious food to our first settlers, it became an important part of the American diet—spreading throughout the entire country—prepared in many ways!

Corn on the Cob

Minnie Lee

Fresh corn is really sweet and delicious if you can boil it as soon as possible after picking. First get your pot of salted water boiling; rush out to the field, pick and husk the corn, and hurry back to the boiling kettle with it. But, should you stumble and drop the ears, go back and pick some more. Corn should boil gently for 8 minutes only. Serve with lots of melted butter, salt and pepper.

And now with the advent of the Microwave, so many years after Nokomis, corn can be even more delicious prepared this way. Wrap each ear in plastic wrap. Cook in Microwave at high heat, 2 minutes for the first ear, plus 1 minute for each additional ear!

Corn Fritters Calumet

1½ cups canned whole kernel corn* with juices	1 tsp baking powder
1½ cups flour	2 eggs, beaten
½ tsp salt	¼ cup water or milk
¼ tsp pepper (white preferred) Pinch freshly ground nutmeg (if desired)	1 Tb melted butter/margarine
	1 tsp vanilla extract (Cognac for the continental)
	2 cups vegetable or corn oil

Sift flour, salt, pepper, nutmeg, and baking powder together. Beat eggs well and add water (milk) and butter/margarine; beat until well mixed.

Add the egg mixture to the flour mixture, stirring until well blended. Add the vanilla (Cognac). Stir in the kernel corn. Batter should be thick enough to drop by spoonfuls. Add a little more flour if necessary.

Heat oil in a deep-fry pan until piece of bread turns golden in seconds. Drop batter from a tablespoon and fry until golden, crisp, and puffy. Drain on paper towel. 4 to 6 servings

Serve hot with lots of butter, honey, or syrup.

*Equivalent of fresh-cooked or frozen corn can be used.

Egg Cheese Grits

Marian Manly

Great for brunches.

1	cup grits, quick *not* instant (ground hominy)	3	eggs, beaten
½	cup (8 Tb) butter/margarine	3	tsp seasoned or garlic salt
¾	lb cheddar cheese, sharp or mild, shredded	1	tsp salt
		1	tsp paprika
		5 to 6	drops hot pepper sauce

Cook grits as directed on package. Stir in butter/margarine until melted. Add the cheese and eggs. Blend in the seasonings.

Bake in a 2-quart greased casserole at 325° for 1 hour. 6 to 8 servings

Golden Corn Bread

Dorothy McReynolds

1	cup sifted all-purpose flour	2	eggs
3	tsp baking powder	1	cup milk
1	tsp salt	¼	cup oil or melted shortening
2	Tb sugar		
1	cup cornmeal, yellow or white		

Sift together into large mixing bowl the flour, baking powder, salt, and sugar. Stir in cornmeal. Make a small pocket in center of mixture and add eggs and milk. Stir flour from sides and beat just until dry ingredients are moistened. Add oil (shortening) and mix.

Lightly oil an iron skillet or a square baking pan and preheat it for about 5 minutes in 375° to 400° oven. Spoon batter into heated skillet (pan) and bake for about 30 minutes, or until top is lightly browned. 4 to 6 servings

Indian Corn Pudding

In Europe this pudding was made with wheat or rye. Our early settlers were taught to use cornmeal by the Indians.

½	cup cornmeal, white or yellow	2	tsp salt
1	qt milk	1	cup dark molasses
4 to 6	Tb suet, finely chopped, or butter	1	apple, peeled and grated (if desired)
1	Tb nutmeg (freshly ground best)		Butter
		2	additional cups milk

Put cornmeal in a large pot. Stir in the 1 quart of milk and let come to a boil. While coming to a boil, add rest of ingredients except the butter and additional 2 cups of milk. Keep stirring until pudding starts to boil. Then let boil until it thickens. Pour into a 2-quart buttered casserole. Bake at 225° for 30 minutes. Take out of oven, stir in 1 cup of the additional milk. Then back into the oven at 250° for 2 hours. Take out again and pour the second cup of milk over the top—do not stir. Back in the oven for 4 hours. Lower temperature from 250° to 225° if cooking too fast. 6 to 8 servings

Pudding will be soft. Serve either warm or cold with a dollop of whipped cream or ice cream.

The Outpost Camp

To a group of islands surrounded by a large chain of lakes, way up in the wilds of Canada, north of Lake Superior Gitche Gumee, the Ojibway family of George Mongoneenee and his wife Hanna Amut migrated. There they made their home and for years were the sole inhabitants of the area—until 1969, when it was "discovered" as a great fishing haven.

Then, George, and his sons—Gordon Tapete and Edward Mossquagh—and his daughters—Irene Romale and Margaret Dalee—with virtually an axe, saw, and hammer, busied themselves in building log cabins for the Iron Range newcomers. Logs were cut from spruce trees, dragged or floated on the lakes, then peeled and clear-varnished. Equipment, supplies, and furnishings began arriving, either flown in or barged by snowmobile during the winter months. Eventually a small village emerged and there on the banks a sign is posted:

JENO'S
WILDERNESS VILLAGE
Jeno F. Paulucci, "Mayor"

Living quarters are equipped and furnished with all the creature comforts from automatic dishwasher, icemaker, clotheswasher and dryer to a sauna! But there is not the first clock in the place.

The Outpost Camp, as it is affectionately called, can only be reached by seaplane. The lakes abound in walleyes and northern pike. Fishing "holes"—dubbed with such names as Oil Can, Mystery Bay, Split Rock—are trolled by motorboats carrying small washtubs for the "catch." And fishing at favorite Termite Rapids is only minutes away by seaplane.

Wild blueberries abound for pies and pancakes. Many of Jeno's guests at the Outpost Camp are gourmet cooks, and busy is the kitchen with such "Chefs" as Frank Befera, Kelly Cardiff, Bob Heimbach, Eddie Muccilli, Tom Stevenson—to mention only a few! All men? No wonder! The Outpost originated as a men's fishing paradise, but now it is shared with the womenfolk, who have proven to be as avid "fishermen" as the men! To date, Lois has caught the largest walleye ever.

A bonus of our first trip was not only flying our catch of walleyes home with us, but getting a selection of terrific recipes from the fellows.

Fish Fry at the Outpost Camp

A favorite recipe for not only walleyes, but also any firm-flesh fish, such as red snapper, perch, halibut, is Kelly J. Cardiff's:

Wash and clean walleye fillets thoroughly; dry with paper toweling. Mix equal amounts of flour and crushed cornflake crumbs and season with salt and pepper.

Beat 4 to 6 eggs (depending on amount of fish to cook) in a bowl, adding a little milk or water. Dip fish in egg batter, then bread with flour and cornflake mixture and deep fry until golden brown, turning once.

At the Outpost Camp I use a large cast iron frying pan with almost 1 inch of safflower oil as the liquid shortening. I've used all kinds, but the safflower seems less greasy with no oil taste. Maintaining a proper oil temperature in frying is a big factor. (A cube of bread browns in seconds.) The fillets seem to require about a minute on each side.

For a change, use equal amounts of *cornmeal* and flour. For 4 to 6 servings:

2	lbs fish fillets	¼	tsp pepper
½	cup flour	2	eggs
½	cup corn flakes or cornmeal	1	tsp milk or water
1	tsp salt		

Baked Squash

Hubbard, acorn, butternut, buttercup, banana, or Mediterranean
Butter/margarine
Salt and pepper

Wash and cut into serving pieces. Remove seeds and stringy portion. Place face down on a foil-lined cookie sheet. Bake at 375° for 30 minutes. Turn cut side up, dot with butter/margarine, season with salt and pepper to taste, and bake until tender (about 30 minutes), brushing often with melted butter.

It was the Indians in Minnesota who introduced our first settlers to a number of vegetables, not only corn but potatoes, pumpkin, tomatoes, and squash.

A typical feast, as for Hiawatha's wedding to Minnehaha, served in bowls made of basswood, with spoons made of horn and bison, included sturgeon, pike, buffalo marrow. They ate pressed cakes of dried meat and fat known in Cree language as Pemican. There was deer and bison meat, yellow corn cakes, and wild rice.

Wild Rice Mahnomonee, is not really a rice, but the grain of an aquatic grass growing on the muddy bottom of streams, lakes, and swamps. "Ricing," done by the women of the Indian tribes, was harvesting the rice by canoe, beating the plants so grains fell partly into the canoe and partly back into the muck to reseed. It was one of the staples in the Indian diet.

With the advent of European settlers, the Indians scattered—many to settle on government-provided "Reservations." There they pitched their wigwams and made and sold souvenir moccasins and beadwork. And to provide them with a source of food and income, the government granted them the exclusive rights to the wild rice. Only they could harvest the crops and auction it off for cash.

This wild growing grain of nutlike flavor was variable, making it a very dear item. However, within the last twenty-five years, cultivation methods have been devised so that the wild rice has been domesticated in many parts of the Great Lakes area.

Cooked wild rice can be enhanced by tossing it with any number of good things: melted butter, minced scallions, sautéed mushrooms, chopped walnuts, pignoli (pine nuts), diced ham, chopped parsley, chives, or just plain salt and pepper.

One cup wild rice will yield three to four cups cooked rice.

Wild Rice Casserole

Lois Paulucci

6 to 8	ozs wild rice, washed and drained	1	cup diced celery
1	Tb salt	1	cup chopped green pepper
1/3	lb bacon, diced (4 to 5 slices)	1	4-oz can mushroom pieces, drained
1/2	cup (8 Tb) butter/margarine	1 1/4	cups chicken broth
1	cup chopped onion		

Cook rice in boiling water to cover (salted with 1 tablespoon salt) in a lidded pot for 30 to 35 minutes. Drain.

Sauté bacon until crisp. Drain on paper towel. Pour off fat and in the same pan sauté the vegetables in melted butter/margarine until onion is soft. Combine all ingredients with broth. Bake in a covered 2- to 3-quart casserole at 350° for 30 minutes. Can be frozen: thaw and reheat. 6 to 8 servings

Wild Rice Dressing Nokomis

This dressing is delicious with turkey, chicken, duckling, and also with game such as pheasant, partridge, grouse, squab, or quail.

Wild Rice:

- 1 cup wild rice
- 1 tsp salt

Wash rice in wire strainer under cold running water. Combine rice and salt with 4 cups water in saucepan. Heat to boil. Cover and simmer over low heat 35 to 45 minutes, or until rice is tender. Drain. 3 to 4 cups cooked rice

Dressing:

1 cup cooked wild rice	¼ cup sliced mushrooms, raw or canned
¼ cup (4 Tb) butter/margarine	1 tsp salt
¼ cup chopped onion	¼ tsp pepper
¼ cup diced celery	½ to 1 tsp sage or thyme

Melt butter/margarine in frying pan. Sauté onion until golden and soft. Add celery and mushrooms; cook 2 to 3 minutes. Add wild rice and seasonings. 2 cups dressing

Lightly stuff bird or birds of your choice. Adjust oven temperature and timing according to type of bird.

Indian Dessert

There is an Indian reservation on Mille Lacs Lake in Minnesota. Mille Lacs (meel lock) means "a thousand lakes" in French.

Surrounding this area are huge areas of maple trees, and Minnesota once produced as much syrup as Vermont. The Indians made huge quantities of maple syrup from these trees.

A favorite treat for the Indians was to pour maple syrup over a ball of snow!

ENGLISH

In the 1880s, when rich deposits of iron ore were found while mining for copper and gold, loggers and miners from surrounding areas and from the East came rushing to Upper Peninsula Michigan.

But it was the Cornish, direct from the coal mines of Cornwall, England, who became the top iron ore miners and captains there. They were born miners, with the experience and expertise to drill, dig, and dynamite the hard, blue-black hematite found underground.

They carried names such as Jones, Smith, and King, but their fellow workers called them "Cousin Jacks." Strong and sinewy, they were great wrestlers, and they brought the sport of curling with them to the Iron Ranges.

When the iron ore rush began on the Vermilion and Mesabi Ranges, the Cornish joined the hundreds of loggers and miners to mine the newly found deposits of ore. However, they could not believe that here the iron ore was a flat deposit of red dust lying on the surface. They were used to drilling hundreds of feet underground, not scooping up a red powder with a steam shovel, which they dubbed "Bloody Ditchdiggers."

One of the great Cornish contributions to the Iron Ranges was the pasty (pronounced pass-tee), meat and vegetables wrapped in pastry. This was the Cornishman's staple of the midday meal, washed down with tea. There are varied stories as to how the miners kept their pasties warm. Some wrapped them in a clean cloth and cached them under their shirts to keep warm; some warmed them on a miner's shovel held over two candles.

Pasties became a favorite food of all nationalities on the Iron Ranges. We used to have pasties and blueberry pie on our picnics. Many churches still make pasties to raise money.

When we think of the English, we think of tea, crumpets, and scones; fish and chips; sandwich plates of roast beef and horseradish; unusual vegetables like sea kale, purslane, and dark blue snap beans; kippered herring; and pies—fruit and meat.

Cheddar cheese, enjoyed everywhere, originated in Somersetshire, England, and spicy Worcestershire sauce was first concocted in Worcester.

Beer and ale date back to Elizabethan days and are still important to the English diet, along with wines from many countries. Wassail! To your health!

The saying, "Mind your Ps and Qs," originated in the English pubs. The pints and quarts of beer and ale consumed on credit by the patrons were marked down on the back of the bar door. When a patron overimbibed, he was reminded of the number of pints and quarts already on his account! Darts was a favorite pub game.

Cheese Apples

Lu Rene Ball

Grate sharp cheddar cheese. Form into tiny balls. Decorate with a small rose leaf and whole clove to form the stem of an apple. Dip cotton in a solution of red food color diluted with water to gently tint each cheese apple. These apples are tasty and colorful on a hors d'oeuvre tray.

Untinted, the tiny balls look like apricots or peaches!

Cheese Balls

Dianne Howard

8	ozs cheddar cheese, sharp or extra sharp, grated	1	cup flour plus almost another ½ cup
½	cup (8 Tb) butter/margarine, at room temperature	65	small pimiento-stuffed olives

Mix cheese with butter/margarine. Add flour, a little at a time, and blend well. Form into 65 small balls, each covering a stuffed olive. Freeze balls. When ready to use, heat oven to 400°. Bake 12 to 14 minutes on a cookie sheet.

Castleford Toad-in-the-Hole

Pat White

When I first met Pat White, her speech prompted me to ask whether she wasn't directly from England. She was; and she was happy to share English family recipes with us—complete with her own comments. Here's one from Yorkshire.

4	lamb chops	2	cups milk
1	cup bread crumbs	1	Tb flour
½	tsp thyme	2	eggs, well beaten
½	tsp chopped fresh parsley		Salt and pepper

Trim off skin and most of the fat from the chops. Grease a deep baking dish; sprinkle bottom with bread crumbs and mixture of thyme and parsley. Lay the chops on bread crumbs. Make a batter with milk and flour, adding the eggs; salt and pepper to taste. Pour the batter over the chops and bake at 350° for 1 hour. 4 servings

Four small steaks may be substituted for the chops. Serve with brown gravy and a green vegetable.

English Shepherd's Pie

Pat White

This is the original from Yorkshire. Monday was always the day for Shepherd's Pie. After Sunday's roast lamb dinner, the leftover lamb was turned into a delicious hot Shepherd's Pie.

2	cups cooked lamb	1	cup gravy or good stock
1	large onion, partially boiled (parboiled)	2	cups well-mashed potatoes
	Salt and pepper		Butter

Put lamb and onion through a coarse meat grinder. Season well with salt and pepper to taste and put in the bottom of a deep baking dish. Cover with gravy (stock), then with the mashed potatoes. Score top of mashed potatoes with a fork. Dot top with butter. Bake at 350° for 40 minutes until top is well browned. 4 to 6 servings

Pasties

(Pass-Tees or Pahs-Tees)

Florence Trepanier

Also known as "Cousin Jacks," a hearty meat-and-potatoes pie.

Pastry:

3	cups flour
1	Tb salt
¾	cup plus 1 Tb (13 Tb) Shortening or lard
	Ice water

Filling:

1¼	lbs top round or flank steak, diced
1	large baking potato, peeled and diced
1	medium onion, diced
4	tb ground suet
	Salt and pepper

Make pastry first. Mix flour with salt. With pastry blender or 2 knives cut shortening into the flour until the size of peas. Sprinkle with water, 1 tablespoon at a time, mixing lightly with a fork until all the flour is moistened. Press into a ball. Divide into 4 portions and set aside. Dice meat and vegetables.

Roll out 1 portion of pie crust into a round (not too thin). In lower half of round, layer in this order:

1	row potatoes
	Sprinkling of salt
1	row meat
1	row onions
	Sprinkling of salt and pepper
1	Tb suet

Fold the top half over the layered ingredients half to form a half moon. Seal edges tightly (moisten and use tines of fork). Make 1 slit on top. Place on a cookie sheet. Repeat with the other 3 pie crust portions. When ready to bake, drop 1 teaspoon hot water in slit of each pasty. Bake at 350° for 20 minutes. Then lower temperature to 325° for 60 more minutes. Remove from oven and cool, covered with dish towels. 4 servings

Serve them hot, but they are also delicious cold. Traditionally served with chow chow relish.

Bake extra pasties. Freeze, after they are cold, in aluminum foil. To serve; thaw and heat at 325° in its aluminum foil.

Steak and Kidney Pie

Pat White

1	lb good beefsteak, cubed	1	large onion, sliced
4	lamb or veal kidneys, sliced	1	tsp fresh chopped parsley
1	cup flour, seasoned with ½ tsp salt and ¼ tsp pepper	1½	cups beef stock or gravy
	Fat for browning	½	cup dry red wine
		½	tsp Worcestershire sauce
8	large mushrooms, sliced, or 1 4-oz can, drained		Salt and pepper to taste
		1	unbaked pie crust

Roll beef and kidneys in seasoned flour and brown them in a greased skillet. Mix the rest of the ingredients with the steak and kidneys and put in a deep casserole dish. Cover with the pie crust. Cut slits in top of crust to allow for steam to escape. Bake at 350° for 50 to 60 minutes until pie is well browned and meat is tender. 4 to 6 servings

Egg Brunch Casserole

Sophie Shoemaker

6 to 8	eggs	1	lb sausage or bacon, cooked and drained
1	cup milk		
	Butter	1	4-oz can sliced mushrooms, drained
6	slices bread, cubed		
4	ozs cheddar cheese, shredded		Additional shredded cheddar

Beat eggs and milk well together. In a large buttered casserole (with cover) layer other ingredients in the order they are listed above, pouring egg-milk mixture over all, and sprinkling with additional shredded cheddar. Refrigerate for 8 hours or more. Bake at 350°, covered, for 45 minutes (325° for glass casserole). 10 to 12 servings

English Breakfast

Vivian Buck

For breakfast or brunch or late night supper.

1	dz eggs	½	cup finely chopped green
⅔	cup milk		peppers
1	cup salad	¼	cup chopped pimientos
	dressing/mayonnaise	½	tsp salt
¼	lb bacon, cooked and	¼	tsp pepper
	crumbled		Parsley sprigs

Beat eggs well. Add milk and salad dressing. Stir in remaining ingredients. Bake in an oblong pan set in a pan of hot water in a 350° oven for about 25 minutes, or until set. Cut into squares and serve on toast. Garnish with parsley sprigs. 10 to 12 servings

This recipe can be mixed and refrigerated the night before and poured into baking pan when ready to bake.

Deviled Crab

1	lb crab meat	½	tsp Worcestershire sauce
¼	cup (4 Tb)	1	tsp salt
	butter/margarine	¼	tsp pepper
1	small onion, chopped		Dash hot pepper sauce
2	Tb chopped green pepper		Dash cayenne pepper
2	egg yolks, slightly beaten	⅓	cup mayonnaise
¼	cup bread crumbs	1	tsp dry mustard
2	Tb dry sherry	¼	cup bread crumbs
1	Tb lemon juice	1	Tb butter, melted
1	tsp chopped chives		

In 4 tablespoons butter, sauté onion and green pepper until soft. Stir in crab meat and rest of ingredients except last four items. Fill 4 to 6 crab shells, ramekins, or a 1-quart buttered casserole with mixture. Combine mayonnaise and mustard and spread over mixture. Combine bread crumbs and melted butter and sprinkle over mixture. Bake, uncovered, at 425° for 5 to 8 minutes (casserole, 15 to 20 minutes), or until hot and browned. 4 to 6 servings

Stone Crab Claws

This type of crab is unique to England and Florida waters. In Florida, stone crab season is closed from May 15 to October 15. During the open season, fishermen are allowed to catch them, break off one claw and return the crab to the ocean. Crabs quickly grow additional claws. They are available, already cooked, either refrigerated or frozen at your fish market.

Stone crab claws are delicious as an entrée with lots of melted butter. Serve them either cold or heated through in the oven. You will need to use a nutcracker as those claws are really hard as stones!

Poached Fillets Lavinia

4 to 6 fillets (any fish)
        Fresh asparagus spears
        Butter/margarine
        Tomato wedges
        Salt and pepper
        Lemon juice
   ¼ cup clam juice or chicken
        broth

Roll each fillet around an asparagus spear. Line cookie sheet with aluminum foil. Butter the foil. Arrange fish on foil surrounding with any additional asparagus spears. Spear a tomato wedge on each fillet. Sprinkle with salt, pepper, and lemon juice. Pour clam juice (chicken broth) over. Cover with aluminum foil and seal tightly. Poach at 350° for 25 to 30 minutes. 4 to 6 servings

Serve with rice and peas.

Fish Cakes From Devonshire, England

Pat White

1 cup cooked fish
1 cup bread crumbs
6 fresh mushrooms, cooked
    and sliced, or 1 2-oz can,
    drained
1 cup shelled and chopped
    shrimp
    Salt and pepper
½ egg-cupful chopped thyme
    (1 Tb)

1 egg, beaten
    Flour
1 egg yolk, beaten
    Bread crumbs
    Fat for frying
½ egg-cupful chopped parsley
    (1 Tb)

Mash the fish with a fork in a bowl. Add the 1 cup bread crumbs, mushrooms, shrimp, salt and pepper to taste and thyme. Bind with the beaten whole egg. With floured hands, form into balls, then dip in egg yolk and bread crumbs. Fry in skillet until golden brown. Drain well before serving. Garnish with parsley. 4 to 6 servings

Steamed Fresh Shrimp

For shrimp that will be pink, juicy and tender.

Bring salted water to cover to a boil in a large pot. Add your favorite seasonings, total 1 Tb per 2 lbs shrimp, plus 1 tsp lemon juice. Add the shrimp. Bring back to boiling. Remove from heat and allow to set, covered, for 5 minutes *only*. Drain shrimp, rinse in cold water, drain again. Shell and devein.

Suggested seasonings: Celery salt, salt, pepper, cloves, mustard seed, bay leaf, mace, cardamom, ginger, cassia, paprika.

Zesty Cocktail Sauce

Combine all ingredients and chill. 1½ cups sauce

1	cup chili sauce	1	tsp Worcestershire sauce
2	Tb catsup	1	tsp pickapeppa
2	Tb lemon juice	4	drops hot pepper sauce
1	Tb horseradish		Salt and pepper to taste

Delicious for shrimp, snow crab claws, Alaskan King crab claws.

Beef Rib Roast

We enjoyed Roast Prime Rib of Beef au Jus, English Yorkshire Pudding, and Creamed Horseradish Sauce at the famous Redwood Room in the Clift Hotel in San Francisco. From huge, gleaming Simpson silver carts, their chefs from London sliced the enormous roasts and served the diners their individual preference in doneness.

        Rib roast (4 to 5 ribs)
        Salt and pepper
½   large onion* (if desired)

Rub roast all over with salt and pepper. Let stand at least 20 minutes. Place roast on a rack in an open roasting pan, fat side up.

According to expert English chefs for a perfect roast:

First sear your rib roast at 500° for a few minutes (about 10) until brown. Then continue roasting at 300° to desired doneness.

With the drippings in roasting pan, prepare Yorkshire Pudding (below) to complement the roast. 4 to 6 servings

*Skewer onion half on top of roast after the searing process.

Yorkshire Pudding

Peg Heathrow

We first tasted this delightful pudding in Vancouver Island, Canada. A search for the recipe only resulted in popover recipes. Here at last is the real thing.

1½	cups flour	1	tsp onion salt or crushed
1½	cups milk		thyme
3	eggs		Drippings from roast

Blend together flour, milk, eggs, onion salt (thyme), and beat with an electric or rotary beater until batter is smooth. Let stand until roast is ready. Batter will thicken.

Remove roast from pan to a warm platter. Degrease the pan by pouring off excess fat. Then pour and stir batter into the meat drippings in the roasting pan. Bake at 375° for 30 minutes or more until puffed and golden. Serve with slices of roast beef. 4 to 6 servings

We have also known of an English custom of baking cooked egg noodles in the drippings.

Horseradish Sauce

1 cup mayonnaise
⅓ cup prepared mustard

⅓ cup horseradish

Whisk ingredients together in a small bowl. 1⅔ cups sauce
Variations:
Fold in ½ cup heavy cream, whipped.
Leave out the mustard.
Serve with cold roast beef, turkey, ham.

Rock Cornish Hens

A miniature chicken crossbred from a British breed and Plymouth Rock chickens. All white meat.

Cornish hens (one per person)
Sage
Thyme
Celery salt
Onion salt

Salt and pepper
¼ cup (4 Tb) butter, melted
Garlic salt
¼ cup dry white wine or water

Lightly sprinkle inside of each hen with sage, thyme, celery salt, onion salt, salt and pepper. Pour melted butter over each bird and sprinkle generously with garlic salt. Refrigerate for about 30 minutes.

Roast in 400° oven for 1 hour, or until brown and tender (shallow pan, no rack, no cover). Remove hens to warm platter.

Degrease roasting pan and pick up juices with white wine (water). Strain if desired. Serve au jus in a gravy boat.

Cornish Hens with Wild Rice Dressing

Cornish hens (one per person)
Salt and pepper
Wild Rice Dressing

Nokomis (see recipe, Indian section)
Butter/margarine, melted

Wash and dry Cornish hens. Salt and pepper cavity. Stuff loosely with rice dressing. Brush with melted butter/margarine. Roast in shallow pan, no rack, no cover, at 350° to 400° about 1 hour until brown and tender.

Watercress

Almost considered a staple in the English diet, watercress conjures up English ladies nibbling dainty watercress sandwiches at teatime. It replaces lettuce in salads and sandwiches, is used as an elegant garnish instead of parsley, and is added to soups. In ancient times it was even known as a love potion.

In England, this leafy plant is grown ideally in the Dorset area, which is abundant in chalk water. (In marshes in Victoria, British Columbia, we picked wild growing watercress.) Proper raising, cutting, and bunching is considered a skilled craft. It is rather a paradox that the best strain of watercress now grown in England was crossbred over the last decade with a variety from this country—after a crop failure wiped out their strain.

Although not very well known and not of the standard English quality, watercress is gaining more popularity in this country. In Italy, rugula is a kissing cousin to watercress.

Watercress Salad

Cordon Bleu Watts

1	bunch watercress	Lemon Dressing
4	raw mushrooms	
2	eggs, hard boiled and chopped	

Wash, drain, and crispen watercress. Arrange on individual salad plates. Slice mushrooms very thin and sprinkle over watercress. Then sprinkle with chopped egg. Pour Lemon Dressing over. 4 servings

Lemon Dressing:

1/3	cup lemon juice	1	Tb prepared mustard
4	Tb wine vinegar	1	tsp salt
2	green onions or shallots, minced	1/2	tsp pepper
1	clove garlic, minced	1	cup vegetable oil (or more)*
2	Tb finely minced fresh parsley		

Whisk all ingredients together, except oil. Whisk in oil gradually until of thin "mayonnaise" consistency. Refrigerate in covered jar. 1½ cups dressing
*Peanut oil is also good.

Bubble and Squeak

Pat White

Leftover cold boiled
potatoes, sliced
Leftover cooked cabbage,
chopped, or Brussels
sprouts

1 onion, partially boiled and
finely chopped
Salt and pepper
Butter or fat drippings
from roast

Melt butter (fat) in skillet. Put in potatoes, cabbage (sprouts), onion. Season with salt and pepper to taste. Fry until golden brown; stir so all sides are browned.

Crispy Baked Potatoes

From the gourmets "down under" in Australia.

Wash and scrub baking potatoes. Heat oven to 450°. Rinse potatoes with water and sprinkle salt all over wet skins. No aluminum foil. No pricking of the skin. Bake for 1 hour.

Stovies

Pat White

2 cups cold mashed potatoes
1 large onion, partially boiled
and chopped
1 Tb butter, softened

Salt and pepper
Flour
Fat for frying

Mix potatoes, onion, butter, and salt and pepper to taste in a bowl. Form mixture into balls with well-floured hands. Flatten balls and fry in skillet on both sides until golden brown. 4 to 6 servings

This is a tasty side dish.

Twice-Baked Potatoes

Bob Heimbach

When asked if he had a name for his baked potatoes, Bob answered, "I just call them Twice-Baked; but maybe you can give them a more glamorous name." Like Shakespeare, "A rose by any other name, etc.," Twice-Baked Potatoes by any other name would be as delicious!

40

Baking potatoes (one half per person)
Butter
Milk or 1 egg
Salt and pepper
Onion, grated
Green pepper, chopped or shredded

Cheddar cheese, sharp or extra sharp, shredded
Crisp bacon bits
Dill weed
Paprika

Bake potatoes (wet skins sprinkled with salt) at 450° for 1 hour. Cool; split in half lengthwise. Scoop out cooked potato and mash in a bowl with butter and milk (egg) until smooth. Season to taste with salt and pepper. Mix in onion, green pepper, half the cheddar cheese, bacon bits, and dill weed. Spoon back into the baked shells. Top with remaining cheddar cheese and sprinkle generously with paprika. When ready to serve, pop them back in the oven at 350° until potato mixture is hot and cheese is melted on top.

A small steak, a Twice-Baked Potato, and a light green salad—whatta meal!

Salmon and Cucumber Sandwiches

Ingeborg Agnes Spalding

An English friend gave Ingeborg this recipe.

1	7¾-oz tin salmon, red or pink
1	Tb malt vinegar
¼	tsp pepper
1	cucumber

1	loaf bread, cut into 20 thin slices
½	cup (8 Tb) butter/margarine, softened

Remove bones and skin from salmon. Add vinegar and pepper; beat well with a fork. Peel cucumber and slice very thin.

Take 2 slices of bread and open so that they match evenly. Spread both with butter/margarine. Then spread 1 slice with salmon and layer with cucumber slices. Cover with the second bread slice. Cut off crusts and then cut each sandwich into 4 triangle pieces. (Cutting after the sandwich is assembled seals the edges and seals in the juices.) 40 triangles

To offset "burpiness," one English lady suggests topping each sandwich with a sprig of fresh mint!

Bee Lee's Grilled Shrimp Sandwiches

1   4½-oz can shrimp or 1 cup
    chopped cooked shrimp
1   cup grated sharp cheddar
    cheese
2   green onions and tops,
    chopped
½   cup diced celery
⅓   cup mayonnaise

1   Tb chili sauce
1   tsp horseradish
1   tsp lemon juice
½   tsp salt
⅛   tsp pepper
8   slices bread
    Softened butter

Mix together all ingredients except bread and butter. Spread mixture on 4 slices bread. Top with remaining slices. Spread with butter. Place buttered side down in heavy skillet. Brown. Press down with pancake turner. Turn sandwiches and brown on other side. 4 sandwiches

Shrimp mixture can also be spread on single slices of bread and put under broiler. For canapés, spread on wafers and put under broiler.

Tea Party Sandwich Loaf

Choice of:

1   unsliced round loaf of
    bread, crusts removed
1   unsliced sandwich loaf,
    crusts removed
16 thick slices white or 8 slices
    each of white and dark
    bread, trimmed of crusts
    Butter/margarine, softened
2   8-oz pkgs cream cheese
¼   cup mayonnaise

Garnishes, choice of:
Pimiento strips
Sliced black olives
Chopped Parsley
Sliced pimiento-stuffed olives

Cut whole loaves of bread into 4 even horizontal slices. Spread softened butter/margarine over inside slices only. Lay one layer of bread or 4 slices side by side on a platter. Spread with No. 1 filling of your choice (below). Cover with layer of bread. Spread with No. 2 filling of your choice. Layer with more bread and spread with No. 3 filling of your choice. Top with layer of bread.

Beat cream cheese with enough mayonnaise to spreading consistency. Frost sides and top of loaf. Garnish. Chill until serving time. Cut into 1½-inch slices. Sandwich loaf may be refrigerated (well covered with plastic wrap) for several hours, even overnight, and then frosted a few hours before serving. 8 to 10 servings

Black Olive Nut:

Combine 1 can (4½-oz) chopped black olives, well drained, with 1 pkg (8 oz) softened cream cheese and ½ cup chopped nuts.

Crab meat:

In a blender, place 1 pkg (3 ozs) softened cream cheese; 2 Tb mayonnaise: 3 green onions, chopped, or chopped onion; 1 can (7½-oz) crab meat, drained and sliced. Blend until well mixed.

Egg Salad:

Combine 6 chopped hard-boiled eggs, ½ cup finely chopped celery, ½ cup mayonnaise, 1 Tb chopped pimiento, 1 Tb prepared mustard, and salt and pepper to taste.

Deviled Ham:

To 1 can (4½-oz) deviled ham, add 2 Tb finely chopped green pepper or drained pickle relish and 1 tsp prepared mustard. Mix well.

Tuna:

Blend together ¼ cup mayonnaise, 1 tsp minced onion, and ¼ tsp salt; add 1 can (6½-or 7-oz) tuna, drained and shredded, ¼ cup minced celery, and 2 Tb snipped parsley.

Liver Spread:

Combine 1 can (4½-oz) liver spread and ¼ cup mayonnaise; mix well. Stir in ¼ cup finely chopped black olives.

Chicken Salad:

Combine 2 cups finely diced cooked chicken; ½ cup green grapes (if available), cut in half; ¼ cup coarsely chopped toasted blanched almonds; ¾ cup mayonnaise; 1 Tb grated onion; 1½ tsp. salt and dash of pepper. Mix well.

Ham Salad:

Combine 1 lb ground cooked ham, ½ cup chopped sweet pickle, ½ cup mayonnaise, 1 Tb grated onion, ¼ tsp salt, dash of pepper. Mix well.

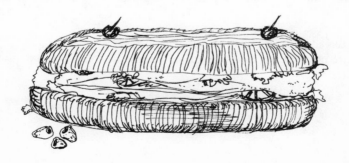

Annie's Cheese Biscuits

So delightful for tea.

2	cups grated cheddar cheese, sharp or extra sharp	½	tsp cayenne pepper
2	cups flour	2	egg yolks
1	cup (2 sticks) butter/margarine, softened		Dash of salt
			Pecan halves
			Paprika

Mix cheese, flour, butter/margarine, and pepper into a soft dough. (No salt is required as cheese and butter allow for it.) Roll thin (¼ inch). Cut into tiny 1¼- to 1½-inch squares and place on cookie sheets.

Beat yolks with salt until very, very frothy. Drop small amount of egg yolk on center of each biscuit. Top with pecan half. Sprinkle with paprika. Bake at 350° for 15 to 20 minutes. 45 medium or 60 *petits* biscuits

Apple Pye

English people relish fruit pies, like blueberry, gooseberry, and "pyes of apples." Dating back to the sixteenth century, tradition is that apples always ripen on St. Swithin's Day.

5 to 7	tart apples*	¼	tsp nutmeg (freshly grated best)
2	Tb flour		
¾ to 1	cup sugar	2	pie crusts (see Mrs. Grider's recipe below)
⅛	tsp salt		
1	tsp cinnamon	2	Tb butter/margarine

Peel apples and slice thin. Mix flour, sugar, salt, and spices. Combine with apples; let stand. Prepare pie crust. Line pie pan with pastry and add apple mixture. Dot with butter/margarine. Cover with top crust; slit top so steam may escape. Bake at 450° about 10 minutes; reduce heat to 375° and bake about 30 minutes longer. 6 to 8 servings.

Delicious served with ice cream or a slice of cheddar cheese on top.
*If apples are not very tart, add 1 teaspoon lemon juice. Grated lemon peel may be added if desired.

Fruit Rocks

Madeline Howard

3	cups sifted flour	½	tsp mace	
7	cups pecans, cut up or chopped (about 35 ozs)	¼	tsp salt	
		1	tsp baking soda	
2½	cups white raisins	2	cups chopped dates, (about 10 ozs)	
1	cup light brown sugar, tightly packed	2	cups diced candied cherries (about 1 lb)	
1	cup (2 sticks) butter/margarine	1	lb candied pineapple, finely diced	
3	eggs			
1	tsp cinnamon	½	oz Cognac (if desired)	

Use 1 cup of the flour to dredge nuts and raisins in an extra large mixing bowl or 8-quart pan. Set aside. Use electric mixer to cream brown sugar and butter/margarine. Add 3 eggs 1 at a time, to mixture. Then add flour, about ½ cup at a time. With a spoon, mix in the cinnamon, mace, salt, baking soda, dates, cherries, pineapple, and Cognac. Pour mixture over the nuts and raisins and mix well with spoon or hands. Drop by the teaspoon on a cookie sheet lined with aluminum foil. Bake at 350° for 15 minutes. Do not over brown. 10 to 12 dozen.

You can use walnuts as well as pecans. Store some candied fruit in your refrigerator (it is a seasonal item). So you can bake them the year around. They're delightful for teatime.

Apple Curranty

Pat White

This is a very old Devonshire dish and has many names. Apple Curranty should be served with thick cream.

4	large cooking apples, peeled and chopped	⅓	cup sugar
¾	lb self-rising flour	¼	tsp salt
½	lb suet, finely chopped or margarine	⅓	cup currants
		⅓	cup raisins
		1	egg, lightly beaten

Put flour into a bowl and blend with suet (margarine), sugar, and salt. Add chopped apples, currants, raisins, and mix together with beaten egg. Add enough extra flour to form consistency of a cake.

Grease a deep dish, put in mixture and bake at 350° for 1 hour. If preferred, put mixture in a greased pudding bowl, cover with wax paper. Place on a rack in a large kettle of boiling water and steam for 2½ hours. 6 to 8 servings

Fresh Blueberry Pie Victoria

4	cups blueberries	1	Tb lemon juice (if desired)
¾	to 1 cup sugar	2	pie crusts (see Mrs. Grider's recipe, below)
4	Tb flour		
½	tsp cinnamon	2	Tb butter/margarine
	Dash grated fresh nutmeg (if desired)		

Mix together sugar, flour, cinnamon, nutmeg, and lemon juice. Lightly toss mixture with the blueberries. Set aside.

Prepare the pie crust. Line pie pan with pastry and add blueberry mixture. Dot with butter/margarine. Cover with top crust; slit top so steam may escape. Bake at 450° for 10 minutes; reduce heat to 375° and bake about 30 minutes longer. 6 to 8 servings

Delicious served with dollop of ice cream on top.

Cherry Pie

Shirley Stein

4	cups pitted tart cherries	2	Tb brown sugar
1	tsp lemon juice	2	pie crusts (see Mrs.
1/2	tsp cinnamon		Grider's recipe, below)
2	tsp cornstarch	2	Tb butter/margarine

Mix lemon juice, cinnamon, cornstarch and brown sugar. Toss mixture with cherries and set aside for at least 15 minutes.

Line bottom of pie pan with one pie crust. Roll out the second pie crust and cut into strips 1/2 inch wide. Add cherry mixture to pan, and arrange strips of crust over it in lattice-work pattern. Moisten edge of bottom crust and seal edges of lattice-work strips to bottom crust. Dot with butter/margarine. Bake at 425° for 55 minutes.

Mrs. Grider's Pie Crust

Emily Grider

Good and rich for dessert pastries and quiche (keesh).

5	cups flour	1	lb shortening or lard
2½	tsp salt	1	egg

With pastry blender or 2 knives, cut shortening (lard) into flour and salt.

Beat 1 egg; place in measuring cup. Add water to make ¾ cup. Sprinkle over flour mixture, a tablespoon at a time, and mix lightly with fork. Press into ball, roll out or keep refrigerated, wrapped in wax paper. 3 or 4 double crusts
Baked Pie Shell:
Roll out dough for one crust. Arrange in pie pan. Crimp the edges. Prick pastry with a fork both sides and bottom to prevent puffing. Bake 450° to 475° for 8 minutes, or until lightly brown.

"Mix-in-Pie-Pan" Pie Shell

Edith Harrison

A sure and easy way to make pie crust when cruising in your boat.

1½	cups flour	¼	tsp cinnamon (for fruit pies)
¼	tsp sugar	½	cup vegetable oil
¼	tsp salt	3	Tb milk or water

Mix flour, sugar, salt, and cinnamon, if required, in pie pan. With a fork, beat together oil and milk (water). Add to the flour mixture and mix well with fork. Pat dough with fingers all over to line pie pan. Bake at 300° for 12 to 14 minutes.

Trifle

A dessert made with custard or pudding, which the Italians adapted and call Zuppa Inglese!

Vanilla Pudding:

1/4	cup sugar	2	cups milk
3	Tb cornstarch	1 1/2	tsp vanilla extract
1/4	tsp salt		

Mix first 3 ingredients together in a saucepan. Gradually stir in the milk and cook over low heat, stirring continuously, until pudding comes to a boil. Blend in the vanilla and set aside.

Pound Cake: see Two Pound Cakes recipe (below)

Filling:

3	bananas, peeled and sliced	2	ozs (or more) brandy or Amaretto
2	cups raspberries		
2	cups strawberries (sliced if large)	1	pt heavy cream, whipped
		1	tsp brandy or vanilla extract
2	cups blueberries		
1/4	cup chopped pecans or walnuts		

Mix fruit and nuts together.

*To assemble:*Slice cake and arrange a layer in a large glass bowl. Top with a layer of fruit-nut mixture and sprinkle with some of the brandy (Amaretto). Continue layers up to nearly top of the bowl. Spread with vanilla pudding, and cover with whipped cream mixed with 1 tsp brandy or vanilla. Chill at least 1 hour. To serve, spoon down through the layers so that each serving includes cake, fruit-nut mixture, pudding, and whipped cream. 10 to 12 servings

Vary it a trifle! Place 1/2-inch slices of pound cake on a platter. Sprinkle generously with brandy or wine. Refrigerate 30 minutes or more. Spread with strawberry or raspberry jam. Cover with second layer of cake. Spread with vanilla pudding and top with a layer of whipped cream. Refrigerate before serving.

Two Pound Cakes

Lois Paulucci

1	lb butter/margarine	4	cups flour	
4	cups sugar	1	tsp baking powder	
10	eggs, at room temperature	1	Tb vanilla extract	

In mixer, beat butter/margarine until fluffy. Add sugar and beat. Add the eggs all at once and beat again. Sift flour with baking powder, then beat in gradually. Add vanilla. Divide batter into two angel food cake pans, lined with wax paper, greased and floured. Bake at 300° for 1 hour, 10 minutes. 2 cakes

IRISH

They were right alongside the Cornish in Upper Peninsula Michigan, the Irish from the salt mines of Ireland. They were a hardy group, experienced miners, who worked well with the Cornish.

For diversion, they liked to fight, and if they could not get the Cornish or the Scandinavians to fight, they fought among themselves. But many an Irishman proudly served on the police force with his *shillelagh*.

They were great entertainers, and when an Irishman belted out" When Irish Eyes Are Smiling," for sure he stole your heart away! They were the people of the shamrock (emblem of Ireland), the four-leaf clover (hope, faith, love, luck), and the Blarney stone. Very sociable, they organized clubs, such as the Literary Society for poetic aspirations, though some claimed that it promoted more alcohol than it did literature.

Irish wakes are legendary. The superstition was that evil spirits would snatch the dead, so the Irish would watch over the body all night long, fortifying themselves with food, spirits, and conviviality. Some wakes lasted two to three days. But what better way to be sure the person was really dead, and to give him a good send-off before putting him in the ground!

The celebration of St. Patrick's Day was traditional on the Iron Range. How we looked forward to seeing who was wearing green that day.

On the Iron Range, we had any number of Irish: Dougherty, Godfrey, Kearney, O'Reilly, and Maloney. But like the Cornish, they turned to other work on the Mesabi Range, as they, too, scoffed at mining iron ore with a steam shovel. They built railroads, became playwrights, politicians, actors, and orators. They were proud of their heritage from the Emerald Isle, the land of potatoes, Irish soda bread, porridge, and whiskey.

Ireland! From the olden days in a thatched cottage with a turf fire in the open hearth, crickets chirping, bastable oven (iron pot), griddle on a trivet, and the dash churn, came the hearty Irish fare, source of rugged health and stamina. Breakfast was oaten porridge—said to put roses in your cheeks and curl your hair—boiled eggs, brown bread, and strong tea. Dinner was a hearty midday meal of soup (to warm the innards on cold, blustery days), potatoes (the daily Irish sustenance), roast meat, greens, and a berry tart. At evening tea, one supped on bacon and eggs, cold meats, salads, and breads (a variety of breads, unleavened, and made with buttermilk and baking soda). Buttermilk was said to be the best antidote for a hangover. Young geese were served on Michaelmas Day, September 29, and the large, matured goose was the customary Christmas dinner. Eggs were fed to everyone, even raw to race horses and greyhounds. Many other foods were traditional: Colcannon and Barmbrach on Hallow's Eve, pancakes on Shrove Tuesday, and plum pudding—you wouldn't dare serve an Irishman Christmas dinner without it!

To the Irish, "beverages" meant anything from hot toddies to soft drinks. But "drink"—that meant stout (Guinness), poteen (an illicit spirit produced in homemade stills in days gone by), and of course, whiskey. Whiskey was drunk straight or with water, but never iced. After all, it was their inner central heating system; it raised the temperature, strengthened, cheered, and even healed when laced with raw garlic cloves. *Sláinte' Gus Saol Agat!* To your health!

Speaking of Irish blarney, do you know what Irish diplomacy is? "The ability to tell a man to go to hell so that he will look forward to making the trip."

Potato Onion Soup Gaelac

After potatoes, onions are the most important cooking ingredient to an Irishwoman.

2	cups thinly sliced onions	1	clove garlic, crushed
3	potatoes, peeled and thinly sliced	1/4	tsp mace
		1/4	tsp thyme
2	Tb butter/margarine	1/2	bay leaf
5	cups chicken stock or milk		Salt and pepper to taste
2	Tb fresh chopped parsley		Chopped chives

Slowly sauté onions and potatoes in melted butter/margarine in a tightly lidded pan until vegetables are soft, but not dried out or browned. Blend in stock (milk); add all other ingredients except chives. Simmer 30 to 40 minutes. Strain soup through a sieve. When ready to serve, reheat, pour into soup cups, and garnish with chopped chives. 6 to 8 servings

Corned Beef and Cabbage

A real Irish dinner fit for the likes of Sullivan, Sheehy, Danahy, O'Brien, Kelly, and Ryan. You can "corn" your own beef, but it's already available corned, beautifully spiced with a number of herbs and seasonings.

3 to 4	lbs corned beef, brisket or round	4	potatoes, peeled and halved
1	cup chopped onion	1	head cabbage, cut into wedges
18	whole peppercorns		Butter
18	whole cloves		Fresh parsley, chopped
1	large turnip, peeled and quartered (if desired)		Horseradish
4	carrots, scraped and cut in half lengthwise (if large)		Prepared mustard

Place corned beef in large covered kettle with water to cover. Bring to a boil and then turn down heat to simmer. Add the onion, peppercorns, and cloves; let simmer about 1 hour.

Add turnip, carrots, and potatoes, and continue simmering about 1 hour more.

To avoid overcooking, keep testing. As vegetables or corned beef are nearly done, remove from pot until all items are nearly ready. Return to pot, add cabbage wedges, and cook about 15 minutes longer.

Slice meat onto a hot platter, surround with vegetables, dot with butter, and sprinkle with parsley. Serve with horseradish and mustard. 4 to 6 servings

Glazed Corned Beef

Joan Feher

3 to 4   lbs corned beef, brisket or
round
2   bay leaves
8   whole peppercorns
2   cloves garlic

Glaze:

½   cup pineapple juice
1   cup dark brown sugar
2   tsp dry mustard

Place corned beef in large covered kettle with water to cover. Bring to a boil. Remove immediately from heat and pour off half the water. Add the seasonings and bring to a boil again. Reduce heat and let simmer for 2 to 3 hours, until meat is fork-tender. Remove beef from water and place in a baking dish.

Blend all ingredients for glaze. Pour over beef. Bake at 400° for 30 to 40 minutes, basting often until browned and glazed. 4 to 6 servings

Scobac Gaelac O'Sullivan

Irish Stew

Authentic Irish Stew was first made from kid (young goat). Then mutton—usually the neck. Now we use any cuts of lamb. Note that real Irish Stew never has carrots in it. Steamed, buttered carrots cut into julienne strips can be served as a side dish.

2   lbs boneless lamb, cubed
6   medium potatoes
2   large onions, sliced

¼   tsp thyme
Salt and pepper

Peel potatoes; slice 2 of the potatoes very thin. Leave the others whole or cut in half, depending on size.

In a greased Dutch oven or large casserole, layer the sliced potatoes on the bottom, then layer with half the sliced onions, and then the cubed lamb. Sprinkle with thyme, salt and pepper to taste. Place remaining onions on top. Cover with the whole potatoes. Season again with salt and pepper. Add 2 cups water. Fit aluminum foil tightly over pot and cover with lid. Bake at 350° about 2½ hours, or until lamb and top potatoes are tender. The bottom sliced potatoes will have "cooked down" to thicken the juice. 4 to 6 servings

Iron Range Lamb Stew

2   lbs boneless lamb or
leftover roast, cubed
3   Tb butter/margarine
¼   cup chopped onion

1   clove garlic, minced
1   cup beef broth or leftover
au jus
¼   tsp rosemary

⅛	tsp thyme	2	potatoes, peeled and cubed
¾	tsp salt	6	small white onions(score
¼	tsp pepper		"x" in root end with knife)
2	carrots, sliced	4	tsp cornstarch

Brown the meat in the melted butter/margarine. Add chopped onion and garlic; cook until onion is soft. Add broth (au jus) and seasonings. Simmer gently until lamb is nearly done. Add the vegetables and cook until meat and vegetables are tender, 30 to 40 minutes. Thicken with cornstarch blended with 4 tablespoons water. 4 to 6 servings

Colcannon

This is a typical Irish dish and at Hallow's Eve you might find a thimble, button, or a coin wrapped in paper in the mixture, denoting spinsterhood, bachelorhood—or wealth.

4	medium potatoes, peeled and halved	1	cup boiled, drained, and chopped cabbage
1	tsp salt	1	Tb butter/margarine, melted
2	Tb butter/margarine		
6	green onions and tops, chopped		Salt and pepper
1 to 1½	cups milk, heated	1	Tb fresh chopped parsley

Cook potatoes in boiling salted water to cover for 20 to 25 minutes until tender, but not mushy. Drain. Shake potatoes in kettle over heat until dry. Mash potatoes with the 2 tablespoons butter/margarine. Mix green onions with heated milk and whip into the potatoes. Toss cabbage with 1 tablespoon melted butter. Blend into the mashed potatoes. Season to taste with salt and pepper. Sprinkle with chopped parsley. 6 to 8 servings

Shortbread

Lourine Messenger

1	cup (2 sticks) butter, softened (*not* margarine)
¼	cup brown sugar
¼	cup granulated sugar
2⅓	cups plain flour

Cream butter and both sugars until fluffy. Add flour and mix well. Knead until the consistency of clay. Press firmly into a 14- x 10- x 2-inch ungreased pan. Prick with fork. Bake at 300° for 30 to 35 minutes, or until golden brown. Cut while still hot into 2- by 5-inch sticks. Cool on wire rack. Store in air tight container. 14 shortbread sticks

Irish Soda Bread

Irish bread baking is the best in Ireland, yet it's the easiest bread to make: leavening is melding baking soda with buttermilk, no rising is needed—just mix and bake. In Ireland, bread was baked either in the bastable oven, an all-purpose lidded iron pot suspended in the open hearth, or on a griddle, much like the crescia in Italy, wherein the flattened dough was baked on an iron plate (griddle) that was placed on a trivet to one side of the hearth with hot coals underneath. The bread was browned on one side, then turned to brown on the other.

4	cups flour	1	Tb butter/margarine, softened
1	tsp baking soda	1	cup buttermilk
1	tsp salt		

Mix flour, baking soda, and salt. With fingers, work in the butter/margarine. Stir in the buttermilk to make a soft dough. Turn onto a floured board and gently knead until ingredients are well blended. Form into a ball and flatten into a circle about 1½ inches thick. Place on a lightly floured cookie sheet. With a floured knife, mark the top into quarters (farls). Bake at 425° about 30 to 35 minutes. The aroma is delectable. And what a thick crunchy crust!

Barmbrack

Years ago it was a tradition in the theatrical world to serve tea and "Gort Cake" (as it was affectionately known then) in the Green Room at the theatre. Barmbrack is the exception to the no-yeast type of Irish baking. It is a fruitcake which is always served buttered. At Hallow's Eve, if your slice of cake had a wedding ring in it, it was wedding bells for you!

4	cups flour	1	packet dry yeast
2	Tb sugar	2	eggs, well beaten (reserve some for glaze)
¼	tsp nutmeg (freshly grated best)	1½	cups seedless white raisins
¼	tsp salt	1	cup currants
2	Tb butter/margarine, softened	⅓	cup candied fruit peel (grapefruit, lemon, or orange)
1¼	cups milk		

Sift together flour, sugar, nutmeg, and salt. With pastry blender or 2 knives, cut butter/margarine into the flour mixture. Heat milk to lukewarm. Dissolve dry yeast in milk. Slowly add beaten eggs to milk. Then beat this mixture into the flour mixture. Batter will be stiff, but elastic. Fold in the raisins, currants, and fruit peel. Put batter in a greased 8-inch cake pan (half full). Cover and let rise until double in size. Brush with reserved beaten egg. Bake at 400° about 1 hour, or until toothpick inserted in middle of cake comes out dry. 10 to 12 servings

Christmas Plum Pudding

To both the Irish and the English, the culmination of Christmas dinner is the serving of Plum Pudding brought to the table aflame with lighted brandy or whiskey! You will understand why once you've treated yourself and yours to it.

½ cup flour	¾ cup white raisins
1½ cups bread crumbs	½ cup candied fruit and peel
1 cup light brown sugar,	mix**
tightly packed	1 cup chopped or slivered
½ tsp salt	walnuts or almonds
½ nutmeg (freshly ground	1 unpeeled apple, cored and
best)	grated
¼ tsp ground cinnamon	1 lime or lemon peel, grated
¼ tsp ground cloves	3 eggs, beaten
¼ tsp mace	½ cup Guinness stout† or ¼
¼ tsp ground ginger	cup brandy
¼ cup suet, finely ground	Juice of 1 lime or lemon
¾ cup currants	Brandy Hard Sauce
¾ cup seedless raisins*	(below)

In a very large bowl, mix flour, bread crumbs, sugar, salt, and spices. Mix in suet with pastry blender or 2 knives. Add currants, both raisins, candied fruit and peel, nuts, apple, and grated lime (lemon) peel. Mix beaten eggs with stout (brandy) and lime (lemon) juice. Blend this into the flour and fruit mixture and mix thoroughly, preferably with the hands, to a soft, moist consistency. Add more stout (brandy) if needed.

Pour into a greased 1-quart mold (a Bundt pan is very good) or coffee can. Cover with wax paper or aluminum foil and place on a rack or trivet in a large kettle of boiling water (or use a large roasting pan with cover). Cover tightly with lid and steam for 5 to 6 hours. Keep boiling water at ¾ level of the mold; replenish as needed.

Remove mold from steamer. Remove wax paper or foil and cover with a dry cloth (Irish linen is nice) to absorb any existing steam.

Unmold on a hot platter, douse with heated brandy or whiskey and some granulated sugar; ignite and serve with Brandy Hard Sauce. 10 to 12 servings

*A plum is a raisin when used in a pudding or cake.

**Old English fruit and peel mix contains grapefruit, lemon, and orange peel; cherry, pineapple, and citron. Buy extra and refrigerate for later use.

† Guinness stout, a dark yeasty ale, is the most popular Irish drink, really a "stout" drink, be gorrah!

If Plum Pudding is not to be served immediately, it can be stored in different ways. Leave the pudding in the mold, covered with cloth or foil, and when cool, refrigerate. Or cool pudding, unmold and wrap in cheese cloth moistened with liquor, then wrap in foil and refrigerate. It can also be frozen after refrigeration. When ready to serve, put back in mold, defrost if necessary, and steam as before for 1 or 2 hours. Always serve hot.

Brandy Hard Sauce:

½ cup (8 Tb) butter/margarine, softened

1 to 1½ cups confectioners sugar, sifted

3 Tb brandy (try a flavored one), Cognac, or Irish whisky

Cream butter/margarine with confectioners sugar until smooth and well blended. Slowly add the liquor to the mixture, being careful not to let it curdle. Chill before serving with Christmas Plum Pudding.

Cafe Gaelac

To the Irish, drinking with friends is a ritual and a pleasure. And what could be more heartwarming than Irish coffee.

Into a warm whiskey glass, pour 1 jigger Irish whiskey. Add strong hot black coffee, to about ¾ full. Stir in plenty of sugar (1½ tsp) until dissolved. Float whipped cream on top or pour heavy cream gently on top over an inverted teaspoon. Delicious—sipping hot whiskey-laced coffee through a layer of rich cream.

GERMAN

German-born Ursula Johannette Bertha Beshere extols the favorite foods of her homeland—sauerkraut, pork roast, wurst (voorrst), potato dumplings, Fleisch Rouladen, sauerbrauten, and red cabbage. And what better "sweet" than Black Forest Cake at coffee time! Beer (bier), quaffed from tankards, the wines, the schnapps of the old country—wunderbar! (voonn-dehr-bar).

We are all familiar with "Ich liebe dich" (ikh lee-buh dikh), "auf wiedersehen" (owf vee-dehr-zay-en), "danke schön" (dahng-kuh shön)—I love you, goodbye, thank you—expressions so beautifully said in German, and which we loved to repeat. How much fun it was to sing along with the oompah-pah of the German bands. Such musik (moo-seek)!

On the Iron Range we heard the names Dietrich, Schmidt, Scheffenacker, Kurtzman, Becker, Drescher, Steffen, and Gourley. We learned from Ursula that in Germany, not only does a child receive a given name, but it is traditional for a firstborn daughter to inherit her maternal and paternal grandmothers' names. The second daughter inherits names of her maternal and paternal great-grandmothers. Boys receive names from their grandfathers in the same manner. What a lovely way to show honor and respect, and to preserve ancestral family names.

The small number of Germans on the Mesabi Iron Range came from the East and from the iron ore ranges of Michigan. They were attracted to the Mesabi Range by the lumber industry. Not many Germans became miners; many set up businesses.

Kraut Perogs

Cabbage Meat Squares

Geneva Hanson

Pastry:

1	packet dry yeast
4	cups flour
1	Tb salad oil
1	Tb sugar
2	tsp salt

Filling:

1½	lbs ground beef
1	medium onion, diced
1	good-sized head of cabbage, shredded
	Salt and pepper

Dissolve dry yeast in ½ cup warm water. Combine with flour, oil, sugar, salt, and an additional 1 cup of warm water. Let rise.

In a greased skillet, fry the meat and the onion until the meat loses its color. Add cabbage, salt and pepper to taste. Cover and simmer until the cabbage is done—about 15 minutes. Cool before putting into the squares of dough.

Roll out and cut the dough into 3-inch squares. Put the filling in between 2 squares and pinch the edges together. Bake in a greased oblong pan at 375° until well browned. 12 or more meat squares

Old-Fashioned Boiled Dinner

A good supper made from leftover baked ham!

2 to 3	lbs smoked ham with bone
5	whole cloves
1	cup diced potatoes
1	cup sliced carrots

½	cup diced rutabagas
1	medium cabbage, cut into wedges
	Salt and pepper

In a 4-quart kettle, cover ham and cloves with cold water. Bring to a boil. Skim off foam as it forms. Reduce to simmer and continue cooking slowly 2 to 3 hours, or until ham is very well done in a reduced rich broth. Strain. Shred the ham and return to broth. Bring to a boil, add any or all of the vegetables, and steam, covered, until vegetables are done. Season with salt and pepper to taste. Serve in soup dishes with chunks of crusty bread. 4 to 6 servings

Ursula's Sauerkraut

Ursula Beshere

How warm and good your kitchen feels with the robust aroma of sauerkraut cooking in its juices, with bacon and onions and wine. My mother's curiosity about sauerkraut got the best of her one time. She opened a can of sauerkraut and the pungency that surprised her nostrils prompted her to throw the whole thing away!

½ cup chopped bacon or 3 Tb
  bacon fat
1 cup chopped onion
1 2-lb pouch sauerkraut
  (canned may be used)
1 cup dry white wine
  (Chablis or champagne)

1 cup chicken broth
1 bay leaf
  Salt and pepper
  Wurst (sausage)
  Boiled potatoes

Render bacon (melt fat) in a large kettle. Add onion and sauté until soft. Add the sauerkraut, wine, broth, bay leaf, and bring to a boil. Then let simmer, uncovered, for about 1 hour. Add more wine or broth if needed. Season to taste with salt and pepper. Easy on the salt!

Continue cooking until juice is cooked down and sauerkraut is tender.

Serve with boiled potatoes (cooked in their jackets) and/or cooked wurst. *Gut appetit!* 4 to 6 servings

Jean's Sauerkraut

Jean Kleffman Clauser

My friend Marsiella out in Wyoming tested this recipe for me. Kraut connoisseurs in her family weren't sure they would like this recipe. Instead they were delighted! Except they found it to be a little sweet. Sweet? Well, no wonder. Not having any dry white wine, she had added a little kosher sweet wine?!

1 medium onion, finely
  chopped
1 medium apple, finely
  chopped.
3 Tb butter/margarine

1 28-oz can sauerkraut,
  drained
2 Tb brown sugar
1 cup dry white wine
  (Chablis)

Sauté onion and apple in butter/margarine until golden. Add the sauerkraut; sprinkle with brown sugar. Add the wine and ½ cup water. Simmer for 1 hour. 4 to 6 servings

Fish Batter Siegfred

Makes a puffy batter to deep fry any kind of fish fillets.

2	egg yolks	½	tsp garlic salt
¾	cup beer	¼	tsp pepper
1	cup flour	2	egg whites

Beat egg yolks until lemon color. Stir in beer, flour, garlic salt, and pepper. Mix until smooth. Beat egg whites until stiff (moist peaks). Fold into the batter. 2 cups batter (sufficient for 2 lbs. fillets)

Fleisch Rolladen

(flysh row-lah-den)

Stuffed Beef Rolls

1½ to 2	lbs boneless beef, sliced ⅛ inch thick (10 to 12 slices)	¼ to ½	cup vegetable or corn oil
	Yellow prepared mustard or Dijon	3	to 4 cups beef bouillon or broth
	Salt and pepper		Raw sliced mushrooms (if desired)
1	cup chopped onion	4	tsp cornstarch
1	cup chopped bacon (6 to 8 slices)		Cooked rice or boiled potatoes
1	cup chopped dill pickle		
	Flour		

Spread mustard on each slice of beef. Sprinkle lightly with salt and pepper and stack on a plate to marinate. Meanwhile, chop onion, bacon, and dill pickle—all the same size—and mix together. Place small amount of mixture on each slice of beef. Roll, tucking in the ends, and secure with a toothpick. Keep small amount of the mixture for the gravy. Dredge roulades in flour; tap off excess flour. Brown on all sides in hot oil, using tongs to turn. Pour off excess fat in pan. Add rest of the mixture. Pour beef bouillon (broth) to cover roulades. Simmer gently, uncovered, until meat is tender (1½ to 2 hours). If liquid gets low, add water or bouillon. Thicken gravy with cornstarch blended with 4 tablespoons water if desired. Serve over rice or potatoes. Raw sliced mushrooms can be added the last few minutes of cooking. 4 to 6 servings

Pork Roast

Marsiella Greenfield

3 to 4 lbs center cut loin
½ large onion
2 to 3 potatoes

4 to 6 carrots
Salt and pepper

Season loin with salt and pepper on all sides. Brown slowly on all sides, starting with fat side, in a roaster on top of stove. (May take 30 minutes.) With fat side up, skewer the onion half on top. Cover and place roast in 325° oven. Wash and peel potatoes and carrots and set aside in bowl of salted ice water. The last hour of roasting, add cut up potatoes and carrots. Turn vegetables after 30 minutes. Bake pork 35 to 40 minutes per pound. Remove roast to a warm platter. Drain off excess fat. Pick up "brownings" with dry white wine or water to make gravy. 4 to 6 servings

Any leftover meat and vegetables make a delectable soufflé! Or, bone off meat; put bones and trimmings in pot with leftover gravy and vegetables. Cover with cold water and simmer 30 to 40 minutes. Strain. Makes additional stock for more gravy to serve over sliced meat.

Wiener Schnitzel

Ingeborg Agnes Spalding

Ingeborg Agnes Eppenauer came to this country from Munich (Munchen) as a bride. Her family enjoys the German dishes she learned to prepare years ago.

4 6-oz boneless veal or pork
   cutlets
½ tsp salt
¼ tsp pepper
½ cup flour

1 egg, beaten
1 cup bread crumbs
6 Tb butter/margarine
Parsley sprigs
Lemon wedges

Pound meat very thin between sheets of wax paper. Sprinkle with salt and pepper. Dip lightly in flour, then in beaten egg, then in bread crumbs. Sauté over low heat in melted butter/margarine until golden and tender. Remove cutlets to a warm serving platter and keep hot until ready to serve. Garnish with parsley sprigs and lemon wedges. 4 servings

This is like Costoletta alla Milanese, except the Italians use loin chops.

Coleslaw

Florence Trepanier

The Holland Dutch called it "koolslaa" back in 1624.

2 to 3	cups shredded cabbage	½	cup mayonnaise
¼	cup sliced green pepper (thin strips)	1	Tb lemon juice or wine vinegar
1	green onion and top, chopped	1	Tb sugar (if desired)
½	carrot, shredded or grated	1	tsp salt
		½	tsp pepper

Combine vegetables. Combine mayonnaise with remaining ingredients and mix into the vegetables until well blended. Refrigerate at least 1 hour to marinate. 4 to 6 servings

Variations:

Use ½ tablespoon lemon juice and ½ tablespoon white or wine vinegar. Add 1 teaspoon prepared mustard.

Kartoffelsalat

Hot Bavarian Salad

Ingeborg Agnes Spalding

1	lb potatoes	¼	cup oil
1	medium onion, diced	1	tsp salt
¼	cup cider vinegar or wine vinegar	¼	tsp pepper

Boil potatoes in their jackets in salted boiling water. Let cool slightly, and peel while still hot. Cut in thin slices. Add onion, vinegar, oil, salt and pepper, and ½ cup boiling water. Toss very gently. Adjust seasonings to taste. 4 to 6 servings

This salad is also served in the mountains of Austria. Add bacon bits and you have the Berlin version.

Potato Pancakes

4	raw potatoes, peeled and shredded	1	Tb light cream (if desired)
	Salt	¼	tsp ground nutmeg
4	Tb flour	½	tsp pepper
1	egg, beaten	2	Tb butter/margarine
		1	Tb corn oil

Sprinkle potatoes lightly with salt; mix well and refrigerate for 5 to 10 minutes. By hand, press out all water from potatoes. Sprinkle lightly with flour; add egg, cream, nutmeg, and pepper. Mix well. May refrigerate at this point until ready to fry.

Form potato mixture into small, thin patties. Fry in hot butter and oil until golden on one side, then flip to brown other side. Drain on paper towel. Serve hot. 4 servings

Rösti Emil

4 potatoes
Salt and pepper
¼ cup (4 Tb)

butter/margarine or bacon
fat

Boil potatoes in their jackets. Remove and let stand until cool, then peel and dry on paper towel. Grate potatoes and season with salt and pepper to taste. Sauté in butter/margarine (bacon fat) until brown; do not stir. Put additional butter in a baking pan and flip potatoes into it. Bake at 400° for 5 to 10 minutes. 4 to 6 servings

Beer Bread

Pat Mestek

Delicious for snacking with cheese, salami, and sausage.

3 cups self-rising flour
1 12-oz can warm beer
2 Tb honey

Mix ingredients together until well blended. Pour into a greased loaf pan. Bake at 375° for 30 to 40 minutes, or until brown. 1 loaf

To make small round loaves for cocktail-size slices, use 2 or 3 empty soup cans (10¾-oz size). With 1 lid removed, grease cans, fill ⅔ full with batter, and bake, standing cans upright in oven.

Carrot-Pineapple Bundt Cake

Judy Goethals

3 cups sifted cake flour
2 cups sugar
2 tsp cinnamon
1½ tsp baking soda
1½ tsp salt
1 tsp baking powder
1 8¾-oz can crushed
pineapple

3 eggs, beaten
1½ cups vegetable oil
2 tsp vanilla extract
2 cups grated and loosely
packed raw carrots
1½ cups finely chopped nuts
Cream cheese

Grease and lightly flour Bundt pan. Mix together cake flour, sugar, cinnamon, baking soda, salt, and baking powder. Drain pineapple, saving syrup. Add pineapple syrup to dry mixture; add eggs, oil, and vanilla. Beat for 3 minutes. Stir in pineapple, carrots, and nuts. Bake at 325° for about 1½ hours. Cool 10 minutes in pan before unmolding. Frost with softened cream cheese. 10 to 12 servings

Husarenkrapferl

Hussar Doughnuts

Ingeborg Agnes Spalding

2½   ozs sugar (approx. ½ cup)
6½   ozs flour (approx. 1⅔ cups)
     Grated lemon peel
5   ozs (10 Tb)
     butter/margarine
1   egg yolk
1   egg, beaten
     Chopped almonds (if
     desired)
     Jam (raspberry is best)
     Confectioners sugar (if
     desired)

Sift together sugar and flour; add lemon peel. With a pastry blender or 2 knives, cut butter/margarine into dry ingredients: Add the egg yolk and knead to a smooth dough. Shape into a ball: chill for 20 to 30 minutes.

Pinch small lumps off the dough and roll into balls between palms of your hands. Place balls on a buttered and floured cookie sheet. With the handle of a wooden mixing spoon (dipped into flour from time to time), make a dent in the center of each ball. Brush with beaten egg. A few chopped almonds sprinkled over the pastry enhances the flavor. Bake at 370° for 10 to 12 minutes, or until golden brown. Remove from cookie sheet while still warm and put small dab of jam in center of each. Dust with confectioners sugar. 1 dozen doughnuts

Schwarzwalder Black Forest Torte

A rich chocolate cake with cherries from the scenic Black Forest along the Rhine River and with kirsch, distilled from the cherries.

2	15- to 16-oz cans pitted tart cherries, drained	2	cups heavy cream
1/3	cup kirsch (cherry brandy)	1/2	cup confectioners sugar
1	pkg chocolate cake mix for 2-layer cake	2	Tb kirsch
3	sqs semi-sweet chocolate	12	maraschino cherries, well drained

Place tart cherries in bowl; cover with the 1/3 cup kirsch. Let marinate for about 4 hours at room temperature; stir occasionally. Prepare cake mix according to label instructions, except pour batter into 3 round greased and floured cake pans. Stagger pans on 2 racks in oven. Bake at 350° for 20 to 25 minutes, or until toothpick inserted in center comes out dry. Cool layers on racks 10 minutes. Remove from pans and cool for 2 hours so they are completely cooled. Prepare chocolate curls and grated chocolate for garnish.

In slightly warm oven or Microwave, soften 2 chocolate squares. With vegetable peeler, shave chocolate into curls. Grate the remaining square of chocolate. Set aside in a cool place, but not in refrigerator. Using a fork, prick all over the top of each cake. Drain cherries well; reserve the kirsch liquid. Sprinkle the liquid over the cake layers. In a small bowl, beat at medium speed the heavy cream, combined with the confectioners sugar and 2 tablespoons kirsch.

To assemble: place one cake layer on a cake plate. Spread with 1/4 of the whipped cream mixture. Top with 1/2 of the tart cherries. Place second cake layer on top and spread with 1/4 of the whipped cream mixture and balance of tart cherries. Top with third cake layer. Frost sides of cake with half of remaining whipped cream mixture. Gently press grated chocolate onto the cream. Use rest of cream mixture to form 12 dollops around the rim of the top layer. Garnish each dollop with a maraschino cherry. Pile chocolate curls in center. Refrigerate. 10 to 12 servings

SCANDINAVIAN

They may be classified as Scandinavians, but a Norwegian is a Norwegian, a Swede is a Swede. There is no lumping them together you will discover, as I did when I once called a very dear friend a Swede. She let me know in no uncertain terms that she was Norwegian, although she did finally admit that on her father's side she had a little Swede in her!

They emigrated from Norway and Sweden to the beautiful wooded areas of Michigan, Wisconsin, and Minnesota, primarily because of the similarity to their homeland. There was good fishing and farming, as well as the iron ore and lumber industries.

The Ericksons, Pedersons, Petersons, Nelsons, Swansons, Andersons, Sundquists, Lundeens, and Hegstadts followed the Cornish, Irish, and Germans to the iron ore mines in Upper Peninsula Michigan in the 1880s. To the Cornish and Irish old-timers, the Scandinavians were "damned furriners." From Michigan they migrated to the mining areas in Minnesota, where many turned to farming and to skilled trades like carpentry, plumbing, and masonry.

They are the people of two tables. The smörgåsbord table is laden in a special order according to centuries of tradition: the herrings, spiced, fried, and pickled; then fish, either salmon or eel; then cold meats and salads, with plenty of sweet pickles and onions. Hot dishes are next, with croquettes, omelets, and meatballs. Finally, lingonberries and hot coffee for dessert.

The second table is a "smörgåsbord" of cakes and cookies served with cups of sweet and creamy coffee. Coffee is taken at all hours of the day and night. In Norway and Sweden, coffee houses are filled with people for coffee breaks at ten in the morning and at four in the afternoon.

Christmas to the Norwegians is lutefisk, lingonberries, and lefse, served with potatoes, melted butter, and cream sauce. Lutefisk and lefse dinners are still served as major church fund-raising events.

Potato dumplings, which go by various names in Scandinavian countries, is a good, heavy food for the long winter evenings. They are made with grated raw potatoes mixed with flour, with side pork hidden in the middle. After a hearty meal of such dumplings, you feel like rolling on the floor.

Aquavit, distilled from grain or potatoes and flavored with caraway seeds, is the Scandinavian answer to Irish whiskey. Icy aquavit, usually served in a cordial-type glass, is raised with a courteous nod to a friend and, with a hearty "Skoal," it is drained in one gulp. What better way of saying happy birthday than in the lilting Swedish "Har den äran på födelsedagen" (hawr-den-AIR-ahn-poh-FO-dell-seh-dawg-en), with a shot of this "water of life."

Norwegian Church Group Dinner

Recently a Norwegian church group on the Iron Range netted $1,500 in a fund-raising dinner.

The grocery list for serving five hundred people at this Lutefisk and Lefse Dinner included:

225	lbs lutefisk	13	large cans green beans
70	lbs ground beef	40	dz rolls
12½	lbs onions	75	pies
16	loaves bread (1½ lb size)	6	lbs coffee
8	dz eggs	700	sheets lefse
3	cans allspice	19	lbs margarine
5	lbs salt	9	lbs butter
½	lb pepper	10	lbs sugar
15	lbs flour for gravy	2	qts cream
1	jar kitchen bouquet	10	qts pickles
1	jar beef bouillon	10	lbs cranberries (for sauce)
160	lbs potatoes	5	qts jam and jelly

Frukt Soppa Svensk

(fruhcht sohp-ah)

As fruits were picked, they were either dried or preserved for the long winter months ahead. A favorite dish made from dried fruits was fruit soup, enjoyed either hot or cold with cod, rye bread, or cheeses. Use any combination of dried fruits you wish, such as: raisins, pitted prunes, apricots, apples, currants, pears, peaches.

1½	cups grape juice*	3	lemon slices
1½	cups orange juice*	1	stick cinnamon
½	cup sugar (or more)	4	whole cloves (if desired)
¼	tsp salt	1 to 2	Tb tapioca (if desired)
2	cups dried fruits		Brandy (if desired)

Combine all ingredients except brandy in a saucepan. Bring to a boil, then simmer gently until fruits are soft, 35 to 40 minutes. Remove cinnamon stick, cloves, and lemon slices. Add a dash of brandy. 4 to 6 servings
*3 cups water may be substituted for the juices.

Sodt Suppe Norsk

Lillie Nelson

This is an old family recipe. Marsiella's mother Lillie served this fruit soup very often.

½	cup sugar	½	tsp salt
3	Tb tapioca		Few drops red food coloring (if desired)
1	cup partially cooked pitted prunes	2	preserved pears, drained and cut up (if desired)
½	cup raisins	2	preserved peaches, drained and cut up (if desired)
1	apple, cut up		
½	orange, cut in half		
½	lemon, cut in half		
2	small or 1 large cinnamon stick		

With 5 cups cold water, combine all ingredients except salt, food coloring, and preserved fruit. Bring to a boil and cook 30 minutes, stirring often. Add the salt and food coloring, if used. Then preserved pears and peaches may be added. Serve either warm or cold. 4 to 6 servings

Potato Balls

Marsiella Greenfield

This recipe was handed down from Marsiella's mother, Lillie Nelson, who came from Norway.

Put a pork shank on to cook for an hour in a large kettle with plenty of water.

Grate potatoes into a large bowl. Stir in just enough flour so you can form into soft balls.

Dice salt pork, or side pork salted by hand, into small cubes.

Work near kettle on the stove and have a pan of cold water handy for dipping your hands between making each ball. Pick up enough potato mixture to hold in your hand. Insert cube of salt pork and then roll it from hand to hand, then drop ball slowly into the kettle of simmering shank. Dip hands in water and continue procedure. Cover kettle and let simmer for about an hour.

This is a hearty winter food. Any leftovers can be fried. The Swedish make potato balls using ham.

Lutefisk

Gunhild Elmquist

Traditionally fish was served as a fasting dish on Christmas Eve. For the Italians it was Merluzzo; for the Scandinavians, Lutefisk.

The processing of lutefisk was a long one. Sun-dried cod was soaked in a solution of washing soda, lye, or slaked lime for at least two weeks before cooking. Now it is available, frozen and ready to cook. Sometimes lutefisk can be purchased sealed in a plastic cooking pouch.

Simply soak lutefisk in cold water for one or two hours, drain, and tie it in a cheesecloth bag or pouch.

To boil: Put fish in a kettle of cold water with 1 tsp salt. When water has come to a full boil, fish is done.

To bake: Place foil-wrapped fish in a roasting pan, cover, and bake at 400° for 15 to 20 minutes.

Serve lutefisk with plenty of melted butter, or a cream sauce, and boiled potatoes.
In Norwegian it's Glaedelig Jul and the Swedes say God Jul.

Kunglig Kött Bollen Svensk
Royal Swedish Meatballs

2	lbs ground round steak	2½	tsp salt	
1	lb ground pork	½	tsp pepper	
2	eggs, beaten	½	tsp *each*: ground nutmeg,	
1	cup mashed potatoes		cloves, allspice, ginger	
1	cup bread crumbs	2	cups light cream	
1	cup milk		Flour	
1	Tb brown sugar		Oil	

Mix together all ingredients except cream, flour, and oil. Form into small, walnut-size balls. Roll in flour. In hot oil, brown the meatballs, one batch at a time. Put meatballs in a casserole. Pour cream over. Bake at 325° about 30 minutes. 6 to 8 servings

Bollen Norsk

Margurite Oslund

This recipe will serve approximately twenty-five people.

Meatballs:

6	lbs ground beef
1	large loaf bread (torn into small pieces)
2	cups finely diced or grated onions
2	Tb salt
1	Tb allspice
1 to 2	tsp pepper
6	eggs

Gravy:

2	envelopes dehydrated onion soup
⅓ to ½	cup drippings from meat, or margarine
1	cup flour (approximately)
2	cups canned milk

Mix meatball ingredients together thoroughly, adding water until able to handle easily (use your hands to mix). Shape into small meatballs. Arrange close together on large baking pans (jellyroll-type works fine). Bake at 375° for 15 to 20 minutes until slightly brown. Pour off any drippings and use for gravy, if not too fat. Transfer meatballs to a large roaster or deep pans.

Mix and cook gravy ingredients together, using small amount of water to make correct gravy consistency. Pour over meatballs and heat thoroughly in oven.
These are nice to serve at a big party; place in a chafing dish to keep them nice and hot.

Skinka Bollen Svensk

Swedish Ham Balls

1½ lbs ground pork
1 lb ground ham
2 eggs, beaten
2 cups bread crumbs
1 cup milk

Butter
1 cup brown sugar
½ cup cider vinegar
1 tsp dry mustard

Mix together meats, eggs, bread crumbs, and milk. Form into small balls and place in lightly buttered casserole. Stir sugar, vinegar, and mustard together with ½ cup water until sugar is dissolved. Pour over meatballs. Bake at 325° for 1 hour. Baste meatballs every 15 minutes. 6 to 8 servings

Candle Salad Norsk

According to the Norwegians, the serving of a Candle Salad was a family tradition. It was usually served at Christmas time.

Lettuce leaves
Pineapple slices
Bananas, peeled and halved
Mayonnaise (can be blended with peanut butter, if desired)
Maraschino cherries, halved
Green pepper, sliced in rings

On a lettuce leaf build up a candle by placing a pineapple ring on the lettuce, then stand a banana chunk in the hole of the pineapple slice. Dab mayonnaise on top of and alongside of the banana to simulate melting wax. Use piece of green pepper ring for candlestick handle. Place a maraschino half atop banana for the "flame."

Lefse

Inger Kaldestad

Lefse is a thin, flat bread baked on top of the stove on an ungreased griddle, cast iron frying pan, or in a modern electric frypan. Long sticks carved like a baton were used to turn them over easily. Lefse are best made from leftover mashed potatoes.

Just add flour to the mashed potatoes, a little at a time, keeping the dough soft. Roll a small ball of the dough paper-thin. Lift it with a knife or lefse stick to the pan and bake at moderate heat. Then turn and bake on the other side. Remove each one to a cloth, and cover.

In the olden days, Lillie Nelson used to polish the top of her wood stove and bake the lefse right on it.

To serve, lay lefse flat, butter it, sprinkle with sugar and cinnamon, or use jam. Then roll it up in the shape of an ice cream cone. *Bra aptit!*

74

Berlinerkranz

Marion Carlson

Scandinavians pride themselves on making the most delicate, rich, buttery cookies. This cookie is a Christmas treat.

1 cup (2 sticks) butter, softened	½ tsp baking powder
½ cup sugar	10 cardamom seeds, shelled and finely crushed
2 cooked egg yolks, mashed	2 raw egg whites, slightly beaten
2 raw egg yolks	Granulated sugar
2 cups flour	

Cream butter and ½ cup sugar. Mix the mashed and raw yolks together and add to creamed mixture. Stir in flour, baking powder, and cardamom. Take a small piece of dough and roll in the shape of a pencil. Cut in lengths of about 4 inches, and form into wreaths. Dip the top in egg white and then in granulated sugar. Place on cookie sheet. Bake at 350° about 8 minutes. 3 to 4 dozen

Krum Kaka

(krum kay-kay)

Marion Carlson

An international favorite known as Scandinavian Krum Kaka, Italian Pizzelle, French Crêpes, and Austrian Oblaten.

3 eggs	½ cup (8 Tb) butter, melted
1 cup sugar	½ tsp ground nutmeg
½ cup heavy cream, whipped	1½ cups flour

Beat eggs; add sugar, whipped cream, butter, nutmeg, and flour. Bake on a Krum Kaka iron.

This iron has two patterned plates hinged together and rests on a ring that is placed on the burner. Heat both plates until a drop of water sizzles. Drop a teaspoon of batter on the center of the bottom plate, lower top plate. Bake a few minutes, turning the iron once. Remove Krum Kaka with a spatula and roll up while still warm. A wooden roller, shaped like a long Christmas tree with a curved handle is available to make perfect cones.

Krum Kaka can be eaten plain or filled with whipped cream, lingonberries, ice cream, or preserves. Krum Kaka can be dried flat. Stack and store in an airtight container in refrigerator or in freezer. 3 to 4 dozen

Peppar Kakor

Marion Carlson

1 cup sugar
1 cup (2 sticks) butter, softened, or shortening
1 cup molasses
1 tsp ground cloves

1 tsp ground cinnamon
2 tsp baking soda in a little boiling water
4 cups flour (or more)
Almond halves or slivers

Cream sugar and butter (shortening). Add molasses, spices, baking soda mixture, and 2 tablespoons cold water; mix together. Add flour and knead into a dough. Chill.

Roll dough very thin, cut with round cookie cutter. Top each with almond half (slivers). Bake at 375° about 8 to 10 minutes. 4 to 6 dozen

Rosettes Svensk

Inga Bjorge

These are Swedish lacy fried pastries, made with a special device. Forms, about 3 inches in diameter and ¾ of an inch deep, are shaped like rosettes, hearts, circles, or stars and are attached to a metal wand with a wooden handle.

1 cup milk
1 cup flour
1 Tb sugar
¼ tsp salt

1 tsp lemon or vanilla extract
2 eggs, slightly beaten
Vegetable oil
Confectioners sugar

Blend first 5 ingredients into the beaten eggs. Beat until smooth. Attach a form of your choice to the wand. Pour oil into a large pan deep enough to immerse rosettes. Heat oil to 375°. Heat form by dipping it in oil; remove and drain on paper towel. Then dip heated form into batter, but not quite to the top of the form. Quick fry in hot oil about 1 or 2 minutes, or until delicately golden and crisp. With fork tines, loosen rosette from form and drain on paper towel. Continue dipping procedure until all batter is used up. Dust cooled pastries with confectioners sugar. 3 to 4 dozen

Spritz

Marion Carlson

1	cup (2 sticks) butter, softened	3	egg yolks
⅔	cup sugar	3	cups flour
		1	tsp almond extract

Cream butter and sugar. Add egg yolks. Gradually add flour and almond extract. Put through a cookie press. Bake on cookie sheet at 400° for 8 to 10 minutes. 6 dozen

A cookie press is an elongated cylinder. Put dough in at the top, turn handle and dough is pressed through patterned discs and onto a cookie sheet. The discs are usually star and circle shapes.

Apple Crisp

Marsiella Greenfield

4	cups chopped or diced apples	¾	cup flour
½	tsp salt	1	tsp cinnamon
1	cup sugar	½	cup (8 Tb) butter, softened

Put apples into a shallow buttered pan; sprinkle with salt. Mix sugar, flour, and cinnamon and cut into the butter until crumbly. Spread over apples. Bake, uncovered, at 350° for 40 minutes. 4 to 6 servings

Green Grapes Delight

Berta Hall

A tasty, cool, crunchy complement for meat or fowl. It is also a delightful dessert that is often served at weddings in Minnesota.

1½	lbs seedless green grapes (in season)	1	cup sour cream
		2	Tb brown sugar

Wash and clean grapes; chill thoroughly. Blend cream and brown sugar; mix with the grapes. 8 servings

Lingonberries

Sigrid Nelson

A low creeping shrub of the heath family bears these dark red berries. Similar to the cranberry, the lingonberry is more transparent and sweeter. Years ago, lingonberries were sold ready-cooked from a keg. They would be scooped into ice cream containers as they used to do with oysters. They are usually found in jars nowadays in specialty shops. If found fresh, they can be cooked just like cranberries.

Heavenly Rice

Marsiella Greenfield

A real old favorite!

2 cups cooked rice
2 cups diced or chunk pineapple, drained
½ cup sugar
1 tsp vanilla extract
½ tsp lemon extract

½ cup miniature marshmallows
10 maraschino cherries, halved
1 cup whipped cream
Almond slivers (if desired)

Heat pineapple and sugar until sugar is dissolved. Stir well and cool. Add rice, extracts, marshmallows, and cherries to cooled mixture. Fold in whipped cream. Chill. Serve with sprinkled almond slivers if desired. 4 to 6 servings

Oatmeal Cake

Lois Paulucci

"Thought you might want this cake recipe. We got it from Kettle Falls, Minnesota, and we just love it." We do, too, Lois.

1 cup quick (instant) oatmeal
½ cup (8 Tb) butter/margarine, softened
1 cup brown sugar
1 cup granulated sugar
2 eggs, at room temperature
1 tsp cinnamon
1 tsp baking soda
½ tsp salt
1½ cups flour

Frosting:

10 Tb brown sugar
6 Tb butter/margarine
4 Tb cream
1 cup shredded coconut

Pour 1½ cups hot water over oatmeal and let stand. Cream butter/margarine with the sugars. Add the eggs and beat well. Mix in the cinnamon, baking soda, and salt. Add the flour and mix well. Beat in the oatmeal until well mixed. Bake in 13- x 9- x 2-inch oiled pan at 350° for 40 to 45 minutes.

Mix frosting ingredients together and bring to a boil; continue to boil until syrup turns brown. Pour immediately over hot cake. 10 to 12 servings

Rhubarb Pie

Lori Paulucci

My first encounter with this domestic pieplant was for breakfast. When I taught school in Parkers Prairie, Minnesota, my landlady Mrs. Berquist would stand over me to see that I finished every bit of my rhubarb sauce. It was good for me, all ninety-eight pounds of me!

3 cups rhubarb, peeled and cut into 1-inch pieces*	6 Tb flour
1 cup strawberries*	2 unbaked pie crusts
1⅓ to 2 cups sugar (depending on tartness of rhubarb)	1⅓ Tb margarine
	Granulated sugar

Mix fruit, sugar, and flour together. Pour into formed pie shell, but do not pile too high. Dot with margarine. Top with second crust; seal edges and make slits on top. Sprinkle with granulated sugar. Bake at 400° for 40 to 50 minutes, or until nicely browned. 6 to 8 servings

*2 cups *each* of rhubarb and strawberries may be used. If rhubarb stalks are tender and pink, do not peel.

Pie Crust Mix

Gerri Patnode

Gerri says that this mixture is good for at least five double pie crusts. Keeps for up to one year in a tightly covered container. It's nice to have the crust already mixed.

6 cups flour	1 lb lard
1 Tb salt	

Sift flour and salt into a bowl. Cut in the lard. For a double crust, use 2 cups of the mixture with 5 tablespoons cold water. Do not add water to the mixture until you are ready to make the crusts. Store dry mixture in your cupboard.

Egg Coffee

Scandinavians love their coffee. The pot was always sitting at the back of the wood stove for mid-morning or mid-afternoon, for meals, for anytime "kaffee klatsches."

And, whether you were Norwegian or Swedish (but don't you dare get the two mixed up) coffee was sometimes savoured by sipping it through a sugar loaf or cube held in the mouth. It was instant dessert for Inger Kaldestad and Marsiella Nelson.

Where today there is Mrs. Olson with her mountain-grown coffee, we had our Mrs. Nelsons with their egg coffee.

Lillie Nelson, Norwegian, would stir one whole egg into the measured coffee (pinch of salt, too) and then cook the coffee in an old-fashioned coffee pot (no percolators) filled with cold water. Sally Nelson, Swedish, uses just the egg white with a pinch of salt. The egg was to settle the coffee grounds to the bottom of the pot. Egg coffee is a delicate clear brew.

I remember egg coffee on one occasion when it was my turn to have the Sewing Club meeting and social. For a couple of hours, it was sewing and chatting (I always did my nails!), and then we would have the "fellas" join us for coffee and cake. My landlady had a huge kettle in which I started to make the egg coffee. Imagine my embarrassment when my guests sniffed a waft of boiling coffee coming from the kitchen—with a lutefisk aroma! My landlady had just cooked lutefisk in that pot. Needless to say, that pot of fishy-smelling coffee was dumped into a snow bank in the backyard.

FRENCH

From the province of Normandy, France, in the 1600s, French settlers came to form the French Colony of Acadia, located along the Atlantic Coast of Nova Scotia, Canada. They hunted and fished and turned the meadows into productive farms.

However, as a result of the French and English wars, Acadia became English in 1713. The French were forcibly deported from their homes; their villages were destroyed by orders of the English Monarchy. Such sadness, such disorder and tumult, as his Majesty's soldiers loaded the evicted onto freighters to banish them from Acadia. Families were separated, never to meet again. Longfellow relates the sad tale of the betrothed Evangeline and Gabriel, who were separated and spent the rest of their lives looking for each other.

The Acadians were scattered over Canada and the entire United States. One group made its way down the Mississippi River to Louisiana, where they became known as the Cajuns.

Up north, they became the Voyageurs, transporting men and supplies between trading posts. They were great woodsmen and navigators.

The Canadian French, who followed the Cornish, Irish, and Germans to the iron ore mines in Michigan and Minnesota, worked on the surface as lumberjacks, making mine timbers and driving the horse teams. In their checkered mackinaws and tasseled caps, one wonders whether the fabled Paul Bunyan with his Blue Ox wasn't one of them! Not so long ago, it was our pleasure to again visit the homeland of the French who emigrated to our land via Canada, and to sample their country food.

On the French Riviera, we visited Nice, known for its pizza "palaces" serving *glaces* (ice creams) boissons (beverages), and fourteen varieties of pizza. We would have liked to visit the open market where pizzas are sold from a cart much like our hot dog or hot bagel carts. However, it was Sunday, so instead, we went to Monte Carlo, where we gambled a few francs at the Royal Casino.

The next day we were in Marseille, the great seaport and the second largest city of the Province of Provence in France. Marseille is synonymous with Bouillabaisse (fish stew). We stopped there for lunch, but since Bouillabaisse takes hours to prepare, we settled for soupe de poissons, which is a clear bouillon with a mélange of fishes and condiments that is strained and served with plenty of saffron and sometimes vermicelli.

We drove through Montpelier and Beziers, arriving at the oldest and best preserved walled city, Carcassonne. There we enjoyed pizzas and Soupe à l'Oignon. The pizzas, simply delicious, lived up to their delectable description: "Our Pizzas are baked in an open hearth banked with burning wood and grape leaves. They are garnished with tomato sauce Provençale [that means with garlic] and perfumed with oregano, grated cheese; garnished with cheese, ham, mushrooms, anchovies, mussels, and shrimps." Crusts were either crisp or soft like bread dough. A good bottle of red wine really topped that off.

We also enjoyed a Crêpe Pizza: "Garnished and perfumed the same as regular Pizzas. The crust, though, is replaced by a crêpe [a thin pancake] and is laced with a Mornay Sauce [egg and heavy cream] plus tomatoes." This type of pizza was lighter in garnishments and seasonings.

Soupe à l'Oignon was delightful topped with Gruyère cheese, a product of Switzerland and similar to Emmantaler cheese. Gruyère is generally used here also on seafood and pizzas.

Another delight was Cassoulet de Carcassonne. This is prepared in an earthen pot rubbed with garlic and then layered with white beans, pork fat, bacon, goose meat and fat, and duck meat and fat.

We visited a wine cellar in the Medoc area where St. Emilion is a popular vintage wine. This particular wine cellar was situated in an old castle estate—very picturesque!

We also visited a distillery in the well-known town of Cognac, sampled the Cognac there and then had lunch. We were delighted with the luncheon, which featured a carrot salad made with shredded carrot, a sprinkling of cognac, and a vinaigrette dressing of oil, vinegar, and garlic.

We also sampled a sauerkraut, onion, and celery dish, and enjoyed a fish fried Tempura-style and served with heated catsup. We found out afterward that the fish was eel—very abundant in this area! At Le Karina Restaurant in Tours, we watched our máitre d' prepare and serve Staeck Tartare: Two patties of raw ground beef were covered with chopped parsley and onions and sprinkled with salt, pepper, and a generous amount of prepared mustard. Next came two raw egg yolks and a generous drizzle of hot pepper, Worcestershire, and chili sauces. This was all mixed together and then the meat was formed back into patties. Toast was served with this. *Bon Appétit!*

We found crêpe and pizza stands in the shopping areas of Tours. We visited a butcher shop—what beautiful young lamb, veal, and rabbit hanging on butcher hooks. And squab! The French equivalent of a quick food is a Croque Monsieur, a sandwich made with ham, Gruyère or mozzarella cheese and sautéed in butter. And Croque Monsieur Norvégien à Cheval (Norwegian on horseback) has a poached egg riding on top!

We enjoyed seeing Mont St. Michel. I think every French textbook includes a photograph of this monk's retreat, surrounded by quicksand. A food specialty in this region is mussels—tiny baby ones steamed in garlic. To eat them you pinch the meat with an empty mussel shell, using it like a pincer. Omlette de Mont St. Michel is a pouffe of fluffy eggs, beaten light and airy in a copper bowl (it has to be copper), and just slightly cooked—the top will still be a foam of raw egg. And L'Agneau Prés Salé is young lamb that has grazed on the salt marshes, which gives the meat a presalted flavor.

We motored through the lush, rolling countryside of the Province of Normandy, whence came the first settlers to form the French Colony of Acadia. This area is famous for its cheese: Camembert, Livorot, and Port l'Evèque. The cows that provide the main ingredient are beautiful brown and white creatures, with dark rings around their eyes that make them look like they're wearing sunglasses, and such long, beautiful eyelashes! A little school boy once described them:

They have four legs, one on each corner, two on one side and two on the other. There is a little hole in the back with a tail that just goes so far. The front legs are for going ahead and the back legs for stopping, and the legs just reach to the ground!

Before we reached Caen, we stopped at St. Laurent, where stands the U.S. Military Cemetery above the very cliffs stormed on D-Day, 1944. It brought back memories of schooldays on the Iron Range, when we would observe Armistice Day by singing the song "My Buddy" and reciting the poem, "In Flanders Field the poppies grow between the crosses, row on row. . . ."

An evening in Paris was a beautiful "illuminations" drive around the city after a sumptuous dinner at Le Grand Hôtel. A meal of Navarin des Poissons aux Petites

Légumes, and Cuisses de Grenouille Provençale. Cuisses de Grenouille are frog legs of a special variety. Our French friend remembers catching frogs by waving a red cloth and "*tuc,* the frogs jump at it and get caught."

We visited Versailles, which was beautiful—such tapestries, furniture, and furnishings. The Hall of Mirrors! The sculptured gardens!

On our last evening in Paris we dined at the Eiffel Tower, high above the beautifully illuminated city. Then it was *au revoir, adieu, à bientôt!*

Cheese Ball Neufchâtel

(noef-shaw-tel)

Jane Cardiff

1   8-oz pkg Neufchâtel cheese
1   4-oz pkg Roquefort cheese
1   cup chopped black olives

Snipped fresh or dried
chives

Combine all ingredients except chives and form into a ball. Cover with chives. Serve with crackers

Neufchâtel comes from the town of Neufchâtel-en-Bray in the historic province of Normandy, France. It is similar in taste and texture to any cream cheese but has less fat and fewer calories.

Croque Madame Diane

For your cocktail buffet.

1   loaf French bread
    Butter/margarine
    Slices of ham

Cheese Topping:

1   egg
⅓   cup beer
½   oz Cognac
1   cup grated Swiss or
    Gruyère cheese
¼   tsp pepper
    Dash hot pepper sauce
    Flour (about 1 Tb)

Slice the bread in half lengthwise and lightly toast it in a slow oven (250°). Butter the slices. Layer with the ham. Mix the cheese topping ingredients together and add just enough flour so mixture is not too thin and easy to spread. Spread cheese topping on ham. Place bread on aluminum foil-lined cookie sheet. Bake at 450° in upper third of oven for 15 to 20 minutes. To serve, slice crosswise into small pieces.

Escargots d' Alsace

(es-kar-go dahl sauce)

Escargots are a mollusk, a gastropod. Originally a French delicacy, they are now enjoyed the world over. A superior variety is grown on special farms in France known as escargotières. Imported snails are available on gourmet shelves in a combination package containing a can of 1 dozen escargots and a plastic tube containing 12 shells. Single cans containing 1½ dozen escargots are also available. Serve 6 escargots per person.

1	can escargots	Escargot shells
1	Tb vegetable or corn oil	French bread
½	oz Cognac	
	Garlic Butter Cordon Bleu	
	(see recipe)	

Wash escargots thoroughly in a sieve under cold water. Sauté them a moment in hot oil. Add Cognac and "flame." Then let them cool.

Into each shell, press some garlic butter. Then 1 escargot, tail last, but do not force. Press in more garlic butter. Place on cookie sheet. Bake in hot oven (400°) and remove as soon as butter bubbles, from 5 to 10 minutes. Serve hot with plenty of French bread to sop up the garlicky butter.

A new method is to stuff the escargots into ovenproof individual ceramic dishes. Some are even shaped like escargot shells.

Oysters Rockefeller Lisette

Antoine's of New Orleans have kept their original recipe a secret to this day. The only tip is that no spinach is used! Now they tell us. However, you will find this recipe with spinach is quite delicious! Serve 6 oysters per person.

12	fresh oysters	
1 to 2	ozs Pernod, Herbsaint, or Anisette liqueur	*Toppings:*
2	Tb butter	Bread crumbs
2	Tb flour	Grated Parmesan/Romano cheese
¼	cup drained, cooked, and slightly chopped spinach (see recipe: Italian Spinach Lisette)	Coarsely grated mozzarella cheese
¼	cup cooked spinach juice	Hollandaise Sauce (see recipe)
¼	tsp salt	
⅛	tsp pepper	
2	drops lemon juice	
	Drop Worcestershire sauce	

Wash and open fresh oysters using beer can opener. Marinate with a drop of Pernod on each. (If fresh oysters in the shell are not available, use canned or fresh shucked; drain and marinate with Pernod. Arrange on individual ramekins or use oyster shells, washed and dried.)

Melt butter, stir in the flour to make a roux. Mix in rest of ingredients.

Spread spinach mixture over the oysters and sprinkle with your choice of toppings.*
Place in baking pan. Bake at 400° for 10 to 15 minutes until hot and bubbly. Add a dab of Hollandaise Sauce. Serve hot.
*Can be frozen at this point; thaw before baking.

For the gourmet touch, place oyster shells on a bed of heated rock salt layered in the baking pan and then bake!

Tuna Pâté

Nancy Kirk

2	6½- or 7-oz cans tuna, drained	2	Tb chili sauce
1	8-oz pkg cream cheese, softened	2	Tb chopped fresh parsley
		1	Tb minced onion
		½	tsp hot pepper sauce

Blend together all ingredients. Pack into a 4-cup mold. Chill at least 3 hours. Unmold and serve with crackers.

Cheese Soup St. Galloise

(sant gal-wahz)

4	slices French bread	4	cups hot beef or chicken broth
4	ozs Swiss cheese		Salt and pepper
¼	cup diced onion		Grated Swiss cheese (if desired)
2	Tb butter/margarine		
1	egg yolk		

Dice bread into small pieces, place on cookie sheet and let dry in 250° oven. Shred the cheese. Sauté onion in butter/margarine until transparent. Beat egg yolk with fork and add a small amount of hot broth to egg. Add remaining broth to sautéed onion and cook together 5 to 7 minutes. Season with salt and pepper to taste. Remove from flame and add egg slowly to broth-onion mixture. Return to flame, add cheese, and mix until cheese is melted.

Layer bread on bottom of soup tureen. Pour soup over bread. Sprinkle grated cheese on top if desired. 4 to 6 servings

Marmite de Cultivateur

(mar-meet d kuhl-tee-vah-tur)

Farmers Soup

2 carrots
2 stalks celery
2 leeks (white part) or
   equivalent in green onions
2 Tb butter/margarine

4 to 5 cups hot beef or chicken
        broth
        Salt and pepper
1 Tb minced fresh parsley or
   2 tsp dried flakes

Cut vegetables in julienne strips, 2 inches long. Sauté in melted butter/margarine until just about tender. Remove excess butter. Add to hot broth. Season with salt and pepper to taste. Sprinkle with parsley. 4 to 6 servings

Potages de France Bonne Femme

(poh-tahj d frahns bun fahm)

From one basic potage, a number of fresh, hearty soups can be prepared.

Potage Parmentier
Basic Thick Potato Soup

3 cups sliced onions and/or
   leeks (white part)
3 Tb butter/margarine
3 Tb flour
4 cups diced potatoes

1 Tb salt (kosher is good)
   Green of 1 leek, sliced (if
   desired)
1 cup milk or light cream

Sauté onions/leeks in butter/margarine until soft but not brown. Stir in flour and cook 2 minutes. Add 4 cups hot water and mix well with flour-onion combination. Add potatoes and salt, then green part of leek. Simmer, partially covered, about 20 minutes. Then add milk (cream); choice is up to you, depending on creaminess desired. Heat through. Serve as is or for a smoother consistency, mash or put through a blender. Serve hot. 4 to 6 servings

Variations using Basic Potage Parmentier
Soupe du Jour

To the Potage Parmentier, add whatever leftover cooked vegetables you might have in refrigerator, such as: green beans, peas, Brussels sprouts, squash, and carrots; also lettuce leaves or watercress. Heat through. Serve hot.

Vichysoisse
Puree Potage Parmentier either through a sieve (tamis) or in a blender or a food mill. Add either sour cream or crême fraîche. Adjust for salt (should over-salt it). Chill and then cover and keep refrigerated. When ready to serve; garnish with chopped chives or parsley. Serve cold.
Swiss Onion Soup
Top Potage Parmentier with slivered Swiss cheese and toasted croutons. Heat in oven until cheese melts. Serve hot.

Soupe à l'Oignon Le Cordon Bleu

(soop ah l'oh-neeyoh)

2	lbs yellow or Spanish onions, thinly sliced	5	cups beef stock or bouillon
3	Tb butter/margarine	4	tsp cornstarch or roux thickener (see recipe)
1	Tb vegetable or corn oil	1½	ozs Cognac
1	clove garlic, minced		Grated Parmesan/Romano cheese
¼ to ½	tsp sugar (for color)		
1½	tsp salt		Croutons
¼	tsp pepper		Swiss or mozzarella cheese
1	cup dry white wine		

Sauté onions in butter/margarine and oil for 15 minutes, stirring occasionally. Add garlic and sugar and continue cooking until onions are golden (5 to 10 minutes). Add salt and pepper. Add wine and bring to a boil. Add stock and bring to a boil, then lower heat and simmer 20 to 30 minutes, uncovered, stirring occasionally. Blend cornstarch with 4 tablespoons water; stir into soup to thicken. Or add roux thickener. Add Cognac. Can set aside at this point.* To serve, reheat and top with grated cheese and croutons, or top with sliced Swiss (mozzarella) cheese and place under broiler until cheese is melted. Use individual ovenware soup bowls. 4 to 6 servings
*Freezes beautifully. Thaw and bring back to a boil. Serve with cheeses and croutons or garlic bread.

Note: For that gourmet rich dark brown color, mix in a few drops of an oriental brown gravy sauce (bead molasses), such as is used to color roasts and gravies. Or a few drops of a prepared gravy mix can be used. Restaurants use carmelized sugar, which comes in quart-size bottles. A drop or two is all you need. Ask your favorite restaurateur for a small amount.
In Carcassonne, France, we savored Soupe à l'Oignon with Gruyère cheese—absolutely délicieux!

Soupe de Poissons

(soop d pwah-soh)

This is a clear fish bouillon which we first savored in the great seaport of Marseille.

3	Tb oil	1	piece orange peel
2	medium onions, chopped		Salt and pepper
2	leeks (if available), chopped		Variety of fish and shellfish
1	bay leaf		(eel, crab, lobster, cod,
1	sprig fresh fennel or ¼ tsp		perch, halibut, red snapper)
	fennel seed	½	lb vermicelli
2	cloves garlic, minced		Saffron
2	fresh tomatoes, peeled and		
	chopped		

In hot oil, sauté onions and leeks until soft. Add bay leaf, fennel, garlic, tomatoes, and orange peel, and cook a few minutes. Pour in 2 qts water, season with salt and pepper to taste, and let come to a boil. Add all the fish and let simmer 20 to 30 minutes.

Strain broth, pressing juices out of all the fish. Boil the vermicelli in this fragrant broth. Serve with a sprinkle of saffron and chunks of crusty bread. 8 servings

Stockpot

Broth for preparing gravies, sauces, soups. Each chef takes great pride in his stockpot. Rival chefs in the same kitchen guard against having a handful of baking soda tossed into their pot!

Beef Stock:

Beef bones
Meat trimmings
Soup meat
Cheap cuts of beef
Leftover roast
Salt
Pepper
Carrots
Onions
Celery
Bay leaf
Thyme

For dark color, brown the meat and bones first in an open roasting pan at 450° for 30 minutes. Transfer to a large caldron and cover with ice cold water. Bring to boiling and as scum appears, skim it off. Add salt, pepper, and any of the vegetables or additional seasonings desired. Reduce heat and simmer for a few hours, or until meat falls off bones. Strain, using a very fine, fine sieve. Refrigerate. When cold, remove layer of congealed fat. May be kept refrigerated for a few days and frozen for couple of months.

Poultry Stock:

Backs, necks, gizzards, wing tips of fowl
Leftovers, bones and all
Proceed as for beef stockpot, only do not brown in oven first.

Pork Stock:

Leftover pork
Trimmings
Bones
Proceed as for beef stockpot, only do not brown in oven first.

Fish Stock:

Fish heads
Fish bones
Shells from shrimp, lobster, crabs
Inexpensive fish like codfish, grouper
Proceed as for beef stock, only do not brown in oven first. Simmer slowly 30 to 60 minutes.

Vichyssoise

(vee-shee-swahz)

An elegant cold soup for the gourmet.

2	Idaho potatoes, peeled and cut into pieces	2	ozs smoked bacon with rind, cut into pieces
1	bunch leeks (white part), washed carefully and diced	1	tsp salt
½	bunch watercress, with stems (if desired)	½	tsp pepper
½	cup diced onion	1	Tb snipped fresh chives
		1	Tb chopped fresh parsley
		1	pt half and half (if desired)

Put all vegetables and bacon in pot with 6 cups water, salt and pepper. Boil 45 to 60 minutes until ingredients are soft like mush. Remove the bacon bits. Blend soup in a blender, then refrigerate till icy cold.* Whisk in chives, parsley, and half and half if desired. Season again to taste. 6 to 8 servings
*May be frozen at this point.

FONDUE

Fondue is a dish made by melting cheese in wine, with a little brandy and seasonings added. The word fondue comes from the French verb *fondre*, which means "to melt." Skewered cubes of bread or ham, also crudités, are dipped into the hot bubbly cheese mixture.

Genuine Switzerland cheese is what makes a good fondue. Emmentaler (Switzerland Swiss) is the genuine cheese with the holes. Other countries export "Swiss" cheese but the only similarity may be in the holes! Emmentaler is formed into wheels measuring about 36 inches in diameter, weighing from 160 to 220 pounds. "Switzerland" is imprinted in red all over the natural rind.

Natural Gruyère is a firm cheese similar to Switzerland Swiss (Emmentaler), but with a more pronounced flavor and with much smaller holes. This cheese is sometimes confused with processed Gruyère, which is a soft blend of Emmentaler and Natural Gruyère shaped into small foil-wrapped portions.

Appenzeller cheese, from the region of Appenzell, has only lately become known outside of Switzerland. Until the advent of refrigerated transport, this delicate cheese could not be shipped any great distance. It has a fine texture combined with tanginess, perfect for "spicing" up a fondue.

Cheddar, Corkscrew & Son Fondue

Dennis and Susan Kirkwood Cheese and Wine Merchants

½ lb Emmentaler, shredded	1 cup extra dry white wine, such as a Frascati
½ lb Natural Gruyère, shredded	2 to 3 Tb lemon juice
2 ozs Appenzeller, shredded	2 Tb kirsch
3 Tb cornstarch	Salt and pepper
1 clove garlic	

Combine the cheeses with cornstarch and set aside. Rub bottom of a fondue pot with garlic. (Pot must be ceramic, not metal). Add wine and heat until small bubbles form on the bottom of the pot. Add lemon juice, then slowly add cheese, stirring constantly until all cheese is melted. If too thick or if wine has evaporated, add more lemon juice. If too thin, add more cornstarch. Just before serving, stir in kirsch and season with salt and pepper to taste. 4 to 6 dinner or 10 to 12 hors d'oeuvre servings

Like a soufflé, fondue must be served immediately.

Lasagne à la Française

The French are prone to do their own thing with any dish.

The French version of Italian Lasagne is layering the noodles alternately with leftover cooked chicken, mushrooms, onions, spinach, also cottage cheese, and spreading the layers with a medium white sauce laced with dry vermouth. On top of the final covering of white sauce, a small amount of a light tomato sauce is spread sparingly and then topped with a heavy layer of grated cheeses—Romano, Parmesan, Swiss.

An interesting tip is to drain the cooked (al dente) lasagne in a colander, rinse with cold water, and then drape the strips around the edge of the colander to separate and cool the pasta.

Classic Quiche Lorraine
(Keesh)

½	lb bacon, cut into 1-inch pieces	¼	tsp ground nutmeg
3	eggs	¼	cup shredded Swiss cheese
1½	cups heavy cream	1	unbaked 9-inch pie shell (see Mrs. Grider's recipe)
½	tsp salt		Grated Parmesan/Romano cheese (if desired)
¼	tsp pepper		

Cook bacon until crisp. Drain on paper towel. Beat eggs, heavy cream, and seasonings together, just enough to blend. Stir in Swiss cheese. Spread bacon on bottom of pie shell. Pour in cheese mixture. Sprinkle top with grated cheese if desired. Bake at 375° for about 35 minutes, or until pie shell is golden brown and filling is firm. Serve as entrée (or as an appetizer) 6 to 8 servings

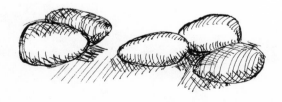

Potpourri Soufflé

(poh-poor-ree soo-flay)

Grandmère Léa
Angoulème, France

Jackie's grandmère taught her how to prepare this delicious casserole made from leftover meats and vegetables, with a golden cheese topping.

Meat Mixture:
- 2 cups leftover meats (any kind) chopped fine or ground
  Gravy (if any)
- 2 eggs
- 1 tsp chopped fresh parsley
- 1/2 tsp garlic salt
- 1/2 tsp onion salt
- 1/2 tsp salt
- 1/4 tsp pepper

Vegetable Mixture:
- 2 1/2 cups leftover potatoes, mashed
- 1/2 cup cooked carrots or other cooked vegetables
- 2 eggs
- 2 Tb butter, softened
- 1/2 tsp salt
- 1/4 tsp pepper
- 1/8 tsp ground nutmeg

Cheese Topping:
- 3 to 4 ozs Swiss or cheddar cheese, shredded

Whip meat mixture ingredients together in a blender. Then whip vegetable mixture ingredients together in a blender.

In a buttered 2-quart casserole, layer the two mixtures alternately, starting on the bottom with the vegetable mixture and ending on top with the same. Sprinkle cheese on top. Bake, covered, at 325° for 45 to 60 minutes until puffy and golden brown. 4 to 6 servings

Red Beans and Rice with Smoked Hot Sausage

To the Creoles and Cajuns this is "Louisiana poor folk's food."

1	12-oz pkg dried red kidney beans	1	bay leaf
¼	lb smoked ham hock or salt pork, cubed (or use both)	2	Tb minced, fresh parsley or 2 tsp dried flakes
2	Tb corn oil or bacon fat		Salt and pepper
2	cups chopped onions		Dash cayenne pepper (if desired)
1	medium green pepper, chopped	3 to 4	cups cooked rice
1	clove garlic, minced	1	22-oz pkg smoked hot sausage

Wash beans. In a saucepan, cover beans with 1qt water. Bring to a rolling boil, turn off heat, and let stand. Meanwhile, in large kettle, sauté salt pork/ham in hot oil (bacon fat) until brown. Add onions and green pepper and sauté until onions are soft. Add beans and water, plus 1½ additional qts water, garlic, and bay leaf. Bring to a boil and then simmer gently, uncovered, 3 to 4 hours, stirring occasionally, until it is reduced to a creamy red sauce. Add parsley. Season with salt and pepper to taste, and cayenne if desired. Serve over hot cooked rice with sausage on the side. 6 to 8 servings

To prepare sausage: Cut sausage in long links. Cook in small amount of water in a frying pan for 7 to 8 minutes (do not boil). Pour off excess water and lightly brown sausage.

La Tourte au Roquefort

(lah toort oh roak-for)

A meal in itself. Serve with a salad.

Marie France

2	lbs potatoes	2	cloves garlic, minced
2	pie crusts (See Pie Crust for Pasties recipe below)	1	Tb butter
		½	cup dry white wine
	Salt and pepper	3	Tb minced fresh parsley
8	ozs mushrooms, sliced	5 to 6½	ozs Roquefort cheese,
5	ozs bacon, finely chopped		crumbled
½	cup chopped onion	1	egg beaten with 1 tsp water
2	green onions or shallots, chopped	¾	cup heavy cream, whipped

Peel potatoes and slice in thin rounds. Rinse them under boiling water (eliminates the starch). Drain and dry with paper towel. Roll out pie crusts and place one crust in deep pie plate (10-in. diameter; 2 in. deep), allowing a 1- or 2-inch overlap. Layer one half of the sliced potatoes on the bottom. Season with salt and pepper to taste.

Sauté mushrooms with bacon bits. Simmer onion, green onions (shallots), and garlic in the butter and white wine until soft but not brown. Layer the mushrooms, bacon, both onions, and garlic over potatoes. Sprinkle with half the parsley and all the crumbled Roquefort. Layer the rest of the potatoes on top. Trim the top pie crust to fit over the potatoes. Brush completely with egg, including the overlap crust. Fold the overlap back over the edge of the pie plate to completely seal the crusts. Pierce top crust, making a small hole. Bake at 450° for 15 minutes, then at 325° for 1½ hours longer.

When cooked, cut the top crust all around to form a lid. Remove lid and spread tourte with whipped cream. Sprinkle with rest of parsley. Replace lid. 4 to 6 servings

Tourtière

(ˈtoor- tˈyair)

French Pie Dish

Florence Trepanier

A traditional dish to celebrate Christmas and New Year's festivities in France and French Canada. Colloquially known as "Toot kay."

2½ lbs lean pork, ground coarse

2½ lbs ground beef

3 large onions, chopped

2 Tb vegetable or corn oil

3½ tsp ground cinnamon

2 tsp ground cloves

2 tsp ground allspice or nutmeg

Salt and pepper

2 cups hot beef bouillon or broth,

5 small Irish potatoes, peeled, cooked, and mashed

6 pie crusts (see Pie Crust recipe below)

Sauté meat with onions in hot oil. When evenly light brown, add spices; season generously with salt and pepper. Add hot beef broth; simmer 15 minutes. Mix in the mashed potatoes and let cool.

Make pie crusts, *doubling* recipe for Pasties and Tourtière. Divide dough into 6 parts. Place 3 bottom crusts in 3 9-inch pie plates.

Divide meat mixture among crusts. Cover with top crusts. Moisten rim of bottom crusts first, then seal tightly. Make 3 slits in each top crust for vents. Bake at 400° for 15 minutes, then at 350° for 15 minutes longer. Serve warm or hot. 3 9-inch pies, 4 to 6 servings per pie

These pies freeze beautifully. Cool thoroughly, wrap in aluminum foil and freeze. To serve, thaw and heat in oven.

Joyeux Nöel et Une Bonne Année!

Pie Crust
for
Pasties and Tourtière

Florence Trepanier

3 cups flour
1 Tb salt
¾ cup plus 1 Tb shortening
(13 Tb)

Ice water (about 9 Tb)

Mix flour with salt. With pastry blender or 2 knives, cut shortening into the flour until the size of small peas. Sprinkle ice water, 1 tablespoon at a time, over mixture, mixing lightly with a fork until all flour is moistened. Press into a ball. Divide into 3 or 4 portions and let rest a few minutes before rolling.

Eggs

In French the word for an egg is oeuf (uhf). The standing joke in my French classes was —

Teacher: Translate - one egg.
Student: un oeuf (uhn uhf).
Teacher: Translate - two eggs.
Student: oeuf, oeuf (uhf uhf).
Actually the singular of egg is oeuf (uhf) and the plural is oeufs (but pronounced uh)!

Omelette Brouillée Lisette

Scrambled eggs for egg lovers and for those who aren't, too!

3 Tb butter/margarine	½	tsp salt
1 cup thinly sliced onion	¼	tsp pepper
1 cup thinly sliced green pepper	6	eggs
		Cubed ham
1 tomato, peeled, cut up, and de-seeded		Mushrooms
		Grated cheese

In butter/margarine, sauté onion until limp. Add the green pepper and tomato and cook until peppers are just soft. Season with salt and pepper. Beat eggs with 2 tablespoons water and stir into mixture; cook until eggs are done but still moist. Cubed ham, mushrooms, or grated cheese can be added to beaten eggs. 4 servings

Fish

Fish should swim thrice
First in the Sea
Then in Butter
And finally in a Good Wine.

Be it Italian Zuppa di Pesce or French Bouillabaisse, the story goes, as in Pierre Loti's Pêcheur d'Islande, that years ago in the spring, fleets of fishing boats would set out to sea—from ports such as in Provence and Bretagne—for the summer fishing season. From a temporary altar on the pier, amid trophies of anchors, fish nets, and oars, reigned the Virgin Mother, the sailors' patron saint. There the women would gather to pray and to bid farewell, "good luck, good fishing" to their loved ones. In August, the fishermen would return with the savory aroma of a Bouillabaisse Sauce simmering in a huge cauldron on shore, awaiting the fish being brought home.

Bouillabaisse is considered such a gourmet specialty, many hesitate to prepare it. Yet, it is a simple "homely" tomato fish stew, easy to prepare.

To the fishermen of Portugal this fish stew is known as Cioppino.

Bouillabaisse Marseillaise

(mar-say-yez)

For those who want to prepare their own sauce, this will make enough for about four to five pounds of fish.

1	cup sliced onions	2	Tb chopped fresh parsley
2	green onions or shallots minced		or 2 tsp dried flakes
¼	cup olive oil	1	bay leaf
4	cloves garlic, minced	½	tsp thyme
1	28-oz can plum tomatoes	½	tsp rosemary
1	8-oz can tomato sauce	¼	tsp fennel seed
1	cup clam juice	¼	tsp pepper
1	cup fish stock or chicken broth	⅛	tsp grated nutmeg (fresh, if available)
½	cup Chianti or dry white wine	⅛	tsp. saffron
		1	slice lemon with peel or 1 tsp lemon juice

In a 6- to 8-quart kettle, sauté sliced onions and green onions (shallots) in olive oil until soft. Add garlic, tomatoes, and tomato sauce; simmer 20 minutes. Stir in rest of the ingredients. Bring to a boil and simmer 40 to 60 minutes. Add fish and cook 10 to 15 minutes or until fish is done.

Bouillabaisse Lisette

(boo-yah-bess)

Such a savory dish as was ever served in France.

1   15- or 16-oz can prepared spaghetti sauce
½   cup Chianti wine
1   Tb lemon juice
1   cup clam juice or chicken broth
½   tsp thyme
¼   tsp fennel seed
¼   tsp rosemary
⅛   tsp garlic salt
⅛   tsp onion salt
⅛   tsp saffron (threads crushed)

2 to 3 lbs assorted fish:
Cod, perch, halibut, red snapper, bass, or flounder, cut into 2-inch pieces
Fresh shrimp, shelled and deveined
Fresh oysters, shucked
Clams in the shell, scrubbed in salted water and well rinsed
Canned oysters, clams, or shrimp, drained

In a large kettle, mix together spaghetti sauce, wine, lemon juice, clam juice (chicken broth), and seasonings. Bring to a boil, then simmer with cracked lid for 30 minutes. May prepare to here and set aside.

When ready to serve, bring sauce to a boil, add fish and cook 10 to 15 minutes. Then add shellfish and cook a few more minutes until shells crack open. Serve in soup bowls with chunks of crusty French or Italian bread. 4 to 6 servings

Leftover sauce can be served reheated over cooked rice or pasta.

Rouille

(roo-ee-uh)

La Calangue

Served with our Bouillabaisse in a Monte Carlo restaurant were tiny rounds of toast spread with this sauce, which was prepared at our table by our garçon.
For each serving:

1	Tb mayonnaise		Dash pepper
1	Tb catsup	3	to 4 drops hot pepper sauce
2	tsp Dijon mustard		(or more)
1	tsp garlic salt		

Mix ingredients together until well blended.

Rouille can be served with chicken and fish (hot tartar) or as a dip for crudités (raw vegetables).

Coquille St. Jacques Manfred

(ko-keey)

4	cups seafood, *chosen from:*			
	1	lb fresh shrimp, shelled and deveined	½	tsp lemon juice
			½	tsp Worcestershire sauce
	2	lobster tails, cut into chunks	4	Tb flour
			4	Tb butter, melted
	6	scallops	1	cup clam juice or fish stock
	2	small filets of sole, flounder, or halibut, cut into chunks	2	ozs dry sherry*
			½	tsp salt
			⅛	tsp pepper
	2	green onions or shallots, minced	¼	tsp garlic salt
			¼	tsp thyme
	2	Tb butter		Pinch crushed saffron
	¾	cup dry white wine		Cooked rice or toast

Sauté green onions (shallots) in 2 tablespoons butter until soft. Add seafood and sauté about 5 minutes, or until shrimp turns pink. Add wine, lemon juice, and Worcestershire sauce. Simmer 2 to 3 minutes. Strain off juice and set aside. Let seafood cool. Mix flour into the 4 tablespoons melted butter until smooth. Stir in 1 cup juice from cooked seafood plus clam juice (fish stock), sherry, and the seasonings. Cook for 5 minutes.

Place seafood in individual casseroles (coquilles) and top with the sauce. Bake at 400° for 5 to 6 minutes until hot and bubbly, or bake in a 1½-quart casserole for about 15 minutes. Serve hot over cooked rice or toast. For a gourmet touch, top with a dab of Hollandaise Sauce (see recipe). 6 to 8 servings
*Try 1½ ozs of Cognac instead of the 2 ozs sherry.

Crab Meat Pie

Ruth Baum Carlton

1 12-oz can snow crab meat,
           drained
½ cup mayonnaise
¼ cup milk or half and half
2 Tb flour
2 eggs, beaten
1 Tb chopped fresh parsley
    or 1 tsp dried flakes

Dash hot pepper sauce
9 ozs Swiss cheese, shredded
⅓ cup chopped green onions
    (scallions)
1 9-inch unbaked pie shell

Mix together the mayonnaise, milk, flour, eggs, parsley, and hot pepper sauce. Set aside. Stir together crab meat, cheese, and green onions (scallions); combine with the egg mixture. Pour into pie shell. Bake at 350° for 40 to 45 minutes. 6 to 8 servings

Crab Meat au Gratin Pontchartrain

1 lb lump crab meat
3 green onions or scallions,
    chopped
½ green pepper, chopped
1 4-oz can mushrooms,
    drained
6 Tb butter

1 pimento, chopped
1 Tb chopped, fresh parsley
½ tsp garlic salt
½ tsp white pepper
½ tsp celery seed or celery salt
3 ozs sherry
½ cup bread crumbs

Sauté green onions, (scallions), green pepper, and mushrooms lightly in butter until soft. Add pimiento, parsley, and seasonings. Add sherry. Gently mix in the crab meat. Then add ¼ cup bread crumbs. Put into 4 to 6 baking shells or ramekins (individual casseroles). Sprinkle with remaining bread crumbs: place under broiler to heat thoroughly. Serve with toast. 4 to 6 servings

Crab Meat Ravigote Louisiane

1 lb lump crab meat
6 strips bacon, fried crisp
1 tsp dry mustard
½ tsp celery salt
½ tsp paprika
½ tsp hot pepper sauce

½ cup chili sauce
1 tsp wine vinegar
    Pinch crushed tarragon
    leaves
1½ cups mayonnaise

Divide crab meat into 4 to 6 individual ramekins or baking shells. Heat in 400° oven. Top with strips of crisp bacon. Meanwhile, blend together mustard, celery salt, paprika, and hot pepper sauce. Mix in chili sauce, vinegar, and tarragon leaves. Blend in the mayonnaise. Spread this sauce over the warm crab meat and glaze under the broiler. 4 to 6 servings.

Sauce also makes a good Thousand Island salad dressing when chilled.

Crêpes

(Krep, as in met)

It is interesting that "crêpe" is the French word for a thin, delicate pancake, which can be used in many ways; made with either sweetened or unsweetened batter. And even more interesting is that many nationalities have their own versions of crêpes: Mexican taco, Jewish blintz, Japanese gyoza, Chinese eggroll, Italian cannelloni. Each version offers a choice of fillings, from using leftovers to the elegant flaming Crêpes Suzette!

Crêpes à la Crab

1	6-oz pkg frozen snow crab or Alaskan King crab meat	1⅓	cups milk
⅓	cup chopped green onions or scallions	⅓	cup grated Swiss cheese
1	cup thinly sliced celery	¼	tsp salt
1	cup chopped mushrooms	⅛	tsp pepper
¼	cup (4Tb) butter/margarine		Dash of ground nutmeg
3	Tb flour	8	cooked crêpes (see crêpes Italian recipe)
			Grated Parmesan/Romano cheese (if desired)

Thaw crab meat and separate into chunks. Retain liquid. Sauté green onions (scallions), celery, and mushrooms in butter/margarine for 2 to 3 minutes. Remove from pan with slotted spoon and set aside. For the sauce, stir flour into the fat in pan until smooth. Add milk and crab liquid and cook until thickened. Stir in Swiss cheese, salt, pepper, and nutmeg. In a small bowl, gently toss crab with the cooked onions, celery, mushrooms, plus ½ cup of the sauce. Adjust seasonings. Spread equal amount of filling across center of each crêpe and roll up or fold over. Place crêpes, in 1 layer only, in shallow baking pan and pour remaining sauce over the top. Sprinkle with grated cheese if desired. Heat at 350° for 10 to 15 minutes. 8 servings

Creole Seafood Gumbo with Okra

Southern Louisiana cooking is part of the heritage handed down from the French and Spanish settlers, the Creoles; from the Cajuns, who are descendants of the Acadian French; and from the Louisiana-born Blacks. It is a potpourri of herbs and spices, of rice and seafood, of savory sauces, and of vegetables such as okra, a vegetable used in gumbo (a soup or stew). Okra is a green pod with a gummy substance that lends a unique flavor.

½	lb fresh shrimp	1	Tb salt pork, minced
½	lb fresh crab meat	1	Tb butter/margarine
3	slices bacon, cut up	1	Tb chopped fresh parsley
1	cup chopped onion		or 3 tsp dried flakes
1	large bay leaf	1	16-oz can tomatoes
2	Tb chopped green pepper	1	8-oz can tomato sauce
1	tsp sugar	3 to 4	dashes hot pepper sauce
1	tsp salt	4	tsp Worcestershire sauce
¼	tsp pepper	1	tsp lemon juice
⅛	tsp thyme	2	cups fish stock or clam
½	lb fresh* or frozen okra,		juice
	thawed		Cooked rice or toast

Shell and devein shrimp and put shells to boil (to add to fish stock or clam juice). In a large pot fry bacon until crisp, add onion and sauté until soft. Add bay leaf, green pepper, and seasonings. When green pepper is soft, add okra. Continue cooking until okra loses some of its gummy consistency. Meanwhile, melt together in another pan salt pork and butter/margarine. Add parsley, tomatoes, tomato sauce, hot pepper sauce, Worcestershire, and lemon juice. Simmer until tomato pulp is cooked down. Add the fish stock (clam juice). Bring to a boil, then transfer to the large pot with the bacon-okra mixture. Simmer slowly for 1½ hours, or until okra is well cooked and sauce has thickened. Stir occasionally. Add shrimp and crab meat. Cook another 10 minutes. Serve over cooked rice in soup plates or over toast. 4 to 6 servings

Small cans of shrimp and crab meat can be used instead of fresh fish.

*If fresh okra is used, wash, cut off ends and slice in small rounds.

Garlic Broiled Crevettes

(kreh-vet)

2	lbs fresh shrimp	¼	cup chopped fresh parsley
½	cup olive oil		or 2 Tb dried flakes
2	cloves garlic, minced		Lemon wedges

Shell and devein shrimp. Arrange shrimp in shallow baking pan. Sprinkle with olive oil, garlic, and half the parsley. Broil about 4 inches from broiling unit from 4 to 6 minutes on each side. Sprinkle with remaining parsley and serve with lemon wedges. 4 to 6 servings

Cuisses de Grenouille Provençale

(qweess d gren-ooy pro-vahn-sahl)

Frog legs are quite a French delicacy and are served in the finest of restaurants. These are specially grown imports, sweet and delicious, having a seafood flavor. They are usually found in the freezer section at fish markets.

1½	lbs small or medium-size frog legs	1	small tomato, peeled, chopped, and de-seeded
½	cup flour	2	ozs Cognac
½	tsp salt	6 to 8	Tb Garlic Butter Cordon
¼	tsp pepper Peanut, vegetable, or corn oil		Bleu (see recipe)

Thaw frog legs and split them into single legs. Wash and squeeze them dry with paper towel. Dredge in flour seasoned with salt and pepper. Brown in small batches in hot oil, shaking pan to keep them from sticking. Add the tomato and Cognac. Cover and simmer 2 to 3 minutes. Stir in garlic butter and simmer until butter is melted. 4 to 6 servings

The drumstick part of chicken wings is delicious prepared this same way.

Shrimp Gumbo Lisette

Gumbo means okra, or a soup thickened with okra. Gumbo is also a French patois spoken by Creoles and Blacks in Louisiana.

1	lb shrimp	1	clove garlic, minced
3	slices cooked bacon, cut into small pieces	1	small bay leaf
1	cup chopped onion	2	Tb minced fresh parsley
1	medium green pepper, cut up	2	Tb Worcestershire sauce
1	15- to 16-oz can or jar spaghetti sauce	1	tsp lemon juice
		⅛	tsp thyme
1	cup clam juice or chicken broth		Dash hot pepper sauce
		1 to 2	cups okra*
			Salt and pepper
		2 to 3	cups cooked rice

Shell and devein shrimp. Render bacon bits; add onion and green pepper and sauté until they are just tender. Stir in spaghetti sauce, clam juice (broth), and garlic. Blend in next 6 ingredients. Sauté gently 30 minutes. Can put aside at this time. When ready to serve, bring back to simmer, add okra, simmer 10 to 15 minutes. Add shrimp and continue to simmer until shrimp turn pink and are cooked (about 5 minutes). Salt and pepper to taste. Serve over rice. 4 to 6 servings
*Wash fresh okra, cut ends off, and slice into ½-inch-thick pieces.

Boeuf Bourgogne

(buff boor-go-nyah)

A great chef's specialty. Serve with rice, parsleyed potatoes, buttered noodles, or chunks of crusty bread. Délicieux!

6	strips bacon, cut into ½-inch pieces	1	bay leaf
3	lbs boneless beef (chuck, London broil)	2	tb chopped fresh parsley or 2 tsp dried flakes
1	large carrot, sliced	½	tsp thyme
1	cup sliced onion	⅛	tsp freshly grated nutmeg (if desired)
1	tsp salt	1	lb raw mushrooms, sliced
¼	tsp pepper	3	Tb butter
3	Tb flour	2	Tb corn oil
2	14-oz cans beef broth or 2½ cups beef stock	¼	tsp salt
2	cups Burgundy wine	¼	tsp pepper
1	Tb tomato paste or 1 tomato, peeled and chopped	18 to 24	small white onions (with knife score "x" in root end)
2	cloves garlic, minced	4	tsp cornstarch

In a heavy 4- to 5-quart kettle, fry bacon until crisp and remove. Brown meat in the bacon fat (in small batches so it will not steam), turning meat often with tongs. Remove meat as it gets brown. In same bacon fat, sauté sliced carrot and onion until onion is soft. Return bacon pieces and meat to kettle. Add salt, pepper, and flour, and stir to coat meat with flour. Measure ½ cup broth (stock) and set aside. Add remaining broth (stock) to beef along with the wine, tomato paste (tomato), garlic, herbs, and nutmeg. Bring to a boil; then cover and simmer gently until meat is "fork-tender" (comes off fork easily), about 1½ hours.

Meanwhile, in large skillet, sauté mushrooms in butter and oil at high heat about 5 minutes, stirring constantly. Season with salt and pepper. Remove mushrooms from skillet. In the same skillet, brown the small onions over medium heat, shaking skillet to brown them evenly. Add the reserved ½ cup broth (stock), cover, and simmer gently until onions are just tender (about 10 minutes).

Thicken the meat and sauce with the cornstarch blended with 4 tablespoons water. Stir over low heat until gravy thickens. Use more cornstarch/water if thicker gravy is desired. Add the cooked mushrooms and onions; bring just to bubbling and serve. 4 to 6 servings

To serve as a stew, add cooked peas, carrots, and potatoes along with the cooked mushrooms and onions. Delicious as reheated leftovers.

Préférence de Monsieur

(pray-fayr-onss d mseeuh)

4 to 6 filets mignons, 1 inch thick
1½ Tb butter
½ Tb corn oil
4 to 6 slices buttered toast
Salt and pepper

2 Tb minced green onion or shallots
⅓ cup Madeira wine or Chablis
Mushroom caps (if desired)

Heat butter and oil in large frying pan until it foams. Sauté filets on each side 3 to 4 minutes to desired doneness. Place steaks on toast on hot platter. Season with salt and pepper to taste. Pour excess fat out of pan, add green onions (shallots) and Madeira wine (Chablis). Boil down, scraping up "brownings." Pour over steaks. Top each steak with raw or cooked mushroom cap. 4 to 6 servings

Steak Diane

This is really a "melting pot" original, using Oriental, Italian, Portuguese, English and French ingredients; plus good old Western beef. Good eatin', Diane!

4 boneless loin strip steaks, ½ inch thick, or 4 filet mignons
Olive oil
Soy sauce
1 2- or 3-oz can or jar fresh green peppercorns* (packed in brine), mashed
2 Tb butter
2 Tb olive oil

Sauce:

1 Tb cornstarch
1 cup beef bouillon or broth
1 Tb chopped fresh parsley
1 Tb chopped green onion or shallots
1 Tb prepared mustard, Dijon, or Diable
¼ tsp lemon juice
¼ tsp Worcestershire sauce
1 oz Madeira wine
½ oz Cognac

Marinate steaks by rubbing with a sprinkling of olive oil, soy sauce, and mashed peppercorns. Brown steaks quickly on each side in hot butter and 2 tablespoons oil. Remove from pan and keep warm while you prepare the sauce.

Combine cornstarch and bouillon (broth). Add, with remaining ingredients, to pan in which the steaks were browned. Stir and cook until sauce is bubbly. Then return the steaks to the pan of bubbling sauce. Serve steaks on hot dishes, pour additional sauce over. 4 servings

For a little French flair, when you add the Cognac to the pan, flame it! With home-made mashed potatoes and buttered peas or carrots, delicious! *Bon appétit!*
*If not available, use a few "grinds" of whole black peppercorns.

Steak au Poivre

(oh pwah-vreh)

2 to 4   lbs sirloin steak, boneless or
with bone cut 1 ½ inches
thick

Salt
Cracked peppercorns or
coarse ground pepper

Trim suet from steak and use to rub inside of frying pan, then sprinkle pan with thin layer of salt. Press cracked pepper into steak on both sides and let stand. Heat skillet until salt starts to get golden. Add steak and sauté on both sides to desired doneness. Steak will be crusty outside, juicy inside. 4 to 6 servings

Tournedos Rossini

Petits filets of tenderloin with sauce and Pâté De Foie Gras. Elegant and delicious. Supposedly created by famous Italian composer Gioacchino Rossini.

4 to 5   filets mignons*
4 to 5   slices bread
        Butter
        Rossini Sauce (see recipe
        below)
2   Tb butter/margarine
1   Tb corn oil

Salt and pepper
4 to 5   slices Pâté de Foie Gras*
        Mushroom caps, fresh or
        cooked
        Sliced tomatoes
        Parsley sprigs

Sauté bread slices in butter until crisp and brown. Keep warm. Prepare Rossini Sauce and keep warm. Fry filets mignons in hot butter/margarine and oil until medium or medium-rare. Season with salt and pepper to taste.

To serve: Place filets on toasted bread slices. Cover with Rossini Sauce. Top with slice of pâté. Top with mushroom cap. Garnish with tomato and parsley. 4 to 5 servings
*Oven roast a whole tenderloin and slice into filets.

*Pâté de Foie Gras can be found in gourmet shops usually in 7-¼ oz tins.

Rossini Sauce:

¼   cup Madeira wine
¼   cup dry white wine
2   Tb tarragon
1   Tb fresh chopped parsley
¼   tsp oregano

1   shallot or 1 clove garlic,
    minced
1   cup beef stock or bouillon
4   tsp cornstarch or roux
    thickener (see recipe)

In covered pot boil first 6 ingredients with 1 cup water until reduced to about ½ cup. Strain the sauce. Add beef stock (bouillon) and thicken with 4 tsp. cornstarch blended with 4 Tb water - or roux thickener.

Émincé de Veau Zürichoise

(eh-man-say d voh zoor-ee-shwahz)

1	lb veal, cut into thin 1½-inch-long strips		Salt and pepper
½	lb sliced fresh mushrooms or 4-oz can drained	1	cup dry white wine
¼	cup (4 Tb) butter/margarine	2	tsp melted butter
2	tsp minced green onions or shallots	2	tsp flour
		2	cups heavy cream
		2	Tb chopped fresh parsley

Sauté veal and mushrooms in butter/margarine. Add green onions (shallots); season with salt and pepper to taste. Add wine and continue cooking until wine is reduced to ½ cup. Thicken with blend of melted butter and flour (roux). Add heavy cream and heat through. Garnish with parsley. 4 servings

Veal Cordon Bleu

12	thin slices veal (uniform size)	½	cup flour
6	thin slices *each* (uniform size):	¼	tsp salt
	Swiss or Gruyère cheese	⅛	tsp pepper
	Ham, prosciutto, or Canadian bacon	1	egg, beaten
			Bread crumbs
		4	Tb vegetable or corn oil

Make a "sandwich" with a slice of cheese and a slice of ham between 2 slices of veal. Press sandwich into flour seasoned with salt and pepper, dip into the egg, and roll in the bread crumbs. Brown quickly on each side in hot oil. Transfer to 425° oven for 10 minutes. 4 to 6 servings

Almond Chicken Ladeva

1 chicken, 2 to 3 lbs, cut into
  serving pieces
1 tsp salt
½ tsp pepper
1 tomato, chopped
½ cup chopped onion
1 clove garlic, minced
2 Tb chopped fresh chopped
  parsley or 2 tsp dried flakes

3 whole peppercorns
3 whole cloves
¼ tsp cinnamon
¾ cup slivered almonds
2 egg yolks, slightly beaten
½ tsp lemon juice

Wash chicken pieces and squeeze dry with paper towel. Simmer chicken, salt, pepper, tomato, and onion with 2 cups warm water in a covered pot, 20 to 30 minutes. Add garlic, parsley, peppercorns, cloves, and cinnamon to chicken and sauce; continue simmering, covered for 5 minutes. Remove chicken from pot and set aside. Strain the sauce, reserve 1 cup, and pour the rest back into pot. Add slivered almonds. Return chicken to sauce and simmer until chicken is tender.

Pour the cup of reserved sauce into a bowl. Gradually add egg yolks, beating vigorously so egg doesn't cook. Pour back into pot. Add lemon juice. Simmer for about 1 minute and serve. 4 servings

Chicken en Brochette

2 large whole chicken breasts
  or 1 large turkey breast
  Salt and pepper
1 8-oz link Italian sausage,
  hot or mild

8 fresh mushrooms
2 Tb butter/margarine
  Chicken livers or small
  pieces of gizzard

Skin and bone chicken breasts; cut into 1-inch pieces. Sprinkle lightly with salt and pepper to taste. Cut sausage into 1-inch pieces; brown and drain. Sauté mushrooms quickly in butter/margarine for 2 to 3 minutes. Sprinkle with salt and pepper to taste.

To assemble, skewer a piece of sausage, a mushroom, a piece of chicken, and a chicken liver; then repeat. Grill, broil, or roast, 7 to 8 minutes on each side. 4 servings

Chicken Jambalaya Orléans

As prepared for lunch by a Creole cook at Hermitage Plantation; 22 hens were used for 225 people.

2	chickens, 2 to 3 lbs, cut into serving pieces	1	cup uncooked rice
	Oil		Salt and pepper
2	large onions, chopped		Garlic salt
			Cayenne pepper

Brown chicken in hot oil. Add onions and sauté until soft and yellow. Add 2 cups water, rice, and seasonings to taste. Bring to a boil, cover, and simmer until rice water is absorbed and chicken is done. Adjust seasonings. 4 to 6 servings

Juicy and Crisp Roast Chicken

The high oven temperature is what does it.

1	fryer, 3 to 4 lbs	1	clove garlic, minced
	Salt and pepper	3	Tb butter/margarine, melted
1	stalk celery, cut into chunks		
2 to 3	sprigs parsley	1	medium onion, diced
1	bay leaf	1	stalk celery, diced
½	tsp thyme	4	tsp cornstarch or roux thickener (see recipe)
2	green onions or shallots, chopped		
1	Tb coarsely ground black pepper		

Preheat oven to 450°. Wash chicken and pat dry. Sprinkle with salt and pepper inside and out. Put the celery chunks, parsley, bay leaf, thyme, green onions (shallots), coarse pepper, and garlic in the cavity or use Mama Paulucci's Meat Stuffing for Fowl (see recipe). Truss chicken by tying legs together, and securing wings with twine. Brush chicken with 2 tablespoons of the melted butter/margarine and place on its side in smallest roasting pan possible. Roast 15 minutes, turn over to the other side and roast 15 minutes, brushing with remaining 1 tablespoon butter/margarine. Reduce oven to 425°.

Remove chicken and cover bottom of roasting pan with diced celery and onion. Place chicken on its back on top of vegetables. Continue to roast and baste often with drippings until chicken is done (30 to 45 minutes). Reduce heat if necessary the last 10 minutes. Remove chicken to a warm platter.

To make gravy, heat vegetables and juices in roasting pan 1 minute. Add hot water and bring to a boil. Scrape and stir "brownings" in pan. Strain. Thicken with 4 teaspoons cornstarch blended with 4 tablespoons water or roux thickener. 4 to 6 servings

Coq au Vin Cordon Bleu

(kok oh van)

1	3-lb. frying chicken, cut up	1	bay leaf
½	cup flour	1	clove garlic, minced
½	tsp salt	1	Tb minced fresh parsley
¼	tsp pepper	2	cups Chianti wine
¼	tsp thyme	2 to 4	cups chicken broth or bouillon
¼	cup olive or vegetable oil		
2	Tb diced bacon	4	tsp cornstarch or roux thickener (see recipe)
6	small white onions		
1	4-oz can sliced mushrooms, drained		

Dredge chicken in flour seasoned with salt, pepper, and thyme. Pat off excess flour. Let stand a few minutes. In a skillet, heat oil and brown chicken until very brown. Transfer to a large pot so chicken isn't stacked. In same skillet, sauté bacon, onions, mushrooms, bay leaf, garlic, and parsley until onion is soft. Add to chicken. Cover chicken with wine and cook until wine is reduced by ½. Cover chicken with chicken broth (bouillon). If needed, add more salt and pepper, and simmer until chicken is tender. Thicken sauce with blend of 4 teaspoons cornstarch and 4 tablespoons water or roux thickener. 4 servings

Coq au Vin Lisette

The melding of chicken fat, salt pork, Cognac, wine and herbs is aromatic. Not an inexpensive dish, but really worth all that Cognac and wine!

2 to 3	small fryers, cut up	2	tsp sea salt (salt crystals; kosher)
	Chicken fat (from the fryers) plus corn oil	½	tsp pepper
8	ozs salt pork, cut into small pieces (rind removed)		Bouquet Garni*
8 to 10	small white onions (with knife score "x" in root end)	2	cloves garlic, crushed and minced
2	Tb flour	1	Tb tomato paste
1	cup Cognac	½	lb sliced fresh mushrooms
2	bottles red wine (Burgundy)	4	tsp cornstarch

Wash chicken pieces and squeeze dry with paper towel. Melt chicken fat with enough corn oil to cover bottom of frying pan (about ¼ inch). Brown chicken until golden and remove pieces to a heavy lidded pot; keep warm.

Brown salt pork in the frying pan, adding the white onions when salt pork is about done; cook until the onions are golden. With slotted spoon, add salt pork and onions

to chicken; add flour and stir to coat chicken pieces evenly. Pour ½ cup Cognac over the mixture, ignite, and let flame. Pour 1 to 1½ bottles wine over chicken so chicken is completely covered. Wine will reduce while cooking, so keep adding more if needed. Add the sea salt, pepper, Bouquet Garni, garlic, and tomato paste. Stir well. Bring to a rolling boil, uncovered. Flame again with remaining ½ cup Cognac and let it burn out. This removes alcohol and excess fat. Add the fresh mushrooms. Cover the pot (cracked lid) and let simmer over low heat. Cook ½ hour or more (usually) until chicken is done. Remove chicken, onions, mushrooms, and keep warm. Bring stock to boil and let it reduce slightly. Thicken stock with 4 teaspoons cornstarch blended with 4 tablespoons water. Return chicken, onions, and mushrooms to pot. Cover and keep warm until ready to serve. 4 to 6 servings
*Combine 2 sprigs parsley, chopped; 1 small bay leaf crumbled; ⅛ tsp thyme.

This is an adaption of Madame Fernande Allard's famed chicken as served in her Paris Bistro. Mme. Allard, whose style of cooking is "Cuisine de Femmes," is rated among France's best cooks.

Creole Fried Chicken

1 to 2	fryers, cut up	⅛	tsp garlic powder
1	tsp salt	⅛	tsp onion powder
¼	tsp pepper		Flour
¼	tsp chili powder	¼	cup vegetable or corn oil
⅛	tsp cayenne pepper		

Mix seasonings together. Sprinkle over chicken parts. Let stand 20 minutes. Roll chicken parts in flour. Let stand 20 minutes and fry in hot oil until crisp and done. 4 servings

Paprika Chicken Ladeva

1	chicken, 2 to 3 lbs, cut into serving pieces	1	clove garlic, minced
½	cup chopped onion	1½	Tb paprika
¼	cup oil	1	tsp salt
1	tsp salt	¾	cup chicken stock or bouillon
½	tsp pepper	1	cup sour cream
1	tomato, blanched, peeled, and chopped	4	tsp cornstarch
1	green pepper, chopped	1	tsp lemon juice

Wash chicken parts and squeeze dry with a paper towel. Sauté onion in hot oil until soft and yellow. Remove from pan and set aside. Brown chicken in hot oil. Season with salt and pepper. Add tomato, green pepper, garlic, and cooked onion. Sprinkle with paprika and salt. Add chicken stock (bouillon). Cover and simmer 30 to 40 minutes. Keep adding stock, if necessary, to have 1½ cups sauce. Remove chicken to a platter and keep in warm oven. Pour ½ cup of the sauce into the sour cream and stir until smooth. Thicken rest of sauce with the 4 teaspoons cornstarch blended with 4 tablespoons water. Then add sour cream mixture and lemon juice to the thickened sauce. Serve chicken with sauce poured over. 4 to 6 servings

Poulet Rôti Lisette

(poo-lay roh-tee)

This is my favorite of all roast chickens. Done on a rotisserie, either open hearth or oven, the chicken is crispy on the outside and juicy inside. Like the French, I don't use stuffing, but do enhance the chicken flavor with herbs and seasonings.

2	small fryers or a 4- to 6-lb roasting chicken	½	tsp salt
2	stalks celery, diced	¼	tsp pepper
2	small carrots, diced	¼	tsp thyme
1	medium onion, diced	¼	tsp crushed sage leaves
1	bud shallot (if available), minced		Lemon juice
1	clove garlic, minced		Salt
			White wine (if desired)

Wash and dry chicken inside and out. Mix remaining ingredients, except lemon juice and salt, together and place in cavity. Truss and skewer chickens. Sprinkle with lemon juice and salt. Roast on rotisserie until done (juices will run clear). Pick up drippings with small amount of water or white wine if desired and heat through to serve over chicken. 4 to 6 servings

For an aromatic stock, cover any leftover chicken, bones, vegetables, and seasonings with cold water and simmer 30 minutes. Leftover meats and seasonings make the best stock.

Cornish Hens aux Gousses d'Ail

(oh goose die)

Garlic can be a very subtle seasoning when used properly. Famous chefs know how to use garlic in quantity, yet subtly, for a delicate flavoring of poultry. The secret is unpeeled, uncrushed garlic cloves! Cornish hens are a miniature chicken crossbred from a British breed of chicken and a Plymouth Rock breed. All white meat, Rock Cornish Hens are a nice size to serve one whole hen per person. Or, try small broilers, or even squab, which is a nestling pigeon—all dark meat and elegant!

Cornish hens or squabs (1 per person)
Salt and pepper
Lemon juice

30 to 40 cloves garlic, whole and unpeeled
Butter/margarine
1 oz Cognac

Preheat oven to 450°. Wash and dry hens inside and out. Sprinkle cavities with salt and pepper. Truss. Rub skins with lemon juice and sprinkle with salt.

Scatter garlic cloves over bottom of a well-buttered (margarine) large roasting pan. Place fowl on top of garlic, breast side up. Place pan in 450° oven, then immediately turn temperature down to 350°. This will start browning the skin without burning the garlic (garlic burns easily). Bake hens for about 1 hour, or until juices run clear when tested. Kitchen will be permeated with a delicious aroma of garlic. Remove hens to a warm place. Run cooked garlic cloves and pan juices through a sieve. Mix together Cognac and 1 teaspoon water and use to scrape up "brownings" in roasting pan over heat. Combine garlic and Cognac mixtures and simmer gently until well blended and hot. Use as a sauce over the hens.

Caneton Rôti

(kah-nay-toh roh-tee)

Roast duckling with either Black Cherry or Peach Sauce is quite a delicacy, yet simple to prepare. Plan ½ duckling (split lengthwise) per person.

2 ducklings, split lengthwise
Salt and pepper

Wash and pat dry. Cut off all excess fat and skin. Salt and pepper the cavity. Prick all fatty deposits all over body with tip of a knife. Sprinkle salt all over the skin. Place on a rack breast side up in roasting pan. Roast at 325° until done and skin is crispy brown (about 30 minutes per pound).

Meanwhile, put necks and gizzards in a pot. Cover with cold water. Add 1 teaspoon salt and ¼ teaspoon pepper. Bring to a boil and then simmer until meat is cooked and you have a generous cup of broth (stock). Strain, adjust salt to taste. Reserve to make sauce.

When ducklings are done, remove to warm platter and degrease roasting pan by tilting the pan and removing fat with a spoon or bulb baster. Pick up brown bits with the duck stock. Continue with preparation of either Black Cherry or Peach Sauce.

Caneton aux Cerises Lisette

(kah-nay-toh oh sir-ees)
Duckling with Black Cherries

2	ducklings, split lengthwise	1	tsp lemon juice
1	16-oz can dark sweet pitted	1	oz Cognac
	cherries in syrup, drained	2	Tb red currant jelly
	(reserve syrup)	4	tsp cornstarch
2	ozs kirsch (cherry brandy)	1	cup duck stock

Prepare ducklings according to recipe above. Macerate (soak) drained cherries in kirsch for 20 minutes. In a saucepan, combine cherry syrup, lemon juice, Cognac, and jelly, and bring to a boil. Simmer 2 to 3 minutes. Drain brandy from cherries and add brandy to sauce. Bring to a boil; simmer 10 minutes. Stir in the 4 teaspoons cornstarch blended with 4 tablespoons water. Simmer a few more minutes. Set aside.

When duckling is done, remove to a warm platter. Degrease roasting pan, and pour in the duck stock to scrape up "brownings" in pan. Add this to the sauce. Bring sauce to a boil and add more cornstarch thickener if sauce seems thin. Then add cherries and cook just until cherries are heated through. Serve sauce in bowl on the side for spooning over duckling. 4 servings

Caneton à la Liqueur de Pêches

(kah-nay-toh———pesh)
Duckling with Peach Sauce

Marie Bretagne

2	ducklings, split lengthwise	1	oz Cognac
1	16-oz can sliced peaches in	1/3	stick cinnamon or 1/8 tsp
	syrup, drained (reserve		ground cinnamon
	syrup)	4	tsp cornstarch
2	ozs peach brandy	1	cup duck stock
1	tsp lemon juice		

Prepare duckling according to recipe above. Macerate (soak) drained peaches in brandy. In saucepan, combine peach syrup, lemon juice, Cognac, and cinnamon, and bring to a boil. Simmer 2 to 3 minutes. Drain brandy from peaches and add brandy to sauce. Bring to a boil; simmer 10 minutes. Remove cinnamon stick. Stir in the 4 teaspoons cornstarch blended with 4 tablespoons water. Simmer a few more minutes. Set aside.

When duckling is done, remove to a warm platter. Degrease roasting pan, and pour in the duck stock to scrape up "brownings" in pan. Add this to the sauce. Bring sauce to a boil. Add peach slices and cook just until peaches are heated through. Serve sauce in a bowl on the side for spooning over duckling. 4 servings.

Goose

For centuries the French have repeated the expression "bête comme une oie" (bet come yoon wah) meaning "stupid as a goose." On the contrary, geese are anything but stupid. True, they honk and babble constantly, but they make good sentinels. It was their shrill cries that warned the Romans of the invading enemy. They are ferocious warriors. My French friend Jackie remembers the old gander that scolded and chased her all over grandmère's yard when she would visit. They have been considered good omens such as when on the day Queen Elizabeth I was dining on roast goose, the good news arrived of the destruction of the invincible Spanish Armada. They are gastronomes choosing to eat only the best—from grains to mollusks and gorging themselves on choice vegetables.

Roast goose was appreciated as a delicacy as far back as the Middle Ages. It is prepared in any number of delectable ways from roast to soups to stews. Every part of the goose is used, the most valued being the foie (fwah). Their fat is used in place of butter or oil; goose down is used for pillows. Years ago, their plumes made fancy ink pens. Even their blood is cooked with parsley and garlic as an entrée.

Since the goose is considered such a delicacy, great care is taken in the raising of geese from fragile chicks to full grown, weighing in at about 10 kilos (22 pounds). In France, it is the farm women who are responsible for their constant care. After the chicks' first month of being fed specially prepared food of nettles and eggs, they are penned in a restricted space. The farm women then force feed them grain through a funnel put in their beak. Surprisingly, the geese come to enjoy this and will clamor loudly should feeding time be a little late. By this method of feeding, the goose develops a liver weighing up to one kilo (2.2 pounds) when full grown.

The foie is prepared in many ways, sautéed or in papillote,* but mostly it is processed as Pâté de Foie Gras (pahtay d fwah grah), which is literally a pie or patty of fat liver. It is savored as a side dish served at room temperature, as a garnish such as on our Tournedos Rossini, or it is eaten with the cheese course. It demands the grandest of wines.

Roast goose is juicy, delicious dark meat. Stuffed with your choice of dressing, it is a festive bird for the winter holidays.
*Papillote (pappy-yoht) meaning "cooked in buttered paper."

Roast Goose

1   goose (average 10 to 12 lbs)
     fresh (if available) or
     frozen
     Salt and pepper

Dressing of your choice or
cut up celery and onion
Angostura aromatic bitters
(if desired)

Thaw goose, wash, and pat dry inside and out. Make little slits (score) all over goose skin (releases the fat). Remove the 2 bags of fat in the back.

Sprinkle cavity with salt and pepper. Stuff with dressing or vegetables and truss the bird. Sprinkle a few drops Angostura over goose and rub into the skin (this is for color). Sprinkle salt and pepper all over the bird. Place on a rack breast side up in an open roasting pan. Roast at 350° to 400° until done, then cut off oven and let roast rest 20 to 30 minutes; this will tenderize the meat.

Any dressing left? Form into balls and place around goose the last 30 minutes or remove as soon as "dumplings" are done.

For gravy, while goose is roasting, simmer the gizzard, heart, and neck in salted water until it makes a thick broth. Strain. Remove goose from roasting pan to a warm place. Degrease pan* and pick up "brownings" with the broth; simmer and add thickener. 10 servings
*Many save the goose grease for cooking.

Turkey Suprême

The best of turkey in a delicious sauce.

1   small turkey (6 to 7 lbs)

Stuffing:

2   stalks celery, chopped
1   small onion, chopped
1   carrot, chopped
1   Tb chopped fresh parsley
¼   tsp thyme
¼   tsp crumbled sage
    Salt and pepper to taste

Combine above ingredients and stuff turkey. Brown turkey in a roasting pan, uncovered, at 450° for 10 minutes. Turn oven down to 325° and continue roasting turkey, covered, until it is done.

Cool. Bone meat off the turkey and set aside. Put bones and vegetables in a pot and cover with cold water. Bring to a boil, skim off foam, and then simmer until you have a nice thick broth. Season to taste, strain, and refrigerate. Spoon off fat when it has congealed on top of broth.

4 to 6	cups boned turkey, cut into small chunks	1	4-oz jar pimientos, cut up
1	cup chopped onion	1	2-oz can mushrooms, sliced or pieces, drained
2	Tb oil	¼	cup dry sherry
	Broth to cover (about 2 qts)	1	cup frozen peas
1	12-oz can shoe peg whole kernel white corn (tiny, sweet kernels)	4	tsp cornstarch
			Hot biscuits or cooked rice

Sauté onion in hot oil until soft. Add turkey and cook a few minutes to lightly brown meat. Pour broth to cover turkey and bring to a boil. Add corn, pimientos, mushrooms, and sherry. Bring back to a boil. Add frozen peas. Simmer gently for a few minutes. Thicken with the 4 teaspoons cornstarch blended with 4 tablespoons water. Serve over hot biscuits or cooked rice. 6 to 8 servings

The sauce is suprême due to the rich turkey broth and sherry wine. This is delightful for a buffet. And convenient, for the turkey and broth can be prepared the day before, leaving only minutes for the final dish.

Ailloli

(i-oh-lee)

From Provence, the French province of garlic! A lovely garlicky sauce to enjoy with meats or fish or to use as a dip. Traditionally it was pounded and mixed by hand in a mortar. A food processor works very well.

1	egg	¼	tsp salt
4 to 6	cloves garlic, mashed with the side of a knife	¼	tsp pepper (freshly ground best)
2	Tb lemon juice	1 to 1½	cups olive oil

Put all ingredients except olive oil in food processor. Using the steel blade, run processor just 3 seconds. Then start again and pour in the olive oil, in a slow steady stream to begin with and then faster as sauce starts to thicken into a mayonnaise consistency. 1 cup sauce

Bouquet Garni

In French cooking this is a standard blend of seasonings. These are wrapped and tied together, or bagged in a piece of cheesecloth—and then the bouquet is removed when the cooking is finished. I mince the parsley and add it to the pot along with the crumbled bay leaf and thyme.

2 large sprigs parsley
1 small bay leaf, crumbled
⅛ tsp thyme
or
2 large sprigs parsley
1 bay leaf
2 celery leaves

Bread Dressing

Basic Recipe

	Quart 4 lbs	2 Quarts 8 lbs	3 Quarts 12 lbs	4 Quarts 16 lbs	5 Quarts 20 lbs
Poultry (in pounds)	4 lbs	8 lbs	12 lbs	16 lbs	20 lbs
Bread crumbs	4 cups	8 cups	12 cups	16 cups	20 cups
Butter/margarine	⅓ cup	⅔ cup	1 cup	1⅓ cups	1⅔ cups
Minced onion	¼ cup	½ cup	¾ cup	1 cup	1¼ cups
Chopped celery	½ cup	1 cup	1½ cups	2 cups	2½ cups
Salt	2 tsp	4 tsp	2 Tb	8 tsp	3 Tb
Pepper	¼ tsp	½ tsp	1 tsp	1 tsp	1½ tsp
Sage	1 tsp	2 tsp	1 Tb	4 tsp	1 Tb plus 2 tsp
Thyme	1 tsp	2 tsp	1 Tb	4 tsp	1 Tb plus 2 tsp
Poultry seasoning	1 tsp	2 tsp	1 Tb	4 tsp	1 Tb plus 2 tsp

In a large bowl, break day old bread *with crusts* (bread crumbs) into ¼-inch to ½-inch pieces.

Melt butter/margarine in large skillet. Add onion and cook until yellow, stirring occasionally. Stir in some of the bread crumbs and heat through. Pour into the large bowl of bread crumbs and add celery and the seasonings of your choice. Mix well. Cool before stuffing the bird.

You can prepare dressing a day or two ahead. Refrigerate, tightly covered, until ready to stuff bird. Pack bird loosely. Put any leftover dressing in a greased pan, dot with butter, cover, and bake separately during last 30 to 45 minutes of roasting time. We like this basic recipe, however, variations in flavor can be made by adding other ingredients, such as drained oysters, boiled chestnuts, sausage, browned and chopped, using about 1 cup of the ingredient per 1 quart of dressing.

Garlic Butter Cordon Bleu

1 cup (2 sticks) butter, softened
1 cup (2 sticks) margarine, softened
1 *whole* cluster garlic cloves, minced
2 Tb minced fresh parsley
1 Tb chopped fresh or snipped dried chives
1 oz Cognac and 1 oz dry white wine
1 tsp salt
¼ tsp pepper

Cream butter and margarine. Gradually mix in rest of ingredients. This keeps well in refrigerator or in freezer. Shape mixture into a sausage-like roll. Wrap in aluminum foil. Slice off required amount.

Use for escargots, Chicken Kiev, for garlic bread and over hot pasta for a Garlic Butter Sauce.

Lemon Butter Cordon Bleu

1	cup (2 sticks) butter, softened	1	tsp chopped fresh or snipped dried chives
4	Tb lemon juice, at room temperature	½	tsp salt
1	Tb chopped fresh parsley	¼	tsp pepper

Mix all ingredients together in mixer or by hand. Shape into a roll. Wrap in plastic or foil. Keep refrigerated.
Use over all fish. Good on steaks, too.

Béchamel Sauce

Named after Louis XIV's Steward Louis de Béchamel.

2	Tb butter	¼	tsp pepper (white preferred)
2	Tb flour		
1	cup chicken broth	¼	tsp paprika
½	tsp salt	½	cup heavy cream

Melt butter over low heat. Add flour and stir until well blended. Remove from heat and gradually stir in the broth. Return to heat and cook until thick and smooth, stirring constantly. Blend in seasonings. Then stir in the cream. About 1¾ cups sauce

Hollandaise Sauce

I approached making Hollandaise Sauce with trepidation, especially after all the cautioning from our chef instructor: "curdles easily, keeps such a short time." However, a classmate gave me this "no fail" recipe—and so it is! (Although a chef would scoff at using a blender!)

4	egg yolks	½	tsp salt
½	Tsp dry mustard	¼	tsp pepper
1	Tb lemon juice	½	cup (8 Tb) butter/margarine, melted
	Dash hot pepper sauce		

Put egg yolks, mustard, lemon juice, hot pepper sauce, salt, and pepper into blender and process at "mix." Mix in melted butter in a steady stream until mixture is completely emulsified (when butter is well blended, "suspended" with the eggs). Refrigerate in tightly covered jar. To heat, place in small bowl over hot water. ¾ cup sauce

Serve over cooked vegetables, such as cauliflower, broccoli, or asparagus, and whenever a recipe calls for Hollandaise Sauce.

Simple Bearnaise Sauce

To Hollandaise Sauce (above) add:

- ½ tsp minced fresh parsley
- ⅛ tsp tarragon leaves
- ⅛ tsp chopped fresh or snipped dried chives

Mushroom Sauce Cordon Bleu

1 lb mushrooms, washed, dried, and sliced	1 cup beef stock or bouillon
2 Tb butter	Salt and pepper
2 Tb margarine	Roux or cornstarch thickener (see recipes below)
2 Tb Madeira wine	

Sauté mushrooms quickly in hot butter and margarine. Drain off fat. Add wine; cook a few minutes. Add beef stock (bouillon) and cook a few minutes more. Season to taste with salt and pepper. Thicken with roux (cornstarch thickener). Two cups sauce

Delicious with steaks and roast meats.

Cornstarch Thickener for Gravies and Sauces

- 4 tsp cornstarch
- 4 Tb liquid (water, bouillon, soy sauce, or wine)

Blend into a smooth paste. Stir into boiling sauce. If thicker sauce is desired, add more thickener mix. This will never "lump" like flour mixture.

Which reminds me. We shared an apartment, three teachers, inexperienced in making gravy. One day Ardelle attempted to make gravy. Her call to dinner: "Hurry up before the gravy hardens!"

Roux Thickener
for Gravies and Sauces

1	cup (2 sticks) butter/margarine	1	cup flour

Melt butter until nearly brown. Stir in flour until smooth. Add a spoonful at a time to boiling sauce for desired thickness. Mold remainder into a "stick." Wrap in aluminum foil or plastic wrap and refrigerate. Keeps for weeks.

Caesar Salad

This is our family clan's favorite. Not only do we use romaine, but we include other greens, as well as cucs, tomatoes.

2	bunches assorted lettuce, torn into bite-size pieces and tossed with desired additions	6	Tb wine vinegar or 4 Tb lemon juice
2	tsp salt	1	2-oz tin anchovies, drained and chopped
½	tsp pepper (freshly ground best)	2	Tb capers
2 to 3	cloves garlic, minced and added to olive oil	¼	cup grated Parmesan/Romano cheese
⅔	cup olive oil	8	bread sticks, in bite-size pieces, or 1 cup croutons or crumbled melba toast
1	egg		

Traditionally, as in the finest restaurants, Caesar Salad is tossed à table with a flourish; ingredients being added and tossed a few at a time. You can do the same. Just line up all the ingredients separately ahead of time. Then proceed. In a large bowl, add to the basic salad the rest of the ingredients in the following order: Salt, pepper, olive oil-garlic; toss gently to coat leaves. Raw egg; toss. Vinegar (lemon juice), anchovies, capers; toss. Cheese and bread stick pieces (croutons); toss.

However, there are occasions when pre-mixing the dressing is warranted (personally, I find it just as delicious). Blend and beat together all the dressing ingredients, except the grated cheese and the bread stick pieces (croutons) and set aside. When ready to serve, toss the salad with the dressing. Then add cheese and bread stick pieces (croutons) and toss again gently. (See also Caesar Salad Dressing Lisette.) 4 to 6 servings

Cucumber Salad Cordon Bleu

    4   cucumbers
         Salt
         Ice water
         Lettuce leaves (if desired)
         Sour Cream Dressing
         Cordon Bleu (see recipe)

Wash, peel and slice cucumbers 1 inch thick. Place in a bowl; sprinkle with salt and cover with ice water. Let stand about 10 minutes (this crispens and "deburps" the cucumbers). Then drain off salt water. Place one layer of slices on lettuce leaves on individual salad plates. Cover with the dressing. 4 servings

Have you tried the "burpless" cucumber? It is a European strain (Concombre Européen) grown in this country mainly in California. Average size is 14 to 15 inches long. No need to peel.

Four Season Salad

A very colorful presentation.

   ½   cup *each* cooked vegetables:
         Sliced beets
         Green beans
         Peas
         Sliced carrots
         Lettuce leaves

Place a mound of each vegetable on a lettuce cup on a large platter or flat tray. Let diners help themselves. Pass the Roquefort Dressing. (See also Salad Dressing Lisette.) 4 to 6 servings

Salade Niçoise

(sah-lahd niece-swahz)

In summer, it's often the main course in France.

1½	lbs potatoes	20	pitted green olives
1	clove garlic	1	onion, diced
½	tsp salt	10	anchovy filets, drained and
¼	tsp pepper		cut in half
6	Tb wine vinegar		Lettuce
7	Tb olive oil		Tomato sections

Boil potatoes in jackets; don't overcook. Rub garlic clove around salad bowl and then mash it. Peel and slice potatoes (while they are still warm) into salad bowl.

Mix together salt, pepper, vinegar, and oil; pour over potatoes. Add olives, onion and anchovies. Toss lightly and chill. Serve on bed of lettuce garnished with tomato sections. 4 servings

Salade de Poivrons et Pastèque

(pwahv-roan eh pass-teck)

Marie de Paris

Watermelon and Green Pepper Salad

An incredible combination—crunchy green pepper, crisp and juicy watermelon, piquant vinegar dressing. Colorful and delightful.

3	green bell peppers	4	Tb white vinegar
1	large chunk watermelon	2	Tb olive oil
3	cloves shallots, minced, or a sprinkle of onion powder	1	tsp salt
2	green onions and tops, chopped	½	tsp pepper

Wash peppers, cut in half lengthwise. Remove seeds and inside white pulp. Cut in fine strips and layer on a large platter. Remove seeds from watermelon and cut off rind. Cut watermelon in bite-size pieces and mound over green pepper strips. Sprinkle with shallots (onion powder) and green onions. Cover with plastic wrap and chill. In a bowl, mix vinegar, oil, salt, and pepper. Pour over salad when ready to serve. 4 to 6 servings

Salad Provençale

(pro-vahn-sahl)

2	heads lettuce (romaine, endive, iceberg, bibb, or Boston)		
			Dressing:
2	tomatoes, cut into wedges	1	tsp prepared mustard or Dijon
1	large onion (Bermuda, Spanish) thinly sliced	2	Tb wine vinegar
2	cloves garlic, minced	7	Tb olive oil
2	Tb snipped chives	1	tsp salt
1	Tb basil	¼	tsp pepper
12	pimiento-stuffed olives		Radishes
12	pitted black olives		

Prepare lettuce: Tear into bite-size pieces in a large salad bowl. Add remaining salad ingredients. If prepared ahead, cover with damp paper towel and refrigerate. When ready to serve, blend the mustard and vinegar and sprinkle over salad. Toss gently. Then add oil, salt, and pepper, and toss. Garnish with radishes. 4 to 6 servings

Fresh Spinach Salad Cordon Bleu

Tossed with a hot vinaigrette, served à table in many haute cuisine restaurants.

1	lb fresh spinach	1	Tb lemon juice
½	cup wine vinegar (headed)	3 to 6	Tb sugar
1	small onion, minced, or 4	¼	tsp salt
	shallots	⅛	tsp pepper
1	clove garlic, minced	3 to 4	slices bacon, cut up fine

Wash and drain spinach. Crispen in refrigerator at least 30 minutes.

Boil the vinegar (this is called "heading"). Add onion (shallots), garlic, lemon juice, sugar, salt, and pepper. Stir and cook until sugar is dissolved. Set aside; keep hot. Sauté bacon bits in skillet until golden brown. Mix bacon and fat into the vinegar base.* Pour over spinach, toss well. Serve immediately. 4 servings

*Vinegar base with bacon can be prepared ahead. Bring to a boil when ready to serve.

Caesar Salad Dressing Lisette

Be sure to make ahead of time.

4	tsp salt	10 to 12	Tb wine vinegar or 4 Tb lemon juice
1	tsp pepper		
4	cloves garlic, minced very fine	2	2-oz tins anchovies (rolled or flat) and drained, cut into pieces
1⅓	cups olive oil		
2	eggs	4	Tb capers

Mix all ingredients together in a quart jar. Refrigerate with a tight lid on jar. 3 cups dressing

When ready to serve, toss dressing with lettuce greens and then add:
½ cup grated
Parmesan/Romano cheese
Broken bread sticks or
croutons

Salad Dressing Lisette

1   cup sour cream
1   cup mayonnaise
½   lb cheese, divided in thirds
     and crumbled
         Choice of:
         Roquefort (French import)
         Bleu cheese (domestic)
         Gorgonzola (that's Italian)
     Salt and pepper

In blender or electric mixer blend sour cream, mayonnaise, and ⅔ of the cheese until smooth. Stir in with spoon the remaining ⅓ of the crumbled cheese. Season with salt and pepper to taste. Refrigerate in covered jar. 2 cups dressing

Dash of hot pepper sauce really spices it up.

Sour Cream Dressing Cordon Bleu

1   cup sour cream
¼   cup finely chopped onion
2   Tb minced parsley
1   Tb chopped fresh or
     snipped dried chives

1   tsp salt
½   tsp pepper
1   Tb lemon juice

Mix sour cream with all ingredients except lemon juice. When well blended, mix in lemon juice. Refrigerate. 1½ cups dressing

Use on cucumber salad.

Vinaigrette Marsielle

(veen-ay-gret mar-see-ell)

1   cup mayonnaise
1   cup sour cream
1   Tb wine vinegar or lemon
     juice
½   tsp Worcestershire sauce
½   tsp salt
¼   tsp pepper

¼   tsp dried parsley flakes or
     dill weed
     Dash hot pepper sauce
3   anchovy fillets, chopped
1   small clove garlic, minced
1   tsp chopped capers (if
     desired)

Blend mayonnaise and sour cream. Mix in rest of ingredients and beat well. Refrigerate in tightly covered jar. 1½ cups dressing

A small amount of water can be added for a thinner consistency.

Broccoli with Cheese Sauce en Casserole André

1	bunch broccoli		Salt and pepper
1	small onion, diced	1	egg yolk
2	Tb butter/margarine	4	tsp roux thickener (see
2	cups milk		recipe)
1	cup grated cheddar or		Grated Parmesan/Romano
	Swiss cheese		cheese

Wash and peel broccoli. Boil in 2 inches salted water, covered, for 5 minutes (will be undercooked). Drain. Sauté onion in butter/margarine until soft and layer it on the bottom of a 2-quart casserole. Heat milk; add the cheddar (Swiss) cheese; salt and pepper to taste. Continue to cook and stir until cheese is melted. Add the egg yolk, stirring rapidly. Thicken with roux. Layer the broccoli over the onion. Pour sauce on top. Sprinkle with grated cheese. Bake in 425° oven until cheese turns golden. 4 to 6 servings

Carottes Raifort

(cah-roht reh-for)

Carol Martin

6	carrots, sliced	½	tsp salt
½	cup mayonnaise	¼	tsp pepper
2	Tb horseradish	½	cup buttered bread crumbs
2	Tb grated onion		

Cook carrots in salted water until just tender. Drain. Arrange in a 1-quart casserole. Combine remaining ingredients except bread crumbs and stir into the carrots. Top with buttered bread crumbs. Bake at 300° for 15 minutes. 4 servings

French Peas Cordon Bleu

1	lb fresh peas or frozen peas, thawed	½	tsp salt
¼	lb bacon, diced	¼	tsp pepper
1	Tb butter/margarine	1	cup water or bouillon (beef or chicken)
2 to 3	leaves of lettuce (outer leaves), cut into small pieces	1	tsp roux thickener (see recipe)

Sauté bacon in the butter/margarine. Add lettuce, salt, pepper, water (bouillon). Transfer to saucepan. Bring to a boil. Add peas; stir. Add roux. Continue cooking 15 minutes. 4 servings

Petits Pois François

(ptee pwah frah-swah)

2 cups fresh peas, cooked, or frozen peas, thawed
¼ cup finely diced celery
1 small onion, finely diced
2 Tb butter/margarine
4 cups hot chicken stock or broth

Salt and pepper
⅛ tsp sugar
1 Tb roux thickener (see recipe)
1 Tb minced fresh parsley

Sauté celery and onion in butter/margarine until soft. Add peas, chicken stock (broth). Season with salt and pepper to taste; add sugar. Thicken with roux if desired. Garnish with a sprinkle of parsley. 4 servings

Stuffed Green Peppers

4 to 5 large, firm green peppers
1 small onion, chopped
1 tsp butter/margarine
1 16-oz can whole kernel corn, drained

Salt and pepper
2 egg yolks
½ cup milk
1 Tb roux thickener (see recipe)

Wash and dry green peppers. Cut stem tops off. Remove inside seeds and white pulp carefully and wash. Chop tops into same size as the corn kernels. Sauté chopped pepper tops and onion in butter/margarine until soft. Add the corn; mix well. Season with salt and pepper to taste.

Combine eggs and milk and bring to a boil. Add roux to just thicken sauce. Add corn mixture to the sauce. Season with more salt and pepper if needed. Fill peppers with mixture.*

Butter a square pan small enough to keep peppers standing up. Can use foil also in between. Bake at 425° about 45 minutes. 4 servings
*This much can be done a day in advance.

Stuffed Peppers Marie

Marie D'Amboise

6	large, uniform green peppers	2	Tb chopped fresh parsley
½	lb leftover cooked pork, veal, beef, or poultry, chopped		Salt and pepper
		2	eggs, beaten
		½	tsp thyme
4 to 5	shallots, chopped, or 2 Tb minced onion	1	cup cooked long grain rice*
		1	8-oz can tomato sauce or 1 cup spaghetti sauce

Wash and dry green peppers. Cut stem tops off. Remove inside seeds and white pulp carefully and wash. Chop pepper tops. Mix together meat, shallots (onion), parsley, and chopped pepper tops. Add salt and pepper to taste, eggs and thyme. Mix well. Add rice.

Fill the peppers ¾ full with this mixture. In Dutch oven, cover bottom of pan with tomato sauce (spaghetti sauce). Crowd the stuffed peppers together. Cover and cook over medium heat until peppers are done. Or bake at 400° for 40 to 50 minutes until peppers are tender.* If tomato sauce reduces, add more sauce or some water to keep peppers from sticking. Serve with remaining sauce poured over peppers. 6 servings

*Do not overcook rice. For faster cooking, you can parboil green peppers about 5 minutes. Cool before stuffing.

Poivrons Français

(poo-wah-vrohn)

Bretagne Anne

This is delicious as a side dish or as an hors d'oeuvre served on thin slices of toast. Serve either hot or cold.

4	medium green peppers	Pepper (freshly ground,
2	Tb hot olive oil	pungent)
1	2-oz tin anchovies, drained and chopped	Black olives

Prepare peppers by scorching them over open flame or under broiler, turning them as their skins blister. Let cool in a closed brown paper bag. Then peel, cut in half lengthwise, remove seeds and stems. Slice in ½ inch lengthwise strips. Layer strips in a shallow bowl, drizzle with hot olive oil. Sprinkle with chopped anchovies. Season to taste with pepper (do not use salt). Top with black olives. 4 servings

Potatoes

Today potatoes are considered valuable in a balanced reducing diet. Great news for a vegetable so maligned over the years as being "fattening," "too starchy." Europeans scorned potatoes for years, claiming them to be harmful to health. Potatoes are really nutritional and contain less calories per ounce than rice, apples, avocados, or even cottage cheese. So, eat potatoes. They can be prepared in so many delicious ways—from baked, mashed, scalloped, fried to gnòcchi and knish!

Pommes Frites

(pohm freet)

In France, when the potato was first introduced, it became the Frenchman's favorite food. Potage Parmentier, a potato soup, was named after one of the first to introduce Pommes de Terre (literally, "apples of the earth")—Monsieur Augustin Parmentier. And Pommes Frites, French Fries, became universal.

There may be differences of opinion in the proper preparation of French fries, but on these points professionals essentially agree:

A deep-fryer with wire basket is best, and a frying thermometer is very helpful. Potatoes are peeled and cut into strips and dried thoroughly. They are never soaked in salted water. Potatoes are fried a few at a time in hot oil and removed to paper towels as soon as they are golden (not brown). This is the first frying. When ready to serve, they are put back into hot oil and fried until brown. Oil may be stored in a tightly covered container, without refrigeration, for reuse.

Oil temperatures vary. The French prefer higher temperatures from 375° to 400°, whereas peanut oil users recommend 320° for the first frying and 375° for the second frying.

After the second frying, one expert drains the fries on a paper towel and salts them. Another removes the potatoes from the fryer onto a hot platter, sprinkles them with salt, and serves them immediately—never draining them on paper towels after the second frying.

Chacun à son goût—every man to his taste—to each his own!

Farmer French Fries

If you like French fries!!

Peel, wash and dry thoroughly 2 to 4 baking potatoes. Cut into ½-inch thick strips. Place on cookie sheet lined with aluminum foil. Bake at 400° for 20 to 25 minutes until lightly browned. Sprinkle with sea salt (salt crystals; kosher). 4 to 6 servings

No cooking oil, fewer calories!

Potatoes d'Or

1½ lbs potatoes, peeled,
   washed, dried, and diced

Salt and pepper
3 Tb vegetable or corn oil

Season potatoes with salt and pepper to taste. Sauté in one layer in hot oil until brown.

Transfer pan to 400° oven for 15 minutes. 4 to 6 servings

Cheese Potatoes en Casserole Georges

4 to 5 boiled potatoes (on hard
   side) peeled and sliced
¼ cup (4 Tb)
   butter/margarine, melted
½ cup milk

½ cup grated Swiss cheese
1 egg yolk, slightly beaten
   Grated Parmesan/
   Romano cheese

Pour butter/margarine into a 2-quart casserole. Layer the sliced potatoes in the casserole. Heat milk, add cheese, and whisk over heat. Remove from heat and whisk in egg yolk. Pour sauce over potatoes. Sprinkle with grated cheese. Bake at 400° until done, about 30 minutes. 4 to 6 servings

Parsley Potatoes Cordon Bleu

4 potatoes, peeled and sliced
   ¼ inch thick
1 medium onion, thinly sliced
1 Tb chopped fresh or
   snipped dried chives
1 Tb chopped fresh parsley

Salt and pepper
¼ cup (4 Tb)
   butter/margarine
1 cup chicken broth
½ clove garlic, minced (if
   desired)

Layer sliced potatoes in buttered 1½ quart buttered casserole. Top with layer of sliced onion. Sprinkle with chives and parsley. Salt and pepper to taste. Dot with the 4 tablespoons butter/margarine. Partially cover with the chicken broth. Add minced garlic if desired. Bake at 450° for 40 to 45 minutes. 4 to 6 servings

Tomates Farcies

Jackie Forget Eldredge

8 large tomatoes
½ lb ground beef, browned, or
   leftover cooked meat
4 shallots, chopped, or 2 Tb
   minced onion
2 Tb chopped fresh parsley
2 eggs, beaten

¼ tsp basil
1 cup cooked rice
   Salt and pepper
   Oil
   Bread crumbs or grated
   Parmesan/Romano cheese
   (if desired)

Wash tomatoes and cut stem top off. Trim out pulp (and reserve) leaving a thick shell. Mix together meat, shallots (onion), parsley, and reserved tomato pulp. Add eggs and basil, and mix well. Add rice. Season to taste with salt and pepper. Fill tomatoes with mixture. Crowd together in small oiled pan. Bake at 350° for 30 to 40 minutes until tomatoes are tender. Sprinkle tops with bread crumbs or grated cheese. 4 to 6 servings

Légumes Mornay Gratinés

(lay-goom—grah-tee-nay)

Marion Carlson

Vegetables:

2	10-oz pkgs frozen mixed vegetables
½	tsp salt
⅛	tsp garlic salt
2	Tb butter/margarine, softened

Mornay Sauce:

¼	cup (4 Tb) butter/margarine, melted
¼	cup flour
2	cups liquid from vegetables, plus chicken broth to make 2 cups
¼	cup grated Parmesan/Romano cheese
1	tsp salt
¼	tsp thyme
¼	tsp freshly grated or ground nutmeg
⅛	tsp garlic salt
2	Tb dry white wine (Chablis)

Topping:

2	cups bread torn into pieces
2	Tb butter/margarine, melted
	Garlic salt

Prepare vegetables per package directions. Drain and save the liquid. Arrange vegetables in a 2- to 3-quart buttered casserole. Season vegetables with the 2 salts and softened butter/margarine, stirring gently.

To make sauce, mix together all ingredients. Pour sauce over vegetables and mix gently.

Top with bread mixed with the melted butter. Sprinkle with garlic salt. Bake, uncovered, at 350° for 30 minutes. 6 servings

Vegetable Casserole Provençale

(pro- vahn- sahl)

1 or 2   tomatoes, sliced ¼ inch thick
½   tsp salt
¼   tsp pepper
1   small zucchini, sliced ¼ inch thick
1   carrot, sliced in thin rounds
1   stalk celery, cut into diagonal pieces
1   large green pepper, cut into strips
½   tsp salt
¼   tsp pepper
½   lb fresh green string beans, parboiled and cut into 2-inch pieces
½   lb fresh yellow wax beans, parboiled and cut into 2-inch pieces
6   small white onions, peeled and cut in halves
¼   cup minced green onion
½   clove garlic, minced
¼   cup chopped fresh parsley
¼   tsp thyme
½   tsp basil
¼   cup olive oil
¼   cup dry white wine

In a greased 2-quart casserole, arrange tomato slices over bottom and sprinkle with salt and pepper. Layer zucchini slices on top. Mound carrot, celery, and green pepper over center part of tomato and zucchini slices. Sprinkle with salt and pepper. Surround carrot, celery, and green pepper with green and yellow beans. Arrange onion halves over the beans. Sprinkle green onions, garlic, parsley, thyme, and basil over all the vegetables. Pour oil and wine over. Place aluminum foil over top and then cover with lid. Bake at 375° about 40 minutes. 6 to 8 servings

Zucchini and Tomatoes Provençale

2 to 3   small or medium zucchini
3 to 4   tomatoes*
2   potatoes (if desired)
  Olive oil
  Salt and pepper
  Onion salt
  Garlic salt
  Parsley, chopped fresh or dried flakes
  Grated Parmesan/Romano cheese
  Bread crumbs

Wash and lightly scrape skin on zucchini. Dry well. Cut in half lengthwise. Wash and dry tomatoes; cut in half. Peel potatoes, and cut into chunks. Grease pan generously with olive oil. Place vegetables, cut side up, in pan. Brush with olive oil. In this order, sprinkle to taste with salt and pepper, onion and garlic salts, parsley, and

grated cheese and bread crumbs. Drizzle with additional oil. Bake, uncovered, at 425° for 30 minutes, or until vegetables are tender. 4 Servings
*If tomatoes are small, use them whole—just slice off the tops.

Zucchini French Fries

2 to 3   zucchini
         Salt

Flour
Corn oil

Wash and dry zucchini. Do not pare. Cut in half lengthwise. With spoon, scrape out seeds. Cut into julienne strips. Sprinkle lightly with salt and let stand 30 minutes. Squeeze water out of strips. Roll in flour and deep fry in hot oil. Drain on paper towel. 4 to 6 servings

Excellent for frying is a new electric deep fryer that comes in baby, daddy, and granddaddy sizes.

Croque Monsieur Louis

Not only is Croque Monsieur a fast-food sandwich served with Pommes de Terre Frites (French fries), but it is delightful with cocktails.
For each sandwich:

2   slices sandwich bread,
    crusts trimmed
    Butter/margarine

2   slices ham
1   slice mozzarella or
    Gruyère cheese

Butter the bread. Place 2 slices of ham with the Mozzarella (Gruyère) in between on the bread. Press down top slice of bread.

Sauté in butter*/margarine until bread is brown on both sides and cheese is melting. Serve hot.
*Butter may be "clarified" first by melting butter and using the clear, yellow liquid off the top and leaving the milky residue. Butter will brown easier in this way, without burning.

To serve as a cocktail canapé, cut each sandwich into four triangles.

Cake Genoise

A famous, rich cake brought to France by Catherine de Medici from the Italian kitchens of Genoa.

1 round angel food cake, cut into 3 layers
1 recipe Cream Filling (below)
1 recipe Bittersweet Chocolate Frosting (below)
1 cup chopped pecans or walnuts

Cream Filling:

⅔ cup sugar
⅛ tsp cream of tartar
5 egg yolks
1 cup (2 sticks) butter/margarine, softened
½ oz Cognac
Confectioners sugar (if needed)

In a small pan, blend together sugar, cream of tartar, and ⅓ cup water. Bring to a boil, stirring constantly until sugar is dissolved. Continue boiling gently without stirring until syrup registers 240° on a candy thermometer (soft ball). Remove from heat and cool 2 minutes. In a large electric mixer bowl, beat egg yolks well. Beat in the syrup in a slow steady stream and keep beating until mixture has cooled. Beat in the butter/margarine, 1 Tb at a time (16), and beat until mixture is creamy and thick. Add Cognac. Refrigerate until firm enough to spread. Confectioners sugar can be added if needed to thicken.

Bittersweet Chocolate Frosting:

6 squares semi-sweet chocolate
¼ cup extra-strong hot coffee
⅓ cup butter/margarine, softened
4 egg yolks
⅓ cup butter/margarine, half firm
3 to 4 Tb confectioners sugar
½ oz Cognac
1 tsp vanilla extract

Melt chocolate in hot coffee over hot water. Pour into electric mixer bowl. Beat in rest of ingredients, one at a time, until mixture is smooth. Refrigerate until firm.

To assemble: Spread cream filling between the layers of cake just up to one inch from the edge. Frost top and sides with the chocolate frosting. By hand, pat nuts around the sides. Refrigerate. 8 servings

Any cream filling and frosting left over can be frozen for another cake.

136

Praline Brittle Pumpkin Pie

(prah-lean)

Praline is a crisp confection made of pecans browned in boiling sugar. It is said to have been named after the debonair Marechal duc de Choiseul–Praslin, a field marshall during the reign of Louis XIII. As a token of affection, he would bestow this confection on his many lady loves.

¼	cup (4 Tb) butter/margarine	¾	tsp ground nutmeg
½	cup sugar	1	tsp cinnamon
1	cup chopped pecans	½	tsp salt
1	envelope unflavored gelatine	¼	cup milk*
½	cup light brown sugar, firmly packed	1	cup heavy cream, whipped*
1	16-oz. can pumpkin	1	baked 9-inch pie shell
			Additional whipped cream for topping

Make pecan brittle by melting butter/margarine in a small pan. Stir in sugar. Add pecans. Stirring constantly, continue cooking over medium heat until sugar begins to turn golden, 2 to 3 minutes. Remove from heat and place on aluminum foil. Cool. Crumble into small pieces. Set aside.

In a saucepan, sprinkle gelatine over ½ cup cold water and stir over low heat until gelatin is dissolved. Remove from heat and stir in brown sugar until sugar is dissolved. Place pumpkin in a large mixing bowl. Add nutmeg, cinnamon, salt and milk, and mix together. Blend in the gelatin-sugar mixture until smooth. Fold in the whipped cream. Sprinkle 1 cup of praline brittle over bottom of pie shell. Spoon pumpkin mixture over. Chill until firm. To serve, decorate with dollops of additional whipped cream and remaining pecan brittle. 6 to 8 servings
*Non-dairy whipped topping may be used instead of milk and whipped cream.

Swiss Apple Pie

2 to 3	golden delicious apples	2	Tb sugar
1	unbaked pie shell	1	Tb flour
	Raisins	½	cup milk
1	egg		Confectioners sugar

Peel and core apples and cut each into 12 sections. Cover bottom of pie shell with raisins. Layer the apple sections over raisins in an overlapping design. Whisk together egg, sugar, flour, and milk, and pour over apples. Bake at 425° for 45 to 60 minutes. Sprinkle top with confectioners sugar. 6 to 8 servings

Bananas Foster d'Agostino

2 bananas, peeled and sliced in half lengthwise
3 Tb butter/margarine
3 Tb light brown sugar
½ tsp cinnamon
1 oz banana cordial
1 oz rum (light or dark)
2 scoops French vanilla ice cream

Place butter in a pan or chafing dish and melt over medium heat. Add brown sugar, stirring constantly until a smooth blend is achieved.

Sprinkle the bananas with cinnamon and add to mixture. Turn up flame until the syrup starts to bubble (not too long or the syrup will carmelize). Add the banana cordial and rum. Tilt the pan away from you to ignite the mixture.

Stir for a final blend, remove from the flame, pick up the bananas with two forks and place around the ice cream, then pour the syrup over the ice cream. 2 servings

Chocolate Mousse Cordon Bleu

A delightfully light dessert.

2 ozs semi-sweet chocolate, shaved
2 egg whites blended with 4 Tb sugar
2 egg yolks blended with 4 Tb sugar
1 oz brandy or Cognac
½ pt heavy cream, whipped

Melt chocolate over hot water or in Microwave oven. Whip egg whites until stiff peaks form. Whisk brandy (Cognac) into egg yolks. Blend melted chocolate into egg yolk mixture. Fold egg whites gently into yolk mixture. Fold in the whipped cream. Chill. 4 servings

Fresh Peach and Brandy Pie

Jean Kleffman Clauser

1 baked pie shell
4 or 5 ripe fresh peaches, peeled and sliced
2 cups peeled and crushed fresh peaches
1 cup sugar
3 Tb cornstarch
1 Tb lemon juice
1 Tb butter
2 ozs brandy or rum
1 tsp almond extract
½ pt heavy cream, whipped
Toasted slivered almonds (if desired)

Line baked pie shell with sliced fresh peaches. In a saucepan, combine crushed peaches with sugar, ½ cup water, cornstarch, and lemon juice. Cook over low heat until mixture is thick and clear. Add butter, cool slightly and add brandy (rum) and almond extract. Cool to medium warmth and spoon over fresh peaches. (If mixture is put over peaches while too hot, they will water slightly.) When completely cool, top with whipped cream and refrigerate 2 to 3 hours. At serving time, you may add toasted slivered almonds for a very special touch. 6 to 8 servings

Glace-Sorbet Flambé

(glahs-sore-beh flahm-bay)

A delightful dessert, beautiful and delicious as enjoyed at Maxim's in Paris.

- 2 qts vanilla ice cream
- 1 qt lime sherbet

Sauce:

- 3 10-oz pkgs frozen or 3 pts fresh strawberries, sliced
- 1 cup sugar, superfine or confectioners
- 1 oz rum, Cognac, or Amaretto
- 1 Tb lemon juice

  Semi-sweet chocolate bar

  Whole strawberries

- 2 ozs Cognac

Line 3-quart mold or bowl with ice cream. Fill center with sherbet. Freeze until firm. Unmold by placing it upside down on a plate. Using hot towels to soften the edges, gently run a knife around edge to separate from mold. Put back in freezer for about an hour. Thaw strawberries, if frozen.

To make sauce, mix together strawberries, sugar, liqueur, and lemon juice. Set aside.

Using a potato peeler (floating blade peeler), form curls from the chocolate bar.

When ready to serve, place ice cream sherbet mold on a service tray or platter. Pour sauce over. Decorate sides and top with chocolate curls, and place whole strawberries around mold.

For the pièce de résistance, heat 2 ounces Cognac in a small saucepan, tilt pan to ignite; then pour the flaming Cognac over the ice cream mold! 12 servings.

You can use berries and fruits in season of your choice as well as your favorite ice creams and sherbets.

Meringue Glacée Cordon Bleu

6 egg whites, at room
temperature

1½ cups sugar
Pinch of salt

Whip egg whites at high speed, adding sugar and salt gradually, until they stand in stiff peaks—so stiff that you can turn the bowl upside down.

Line cookie sheet with foil. Drop spoonfuls of egg whites in a circle (or in a mound) and make a well in each with back of spoon. Bake at 250° to 270° for about 1 hour and 10 minutes. Cool.

Serve on cold plates; fill with ice cream or fresh berries, and top with whipped cream or various sauces. 4 or more servings

FINNISH

Of all European nationalities that emigrated to the Mesabi Range, the Finnish People were the most numerous in the 1900s—over 7,000 Finns.

My many Finnish friends had names such as Salo, Rimpila, Leino, Kuusisto, Lampi, Wirtanen, Kojola, Luoma, Maki, Pakkanen, Niemi, Panula, and Valo.

Eleanor Haila Adamic (we grew up together) believes that most of the Finnish migration to America in the early twentieth century was motivated by political, religious, and economic reasons.

Finland was a part of Russia until 1918. The Finns had been allowed to call out and train their own men for the military in Finland. But when Nicolas II came into power, he decreed that the men were to be shipped to Russia and become a part of the Russian Army. To avoid that, many Finns fled to America. Those who stayed behind were well trained in the Russian Army. Finland won her independence in 1918, and in World War II, her people fought off the Russians with some of the same generals and soldiers that Russia had trained!

Church and State were under one rule in Finland. They took monies and crops away from the common people, leaving them very poor. For this reason, many Finns who migrated to America shunned the church.

Finland is a land of 60,000 lakes—"If you don't see water, you are not in Finland." No wonder the Finnish people emigrated to Minnesota, land of 10,000 lakes! There is an old Finnish proverb: "Oma tupa, oma hupa"—own your own land, be your own master. And that's what the Finns did. Since they didn't care for mining, they acquired land near the iron mines and became farmers.

Like the old tale that farmers first built barns to house their cattle and grain before building a home for the family, so the Finns were said to build their sauna (in Finnish it's sah-oo-nah) first and their living quarters later. We have all become acquainted with this type of bath over the years. In fact, it has become an American way of life.

There was a public sauna in our neighborhood that all nationalities patronized. Saturday night was a big night: pay your fee, pick up towels, buy a couple of bottles of pop, enjoy a steaming, relaxing bath, and then out into below zero weather.

Finnish people conducted all their community activities—religion, labor, cooperatives, music, social,—in their "Finn Halls." In later years, they even had a winter Little Finland in West Palm Beach, Florida, complete with a mayor and a Finn Hall.

As kids on the Iron Range, we would learn expressions in each other's languages, My favorite Finnish ones were:

Minule tul tikku (meenoole toolee teekoo): Please give me a match.
Mina rakastan sinua (meenah rahkahstahn seenooah): I love you.

Like its Scandinavian neighbors across the Gulf of Bothnia, Finland has an abundance of fish. Fish is so fresh that you buy it swimming in tanks at the fish market. The favorite is crayfish, during its short season in July and August. Steamed, its succulence is enjoyed with noisy gusto and slugs of vodka. Finns are noted for their baking: cakes soaked in fruit juices with beautiful marzipan flower decorations, the richest of pastries, and sour rye bread. They consume much butterfat, and beef and pork fats (insulation against the cold weather?). As in Scandinavian countries, meat is expensive and tough as there is little grazing land. So meat is cubed for stews, ground for meatballs, or pounded for roulades. Seasonings most used are caraway seeds and dill.

Finnish Cabbage Rolls

Signe Rimpila

1	large head cabbage	1	cup cooked rice
1	Tb salt	1½	tsp salt
¼	cup bread crumbs	1	tsp caraway seeds
½	cup light cream		Butter
½	lb ground pork	½	cup honey
½	lb ground beef or veal		

Remove core from cabbage and steam cabbage in water salted with 1 tablespoon salt until leaves begin to wilt. Separate leaves. Soak bread crumbs in cream. Mix meat with the soaked bread crumbs, rice, salt, and caraway seeds. Place small amount of meat mixture on individual leaves, roll, tucking in the ends. Place rolls, seam side down, in a buttered casserole. Brush with honey. Bake at 350° until rolls are golden. Pour small amount of boiling water over rolls. Cover with lid and continue baking for about 1¼ hours. 6 to 8 servings

Kalahia Mojakka

(kah-lah-hee-ah moy-yah-kah)

Hazel DeSanto

When I wrote to Hazel for the correct spelling, she not only gave it to me, but also included her mother's fish soup recipe. In loving memory of Mother Kolu, here, in part, is Hazel's letter:

I looked up Mojakka in a cookbook Mother gave me. I don't remember her putting tomatoes in hers, so I'll give you her Finnish version. Mother used quite a bit of onion. Since she preferred a milk broth, Mother would drain off the potato water when the potatoes were almost done. Then she would add the fish and cover the fish with milk to finish cooking. In Finland, this fish soup is known as Kalahiakeitto.

1½ to 2	lbs fish filets (any choice)	1	bay leaf
4 to 5	medium potatoes, peeled and cut into chunks	¼ to ½	tsp ground allspice
			Salt and pepper
1	medium onion, chopped	4	tsp cornstarch
2	carrots, sliced (if desired)		Butter

Place potatoes in a kettle along with the onion and carrots and cover with water. Cook until potatoes are almost soft. Add bay leaf, allspice, and salt and pepper to taste. Add fish and cook a few more minutes until fish is done. Thicken with 4 teaspoons cornstarch blended with 4 tablespoons water. Serve with a chunk of butter floating on top. 4 to 6 servings

143

Paistettu Norsia

(pahees-tee-too norseeah)

Fried smelts, an Iron Range favorite! In the springtime, they would gather down at Park Point on Lake Superior for the smelt runs. Big bonfires with outdoor grills—fish fry!

1 to 2	lbs fresh smelts (available frozen at your fish market)	¼	tsp pepper
1	cup flour		Oil
1	tsp salt		Finnic Sauce (recipe below)
			Lemon wedges

Clean, wash, and dry smelts. Put flour and seasonings in a bag and shake a few smelts at a time in it. Heat oil (about 1 inch high in pan) until bread cube browns in seconds. Fry fish until golden. Drain on paper towel. Salt lightly. Keep warm, uncovered, in oven. Serve either hot or cold (like eating popcorn). Garnish with Finnic Sauce if desired or with lemon wedges. 4 to 6 servings

Smelts can be rolled in other ingredients. First dip in beaten egg, then roll in bread crumbs, crushed corn flakes, or in cornmeal.

Finnic Sauce

2	lemons	1	Tb minced fresh parsley or
3	Tb butter/margarine		1 tsp dried flakes
2	Tb lemon juice		

Cut lemons in half and juice them. Scrape out pulp and white skin. Cream butter/margarine until soft. Gradually stir in lemon juice. Mix in the parsley. Beat until smooth. Fill lemon shells with mixture. Serve with fish. 4 servings

Hampurin Pihvi

Hamburger Steak

Verna Niemi

This is an old Finnish method of cooking hamburger.

1	lb ground beef	½ to 1	tsp salt
1	medium onion, chopped	¼	tsp pepper
2	Tb butter/margarine		Buttered bread slices

Sauté onion in butter until soft and yellow. Mix salt and pepper well into ground beef. Add meat to the onion and fry, stirring with a fork to break up hamburger. When cooked, spread hamburger immediately on buttered bread so that hot meat melts the butter. Serve while hot. 4 servings

Hillopannukakkuja

(heeloh pahnookah kooyah)

Spells Finnish pancakes, akin to Krum Kaka and Crêpes.

⅔ to 1	cup flour	1	Tb sugar
1	cup milk	⅛	tsp salt
2	eggs, beaten		Jam or preserves
2	Tb butter/margarine, melted and cooled	1	cup heavy cream, whipped
			Fresh berries (if desired)

In bowl, combine first 6 ingredients. Beat well until blended (use rotary beater). Batter should be thin. Heat griddle (grease, if required). Spoon batter on griddle, and turn once when pancake starts to bubble. Stack the pancakes, spreading jam or preserves between the cakes. Top with whipped cream. Use fresh berries along with the preserves if desired. 12 to 18 pancakes

Coffee Cake

Goldie Brunner

2	packets dry yeast	5	cups sifted flour (about)
1	cup milk	2	eggs, beaten
¼	cup (4 Tb) butter/margarine		Confectioners sugar icing*
½	cup sugar		Maraschino cherries
1½	tsp salt		Nuts

Soften yeast in ¼ cup lukewarm water. Scald milk; add butter/margarine, sugar, salt, and cool to lukewarm. Then add enough flour to make a thick batter. Add yeast and eggs and beat well. Add more flour, enough to make a soft dough. Turn onto a lightly floured board and knead until smooth and satiny. Place in a greased bowl, turn it over to grease the top. Let rise until double (2 hours). Place in two 13- x 10-inch greased pans or in greased muffin tins and let rise again until double (approximately ½ to ¾ hour). Bake at 350°; coffee cakes for 25 to 30 minutes, rolls for 20 to 25 minutes.

Cool, spread with icing and top with maraschino cherries and nuts. 2 coffee cakes or 3 dozen medium-size rolls.

*For confectioners sugar icing, combine 2 cups confectioners sugar with enough water to make a soft paste. May use canned, ready-to-spread icing.

145

Cranberry Putinki

Dagmar Panula

In the olden days, the pudding was whipped in a bowl immersed in snow.

1	cup cranberries	¼	tsp salt
1	cup sugar		Ice
½	cup farina (ground wheat or potato)		Light cream or whipped cream

Bring cranberries and 4 cups water to a boil; cook gently 20 minutes. Put through a strainer—squeeze cranberries to get all the juice. Mix juice together with sugar in a saucepan and bring to a boil. Add the farina and salt. Cook about 15 minutes, stirring occasionally. Remove from stove. Cool slightly. Put saucepan in bowl of ice and whip pudding with a whisk or spoon until light and fluffy. Cover with plastic or foil wrap; refrigerate. Top with cream. 6 to 8 servings

Finnish Coffee

Eleanor Haila Adamic

Coffee was mixed with a beaten egg, tied in a cloth bag, and dropped into boiling water. The aroma was wonderful and the clear brew tasted delicious.

Sugar lumps (hard ones) were broken in two and put between the teeth and coffee was sipped through the teeth. Many poured coffee into saucers and then sipped it.

ITALIAN

On our first visit to Italy with Mama Michelina, we flew to Rome, stayed there a few days, and then started out with our driver-guide Aldo to journey to Mother's and Father's birthplace, Bellisio Solfare (Pesaro).

We took the Autostrada del Sole, a superhighway that extends from Naples to northern Italy. We stopped frequently for gas and refreshments at Pavessi stations, a chain of beautifully constructed combination stores, bars, and restaurants.

We left the Autostrada to head northeast and passed the outskirts of villages built on top of the highest peak of land, walled like old medieval castles. There was Rietti, Terni, Spoleto (the town that has an exchange program of cultural festivals with Charleston, S.C.), Folignio, and Fabriano.

We drove through the most beautiful countryside. The closer we got to Bellisio, the more excited Mother became. She was taking us to see her homeland. Mother kept nudging us. "Look, look, see the olive trees, see the grape vines, see the cows, see the sheep. Look, look, look."

And it was impressive and emotional to approach little Bellisio Solfare, a small village with a few homes fanning up on either side of a winding mountainous road that goes on through to Pergola and Ancona. As we arrived at the railroad overpass, we glanced up and there high on this mountainous rock, sasso (sah-soh), was the church La Madonna del Sasso. Since that visit, my brother has built the Villa Paulucci on that same rock, halfway up to La Madonna del Sasso.

Bellisio Solfare was a mining town of solfara (sulfur). Most of the townspeople—the Paoluccis (Paulucci), Burattis, Pagliarinis, Borbiconis—worked in the mines. It was when the mines were depleted of sulfur that the miners emigrated to the iron ore mines in America—to Minnesota, to the Mesabi Iron Range.

The surrounding rolling countryside of Bellisio abounded in vineyards, orchards, and olive trees. They raised their own livestock, but no horses, as land was too precious. Even to this day, there are no markets in the town, only a weekly fish and bread peddler.

In the tiny town square stood the community oven, where Mother, on her first trip back, showed her relatives how to bake the cake mixes she had brought from America.

In Bellisio we met cousins and more cousins—Zuara, Maria, Angela, Silvana, Egitto, Filiberto, Cesare, Luigi, Ugo, Colomba, Dardo, Marcello, Guiseppina, Otello, and our dear Zia (aunt) Argenta Paolucci Buratti. Mother (Michelina Buratti Paulucci) and Argenta had been girlhood pals. Zia had a brother, Ettore. Michelina and Ettore were childhood sweethearts. We were shown their homes, next door to each other, where they used to flirt through the upstairs shutters.

Shopping in Bellisio, or rather in Pergola, the neighboring town, was an adventure. Just as in France, one must go to separate stores to take care of one's grocery list: the Macelleria (mah-cheh-lehr-EEah) for meat, the Pescheria for fish, the Panetteria for bread, the Pasticceria for pastry. The state-owned Tabaccheria e Sale shop was interesting; it sells tobacco products and salt for state revenue.

In Pergola, we went to an open market which is held every Saturday morning. Everything from pots and pans to linens, furniture, and wearing apparel is sold in the streets. At noon these merchants pack up and move on to the next town.

Dining out was such a joy. We drove on a road winding around the mountainside, way up to the top, to the Castello, a walled castle abandoned years ago. There in a cavernous structure of rock, we watched the women prepare crescia and roast meats in a gigantic open fireplace. We enjoyed soup with tortellini, pasta with tomato sauce, roast young lamb, squab, partridge, insalata misto, crescia, cheeses, fruit, and plenty of wine!

We spent three days in Rome with cousins Filiberto and Angela Buratti. What meals, mama mia! For noon dinners, as is customary in Italy, we had gnòcchi, polenta, pasta, pollo, and for dessert, crèma and macedònia!

Then it was time to go home. Arrivederci Roma. Ciao!

Ciao is an Italian colloquialism meaning "hello," "so long," "goodbye." What's interesting is that on the first visit Mother made back to her native land, she heard this word for the first time. Could it have been adapted from the American military expression for mealtime—food? Chow—ciao!

Each year members of the Paulucci and Buratti families from America and Europe return to Italy to join the Bellisiani in celebrating the Festival of La Madonna del Sasso, which is usually held on the last Sunday in May, and is under the direction of the Parish Priest, (presently, Don Luigi Merolli).

A procession begins early in the morning; young and old walk hundreds of feet up the winding steep path to the little church. A band accompanies the worshippers, and an oil painting of the Madonna is carried on a rack on men's shoulders.

After a short service, everyone gathers around the well in the courtyard to imbibe in a glass of wine from five-gallon raffia-wrapped jugs, to wash down hard-crusted bread and prosciutto.

The procession then returns down to the village, where mass is celebrated in the village church. Then the priest serves dinner to the visiting Americans and the priests from surrounding villages.

Late in the afternoon, the festivities get going—sack races and greased-pole climbing for prizes, and souvenir baskets of candies and fresh fave for all. More wine, prosciutto, hard-crusted bread, cheeses, and olives are enjoyed.

At dusk, a procession with lighted torches slowly climbs the mountainside again, and what a beautiful sight it is to see the twinkling lights and to hear the gentle murmur of voices. After a display of fireworks, the procession ends back down at the village square where the dancing begins. The band members, led by cousin Balilla Buratti, honored us by playing the one American song in their repertoire, the "Beer Barrel Polka."

The Madonna del Sasso probably dates back to the early part of the twelfth century, when the Avellanti hermits built a monastery and church to replace the first primitive cells there on the sasso.

Jurisdiction of the monastic commune was directed by a priore, and their lives were dedicated to "ora et labora," prayer and labor. The most noteworthy priore of the Madonna del Sasso was Father Innocenzo Marchesi from Forli, who commissioned the painting of *La Madonna and Her Divine Son* in 1710. Subsequently restored and reframed, this painting is treasured to this day.

One of the first miracles recorded and attributed to La Madonna was during church services on June 3, 1781, Pentecost Sunday, when Pergola, Caglia, Frontone, and Serra were destroyed by a violent earthquake. Yet, the people from Pergola, on a pilgrimage to the Madonna del Sasso, suffered no earthquake shock or injuries. These Pergolesi, in recognition of their escape from danger, donated to the Madonna a heart of silver with an inscription, which is still kept in the Sanctuary. A procession was formed to honor Her. The Madonna's portrait was carried to

Pergola and was exposed to the invocations and veneration of the faithful. After eight days, the psalm-singing procession returned the Madonna to the Sanctuary.

Many miracles have been attributed to her since then. Great Uncle Paolucci cried to her for help when, working on the railroad overpass, he lost his balance and started to fall several hundred feet to the ground. He landed on his feet—unhurt. And, during World War II, the women of Bellisio prayed to La Madonna del Sasso to bring back all their loved ones. They might have been captured or wounded, but eventually all the men returned home! In the courtyard of La Madonna del Sasso stands a shrine built by those men to honor and thank her.

To this day the Church of the Sasso maintains its original structure. A statue at the cloister entrance confirms this. It represents S. Romualdo robed in a cowl, with flowing beard and droopy mustache, standing and directing a vigorous glance toward Mt. Catria. In his left hand is the symbolic walking stick, and in his right hand he holds a model of the church. The interior of the church is one big nave with three altars; the major one being a niche completely frescoed with sacred images and inscriptions, the other two, artistically done in baroque design.

Any ancient inscriptions concerning restorations of the Sanctuary have been lost. Only recent ones remain. In one window is the date 1914. In the portico of the Cloister is recorded the restoration in 1934 by the Combattant Section of Bellisio Solfare. Inside the Church the most recent restoration of the splendour of the Sanctuary is recorded with the inscription:

Per Onorare
I Genitori La Tradizione E La Terra D'Origine
Gino Francesco Paolucci
Ha Restaurato Questo Santuario
MCMLXXII

(In Honor of His Parents, Tradition and Land of Origin, Jeno Francis Paulucci Restored This Sanctuary, 1972.)

Upon entering the Sanctuary, the devout are drawn to the faces and animated eyes of the *Madonna and Her Divine Son*. Kneeling at the feet of the Heavenly Patron Saints, visitors recall the pilgrimages, the ceremonies, and the choral voices singing hymns of praise to the first Hermits and to their own ancestors. The Bellisiani jealously guard the Sanctuary of the Sasso, proud of the history and traditions of nearly one thousand years.*

*Translated and compiled from a documentation "Il Sanctuario della Madonna del Sasso, presso Bellisio Solfare" by Sandro Sebastianelli, as commissioned by Celso Paolucci, Bellisio Solfare (Pesaro), Italia.

Some Italian names on the Iron Range were Albani, Gallo, Calliguri, Fena, Antonelli, Pittarelli, Tomassoni, Pecci, Gambucci, Marinucci, Pietrosanti, Digiambattista, Dominichetti, Romani, and Pagliarini.

Typical Italian fare is minestre in brodo (soups eaten with a spoon), like tortellini and capelletti; minestre asciutte (dishes eaten with a fork), including pasta, risotto, polenta, and gnòcchi; also antipasto, pizza, crescia, insalata mista, fruits, cheeses, cafe espresso, and crusty bread. Olive oil, pancetta (bacon fat), salt pork, tomatoes, cheeses, wines, and herbs—such as basilico, oregano, and rosmarino—are all important in Italian cookery.

And, of course, garlic. The Chinese and Greeks may have extolled this exotic bulb as far back as 3,000 B.C., but it must have been the Italians who first introduced it on the Iron Range, because we were known as the garlic and wine people, usually in a disdainful way. How tastes do change!

And wine, it was the beverage of the Italians as coffee was to the Scandinavians and tea to the English!

So, regardless of Congressman Andrew Volstead's Prohibition Law (1919–1933), every family had its supply of wine in the cellar. Grape vendors (like Mondavi and Mattiacci) would go to California, and ship back carloads of grapes. The freight cars were usually unloaded in the dark of night. Why? I don't know, as buying one carload of zinfandel grapes per family was really not illegal!

Then, down in the cellar, undercover, the grapes would be mashed. We had a huge grape press that mashed as you turned the crank. The empty boxes were knocked down for firewood. There were rows of aged whiskey barrels, some horizontal, some vertical, ready for the various stages of processing and fermentation of the wine.

Jeno and I didn't much care for wine, but we did like home brew. This was made in a huge crock kept behind the kitchen stove. Malt, hops, sugar, potatoes, and fresh yeast would ferment until bottling time. It was my job to go to the bakery to buy the needed five pounds of fresh yeast—with the story that we were doing a lot of baking! Sometimes when we would add too many potatoes (to give the brew "kick"), bottles would explode and spew the brew all over the place.

Most recipes in this section were inspired by Mama Michelina's cooking. And someone had to record her culinaria as well as that of other paisanos!

Antipasto

Michelina Paulucci

Delicious served cold as an hors d'oeuvre or as a side dish. Years ago, this was a whole day's work, preparing the vegetables and sauce, and filling sterilized jars for preserving. Now, just keep refrigerated.

½   cup olive oil
1   cup chopped onions
2   cloves garlic, minced
1   16-oz can tomatoes, slightly chopped
2   Tb chopped fresh parsley
1   cup celery (cut bite-size)
1   cup green pepper (cut bite-size)

1   cup whole baby carrots (or regular size, sliced)
1   cup green beans (cut in 2-inch pieces)
1   cup cauliflower florets
¼   cup cider vinegar
½   cup catsup

The following ingredients are all drained of oils or juices (use any or all):

2   2-oz tins anchovies
¼   cup capers
1   14-oz can artichoke hearts
1   3¾-oz tin sardines
1   7-oz can tuna
1   6-oz jar cornichons (baby ear corn)
1   4-oz jar pimientos or roasted red peppers, cut up

1 to 2   cups assorted olives
1   4-oz can sliced mushrooms or ¼ lb fresh, sautéed
1   5-oz jar cocktail onions
1   8- to 10-oz jar gherkin (midget) pickles, sweet or dill

In a large pot, heat oil and sauté onion until soft. Add garlic, tomatoes, and parsley; sauté 3 minutes. Add celery, green pepper, carrots, green beans, and cauliflower, and cook gently 5 minutes until vegetables are just tender, but still crisp and crunchy. Add vinegar and catsup. Then mix in any or all of the remaining ingredients and let simmer a few minutes to meld and heat through. Chill before serving. About 4 quarts

Brasciòle

(bra-zho-lay)

Hazel DeSanto

One slice of flank steak (about 1½ pounds) flattened thin. Sprinkle with garlic powder and black pepper. Layer with thin slices of ham or prosciutto. Sprinkle with grated Parmesan/Romano cheese. Roll up tightly into a long "jellyroll." Secure with twine as you would a salami. Roast at 375° (½ hour per pound or until well done). Chill. Slice thin for hors d'oeuvre.

Harry's Bar

One afternoon as we were strolling along Calle Vallaresso in Venice, we found ourselves in front of the frosted glass doors of Harry's Bar. Harry's Bar was named after an American who helped start the place back in 1931; but it was Giuseppe Cipriani (gew-sehp-peh chee-pree-ah-nee) who made it, he and, later, his son Arrigo (ah-ree-go), Harry.

It was the watering hole of celebrities, notables, royalty, and plain folk. After World War II, Cipriani devoted himself to "la cucina" (lah coo-chee-nah), and Harry's Bar became renowned for the best Italian food in Italy, distinctly Cipriani!

We slipped into Harry's Bar for a Bellini. The bar was conveniently close to the frosted glass doors and well lighted; the dining room, simple with tables and chairs.

Our last evening in Venice we took a taxi (motor launch) to the luxurious Hotel Cipriani. (I have never seen such a huge swimming pool.) There we dined al fresco on Cipriani's delectable tagliatelle, polenta, scampi, and zabaglione. We savoured a raw beef appetizer which Cipriani had concocted for a contessa who could not eat cooked meat. This creation of Commendatore Cipriani's has been a well-guarded secret for years.

Carpaccio

(car-pah-chee-oh)

Vittore Carpaccio was a Venetian Master Painter whose use of brilliant colors inspired the name for this unique antipasto or late night sup. Here is our version.

1 lb beef (lean filet or London broil)	½ tsp dry mustard
	½ tsp hot pepper sauce
1 cup egg mayonnaise	¼ to ⅓ cup cold strong beef broth
1 Tb Worchestershire sauce	

Slice beef paper thin into 3- x 2-inch slices. (Put meat in freezer until partially frozen before slicing.) Arrange 3 or 4 slices on individual plates. Blend together mayonnaise, Worcestershire sauce, mustard, and hot pepper sauce. Gradually mix in beef broth until sauce is of a thick consistency. Spoon sauce over beef slices, allowing some red meat to show through. *Squisito!*

Celery Dip

Angela Buratti

1 Tb olive oil	½ tsp pepper
1 tsp salt	

Mix all ingredients together in individual, tiny dishes. Use to dip crisp celery stalks, also any other raw vegetables like carrot sticks, radishes, and cauliflower florets. A drop of wine vinegar and/or chopped anchovies can also be added.

Mozzarella DeLucca

Cheese snack delicious!

Cut a long loaf of French or Italian bread in half lengthwise. Cover both pieces with slices of mozzarella cheese. Put under broiler until cheese melts and bread is slightly toasted. Cut crosswise into serving slices. For added "spice," sprinkle with onion or garlic salt.

Olives à la Romana

Drain brine off a jar of green olives; either pitted or unpitted, plain or pimiento-stuffed.

Place olives in a small bowl; drizzle olive oil over so olives are well coated. Sprinkle with minced fresh garlic or garlic powder. Let marinate at least an hour before serving.

Pesce Piquante

(pay-shay peee-kahn-tay)

Spicy Fish Delite

Michelina Paulucci

3 lbs fish (white, haddock, pike, or halibut)	8 green Greek peppers in vinegar, finely cut
1 tsp salt	2 cups cider vinegar
½ tsp pepper	3 2-oz tins anchovies (flat or rolled), partially drained
1 cup olive oil	2 tsp capers
6 cloves garlic, chopped	
6 sprigs parsley, chopped	

Boil fish in small amount of boiling salted water for 2 to 3 minutes. Drain. Cut into small pieces. Sprinkle with salt and pepper.

Heat olive oil, garlic, and parsley until garlic is soft. Add green peppers and sauté for a few minutes. Pour in vinegar and bring to a boil. Boil 5 to 10 minutes. Add anchovies and capers. Cool.

Cover bottom of 6 pint jars with a little sauce, then layer fish and sauce alternately, ending with sauce to cover the fish. Twist lids on tightly and refrigerate. Serve cold.

Prosciutto e Melone

(pro-shoot-oh ay meh-lohn-nay)

A very special Italian antipasto.

1	cantaloupe (chilled), peeled, halved, and de-seeded	½	lb thinly sliced prosciutto

For cocktails: Cut melon into cubes. Wrap a small slice prosciutto around each cube and secure with toothpick.

For antipasto: Cut melon in wedges and drape a thin slice of prosciutto on top. The cool, juicy melon blends tastefully with the salt in the prosciutto. Fresh figs (fichi) are also served with prosciutto.

Cappelletti in Brodo

(kah-pay-lay-tee in brod-oh)

Ida Dominici

Tiny meat-stuffed dumplings shaped like little brimmed hats (cappèlo) in broth.
Meat Filling:

1	lb boned veal or chicken breasts	¼	tsp marjoram or freshly grated nutmeg
1	lb lean pork steak or butt	¼	cup (4 Tb) butter/margarine, softened
½	lb beef sirloin steak	4	Tb bread crumbs
¼	cup finely chopped salt pork	3 to 4	Tb grated Parmesan/Romano cheese
2	Tb chopped onion	1	egg
1	tsp salt		
¼	tsp pepper		

Cut meat into large chunks. Render salt pork; add onion and cook until soft. Sauté meat in the salt pork and onion over medium heat for 1 to 2 hours. Season with salt, pepper, and marjoram (nutmeg). By now the meat will have absorbed most of the meat juices; meat should be tender and moist, not dry. Cool.

Grind meats fine and place in a large bowl. Add rest of the ingredients and mix well as for a meat loaf. Cover and refrigerate for about an hour.
Pasta:

4 to 5	cups flour (approximately)
1	tsp salt
6	eggs, at room temperature
	Chicken or beef broth

Place flour and salt in a bowl and make a "well." Beat eggs until frothy, stir eggs into flour, gradually adding 2 tablespoons lukewarm water to form a firm dough.

Let dough rest about 5 minutes, covered completely. Knead dough on lightly floured surface until smooth and manageable. Cut dough and form into balls. Roll out 1 ball at a time so that pasta will not dry out. With rolling pin, roll into a thin sheet on a lightly floured board; immediately cut into rounds with a 1½-inch cutter.

Place ½ teaspoon meat filling toward center of each round; fold 1 side over. Press dough all around sides to seal firmly, then pinch the two ends together to form little hats. Makes about 650 cappelletti.

To serve: Drop cappelletti in rapidly boiling chicken or beef broth. To 1½ quarts of broth, use 100 cappelletti. Let broth come back to a boil, let boil 5 minutes, then turn heat down to medium and continue to boil gently another 5 minutes, or until dough is tender. 10 to 12 servings

This meat filling makes delicious stuffing for ravioli, too!

Lentil Soup

I call this the Italian version of Mexican chili, hot and zesty. No need to soak the lentils.

2 cups dry lentils	2½ tsp salt
½ lb *each* mild and hot sausage (if desired)	½ tsp oregano
	¼ tsp sage
2 cups chicken broth	¼ tsp cayenne pepper
8 ozs pepperoni, thinly sliced	2 medium carrots, sliced
1 cup chopped onion	2 stalks celery, diced
1 16-oz can tomatoes	

Wash lentils in a colander. Cut sausage into small pieces and fry. Drain. In a 6-quart caldron, combine lentils, sausage, 8 cups water, chicken broth, pepperoni, onion, tomatoes, salt, oregano, sage, and cayenne. Bring to a boil. Reduce heat; cover and simmer for 30 minutes, stirring occasionally. Add carrots and celery; cover and simmer 40 minutes more. 6 to 8 servings

Great-Grandmother Paulucci's
Minestrone Soup

This soup comes from my ancestral home in the Marche region of Italy, Bellisio Solfare (Pesaro).

½ cup dry navy beans
1 cup finely diced carrots
½ cup finely diced turnip
1½ cups finely shredded cabbage or 1 cup fresh string beans
½ cup peas (fresh or frozen)
3 tsp salt
¼ tsp pepper
1 tsp oregano
3 Tb butter/margarine

¼ lb salt pork, minced ("batutto")
1 medium onion, sliced
¼ cup minced fresh parsley
1 28-oz can plum tomatoes, slightly chopped
½ cup finely chopped celery
1 large clove garlic, minced
½ to 1 cup spaghetti, broken into 2- to 3-inch pieces, or small elbow macaroni

Soak navy beans overnight and drain, or bring beans to a boil in water to cover and drain. Combine beans, carrots, turnip, cabbage (string beans), and peas* in a large soup kettle. Add water to cover (about 2½ quarts), salt, pepper, and oregano. Bring to a boil, uncovered, and boil for 30 minutes. Meanwhile, melt butter/margarine in a large pan. Add salt pork; render; then add onion. Sauté gently until softened. Add parsley, tomatoes, celery, and garlic. Simmer for a few minutes. Add tomato mixture to the broth and cook for 1 to 1½ hours. When soup is almost done, add spaghetti (macaroni) and boil 8 to 10 minutes until spaghetti is al dente (a little firm when you bite it). 6 to 8 servings
*If using frozen peas, thaw and add them last.
Serve with crusty bread, a green salad, and a glass of wine.

Sausage and Escarole Soup

1 lb mild Italian sausage, cut into small pieces
1 lb hot Italian sausage, cut into small pieces

3 bunches escarole*
1 Tb salt
Salt and pepper

Sauté sausage in an ungreased 12-inch pan until thoroughly cooked. Drain off excess fat and set pan aside. Wash and separate escarole leaves. Bring 4 cups water to a boil in an 8-quart caldron, add 1 tablespoon salt, and drop in the escarole gradually, stirring until all the escarole has been added. When water has returned to a boil, cover and simmer 10 minutes. With a fork, lift the escarole dripping with the water in which it has been cooked into the pan with the sausage. Cook over low heat for 5 minutes. Salt and pepper to taste. 6 to 8 servings

*Escarole, like spinach, reduces greatly in cooking.
Serve with crusty Italian or garlic bread.

Stracciatella

Egg Drop Soup

3 cups chicken broth	Pepper (preferably white)
2 tsp cornstarch*	Grated Parmesan/Romano
1 green onion, chopped	cheese
1 egg, well beaten	

Bring the chicken broth to a boil. Add cornstarch blended with 2 tablespoons water slowly to broth, stirring constantly. When the broth is thickened, add the green onion. While stirring the soup rapidly, gradually add the beaten egg. Remove from the heat immediately and season to taste with pepper. Sprinkle with grated cheese. 4 servings
*Some use pastina or flour to thicken the broth.

Crêpes Italian (Cannelloni)

(kah-nell-oh-nee)

Michelina Paulucci

1¼ cups flour	Filling of your choice
⅛ tsp salt	Spaghetti sauce of your
3 eggs, beaten	choice
1½ cups water or bouillon	Grated Parmesan/Romano
(beef or chicken)	cheese
2 Tb olive oil	

Place first 5 ingredients in mixer or blender and blend well. Let batter stand for 1 or more hours.

To cook crêpes, follow directions of the crêpe pan manufacturer with these precautions: If pan is either too hot to too cold, batter will not adhere. If crêpes are too thin or have a lacy appearance, add more flour to batter. Crêpes may be prepared in advance and refrigerated or frozen. Allow crêpes to stand at room temperature before separating. Makes 18 to 20 crêpes.

Use Liz' Spaghetti Sauce with Meatballs recipe or Pasta Bellisiana spinach mixture for filling. Spoon crumbled meatballs or the spinach mixture on each crêpe, and then roll. Spread spaghetti sauce on the bottom of a large baking pan. Arrange rolled crêpes on top of sauce, in one layer only. Spoon additional sauce on top. Sprinkle with grated cheese. Bake at 350° about 15 to 20 minutes until hot and bubbly. 4 to 6 servings

Pans of rolled crêpes can be prepared ahead. Refrigerate or freeze. Thaw before baking in oven.

Enrico's Spaghetti Carbonara

On one of our first trips to Italy, we noticed roadside signs with "Pasta Carbonara." When we asked our driver, Enrico, what that was, he gave us this recipe, which he prepares quite often.

1	lb spaghetti	6	slices bacon, finely diced
2	Tb salt	2	Tb olive oil
3	egg yolks, at room temperature, beaten	1/3	cup dry white wine
1/3	cup grated Parmesan cheese		Freshly ground black pepper
1/3	cup grated Romano cheese		

Cook spaghetti in 4 to 6 quarts boiling water salted with 2 tablespoons salt about 7 to 8 minutes, until done al dente (a little firm when you bite it). Beat egg yolks with grated cheeses. Fry diced bacon in olive oil until crisp; add wine and continue cooking until wine evaporates. Keep hot. Drain spaghetti and add to bacon-oil mixture. Add egg-cheese mixture. Stir rapidly, so that egg mixture cooks onto hot spaghetti. Serve on *hot* plates. Sprinkle with plenty of black pepper for the carbonara (charcoal) look! 4 to 6 servings

Fettucine Alfredo

(fet-too-chee-nay)

Alfredo L'Originale Imperatore

Alfredo's in Rome, Italy, is renowned. People of worldwide fame have dined there, and autographed photos hang on the walls to prove it. The *pièce de résistance* is Alfredo's Fettucine, and well honored may you be should the Master himself serve it for you.

The first time there, we didn't know all this, so, when the waiter suggested we start our dinner with Fettucine Alfredo, we declined, as we wanted to skip eating pasta. Well, Alfredo himself came to our table, his handlebar mustache bristling. Nobody turned down his Fettucine. Needless to say, we had Fettucine, tossed at our table personally by Alfredo. He flourished a gold fork and spoon engraved: *To Alfredo, King of Noodles. Mary Pickford and Douglas Fairbanks.* July, 1927, and gallantly presented them to one of the ladies in our group to use.

Since then we have become old friends and frequent diners at Alfredo's. Just recently we again enjoyed the Fettucine Alfredo and again I was honored to use the famous gold spoon and fork. Not only were we welcomed as dear friends from America, but we were especially privileged that evening to be invited to the kitchen to watch the chef prepare the Fettucine.

On a huge black stove there were many pots of various sizes filled with boiling salted water. Directly across, on a large table, there were two big tubs: one filled

Sausage and Escarole Soup, p. 158

PHOTOGRAPH BY RICHARD JEFFREY

Fresh ingredients will make all your cooking taste better!

Potica, p. 204

*Kungling Kott Bollen Svensk
(Royal Swedish Meatballs), p. 73*

with grated cheese, the other filled with scoops of butter, and all that lovely pasta was on a large tray.

As soon as an order came in for Fettucine Alfredo for three, in went the noodles, in a pot sized for three servings. As the noodles cooked, the waiter stood by with a warm platter which the chef covered with butter; noodles were then tested for doneness *(al dente)*, the pot was removed to the sink, drained into a long-handled colander, the fettucine emptied onto the platter and covered with cheese. Off hurried the waiter to the diners' table to toss and serve the hot, buttery, covered-with-melted-cheese, Fettucine Alfredo!

We were given valuable tips:

> Use only sweet cream
> butter.
> Boiling water is salted with
> coarse salt.
> Parmesan cheese is fresh,
> not aged, and grated very
> fine.
> Noodles are made with
> eggs and semolina.
> Cream is never used

Fresh Parmesan is difficult to find as it is aged before being shipped overseas, but a good aged Parmesan will do very nicely. One pound of fettucine will serve 4 generously. Use plenty of boiling water (4 qts with 2Tb salt). Be very generous with the butter and cheese. Serve hot!

For Fettucine alla Romana, just add cooked peas and shredded prosciutto or ham.

Gnòcchi

(neeo-key)

Polenta and gnòcchi are my favorites of all pasta (pah-stah).

Gnòcchi are little potato dumplings served with spaghetti sauce. I remember how Mother always used to caution me about using too much flour, which would make the gnòcchi tough. The first time I made them, I was careful to use very little flour. To my dismay, my gnòcchi completely disintegrated when placed in the boiling water! Good thing I had a package of spaghetti on hand!

Here is a foolproof recipe:

2½ cups cold mashed potatoes	Spaghetti sauce of your
1½ cups flour	choice
1 egg	Grated Parmesan/Romano
½ tsp salt	cheese
¼ tsp pepper	

Mix first five ingredients together in bowl, then knead gently on a floured surface. Cut dough in half and roll each piece into a long rope, about 1 inch in diameter. Cut into 1-inch pieces. With finger, indent and roll cut sides in flour. Lightly flour them and let them sit on a floured surface, not touching each other, for at least 30 minutes. Keep turning them over so they can dry. Makes approximately 70 dumplings.

Place gnòcchi in large kettle of rapidly boiling, salted water. Boil gently for about 8 minutes, or until gnòcchi are cooked (not gummy). Drain. Serve with spaghetti sauce and a sprinkling of grated cheese. 8 to 10 servings

Make gnòcchi ahead and refrigerate or freeze them on floured wax paper. They can go straight from the freezer into the boiling water.

Lasagne

Michelina Paulucci

1 lb ground beef	1 6- to 8-oz pkg thinly sliced
4 cloves garlic, minced	mozzarella cheese
3 cups prepared spaghetti sauce	1 16-oz carton ricotta cheese
1 8-oz package lasagne noodles (9 to 11 strips)	Grated Parmesan/Romano cheese

Sauté meat and garlic slowly until meat is browned. Pour off excess fat from the pan. Add the spaghetti sauce and simmer for a few minutes. Cook lasagne noodles in boiling salted water per package directions. Drain. Pour a thin layer of sauce on the bottom of a large baking pan (about 9½ x 13½ inches). Alternate layers, starting with lasagne strips, 2 slices mozzarella, ricotta cheese, and some of the sauce. Repeat layers, ending with sauce. Sprinkle grated cheese on top. Bake at 350° about 45 minutes. Let stand 15 minutes before cutting into squares. 10 to 12 servings

Manicotti

Michelina Paulucci

Prepared like cannelloni, except egg pasta is used instead of crêpes.

Make a batch of egg pasta as for Ravioli (see recipe). Roll dough very thin. Cut pasta into 4- x 6-inch rectangles. Cook in a large kettle of boiling salted water with 1 tablespoon olive oil added. Cook about 5 minutes. Drain. Place pasta pieces between kitchen towels.

To fill, spoon a small amount of your chosen filling on the bottom third of each rectangle. Fold dough over twice.

Proceed as for Crêpes Italian (Cannelloni).

Manicotti shells can be purchased.

Pasta Bellisiana

½	lb ground beef	1	tsp salt
2	cups prepared spaghetti sauce	¼	tsp pepper
2	10-oz pkgs frozen creamed spinach	⅛	tsp grated fresh or ground nutmeg
15 to 16	ozs ricòtta cheese or cottage cheese mixed with a raw egg	1	pkg (48 count, 12 ozs) jumbo macaroni shells
8	ozs mozzarella cheese, shredded		Grated Parmesan/Romano cheese

In a large skillet, slowly brown ground beef. Pour off excess fat. Stir in spaghetti sauce and simmer a few minutes. Set aside. Cook frozen spinach per package directions. Put in a large bowl and let cool. Then mix in ricòtta (cottage cheese/egg) and mozzarella cheese, salt, pepper, and nutmeg. Cook macaroni shells per package directions.* Drain well. Stuff each shell with 1 tablespoon of the spinach mixture. In 2 large baking pans cover bottoms with some of the spaghetti sauce. Place stuffed shells in the pans, in one layer only. Spoon spaghetti sauce over. Sprinkle with grated cheese. Bake at 350° for 30 minutes until hot and bubbly. 10 to 12 servings

Stuffed shells may be frozen before baking, covered tightly with aluminum foil. When ready to serve, remove foil, thaw, and bake at 350° for 30 minutes; or bake frozen, foil-covered, at 350° for 50 minutes, or until bubbly.

Use this basic recipe for filling manicotti shells, ravioli, or crêpes.
*For best results, add a teaspoon of oil to the boiling water. Boil pasta gently, stirring carefully so shells don't break. Drain and immediately separate the shells to keep them from sticking together.

Polenta

(poh-len-tah)

One of my favorites. I remember as a kid that some old Italian families had a large community serving board, which would be spread with the mush and sauce. It was put in the middle of the table, and members of the family would gather around and eat their portion directly from the board.

1   cup yellow cornmeal
1   tsp salt
    Spaghetti sauce of your
    choice

Grated Parmesan/Romano
cheese

Combine cornmeal, salt, and 1 cup cold water. Gradually pour this into 3 cups boiling water, stirring vigorously. Return to a boil, stirring constantly. Lower heat and partially cover the pot. Continue cooking over low heat about 5 minutes, stirring frequently. Caution: polenta bubbles like molten lava.

Spread mush on a large platter or on individual plates. Pour hot spaghetti sauce over; sprinkle with grated cheese. 6 to 8 servings

Ravioli

Michelina Paulucci

Pasta filled with cheese or meat filling and served in a savory tomato or white sauce.

2½ cups flour (approximately)
4   eggs
1   Tb olive oil
1   tsp salt
    Meat or cheese filling of
    your choice

Spaghetti sauce or
Béchamel Sauce (see
recipe)
Grated Parmesan/Romano
cheese

Beat eggs lightly with the olive oil and salt. Put flour in a mixing bowl and shape into a "well" with a hole in the center. Pour egg mixture into the center and blend flour into the eggs with your hands (better than a spoon), working the flour from the inside all around the wall until all flour is mixed in. (The experts can do this on a flat surface without breaking the dike and having an egg flood!) Form into a ball and knead it on a floured surface until pasta is smooth and elastic. Then shape it into a ball, brush lightly with olive oil, and let rest in a bowl covered with a dish for 30 minutes.

Take half the dough; pull and stretch it to start shaping into a rectangle. On a floured surface, roll it with a rolling pin (the long kind is better), back and forth with pressure (dough is elastic and not like a pie crust), until dough is *very* thin. Your finished ravioli will be of double thickness so it is important that dough be rolled thin.

Place 1 tsp filling, 4 inches down from edge of pasta and in a row 1½ inches apart. Pull dough over filling to cover, press with fingers. Cut with serrated roller, and seal with floured tines of a fork on all three sides of the "pillow." If you use a pasta machine to roll the dough, place dollops of filling on one strip and cover with a second strip and proceed as above, sealing all four sides. Turn ravioli onto a floured surface, sprinkle with flour and let dry before cooking. If storing ravioli, be sure they are well floured on both sides; refrigerate, to keep for a couple days, or freeze in serving portions. Makes approximately 3 dozen.

Place ravioli in a large kettle of boiling salted (2 to 3 Tb salt) water. Boil gently with "cracked" cover from 10 to 15 minutes, or until pasta is just tender but not gummy. Drain ravioli, arrange on a platter. Cover with favorite sauce. Sprinkle with grated cheese. 6 to 8 servings

Frozen ravioli can go directly from freezer to pot of boiling salted water.

Egg Pasta recipe can be used to make egg noodles, like fettucine. With rolling pin, roll out dough flat and thin. Then, starting at edge nearest you, fold and roll the dough away from you into a tube. Cut crosswise into desired widths. Shake apart and let dry on a floured surface. Or hang noodles on a pole to dry—just like in Italy.

Mama Michelina is proud that Jeno's prepared frozen Italian Entrées now on the market include not only Lasagne with Meat Sauce, Manicotti and Cappelletti, but Cheese Ravioli and Meat Ravioli, as well.

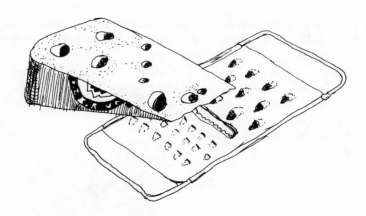

Ravioli Fillings

Michelina Paulucci

A combination of cooked meats and poultry, finely ground, seasoned with spices, and mixed with eggs, spinach, and cheese. Many use leftover meats. There are different methods of cooking the meat. Mother cooks the meat in tomato sauce. Others braise or roast it.

Meat Filling:

    1 lb turkey or chicken breasts
       with skin
    1 lb lean pork
    1 lb lean beef
    1 lb veal or additional beef
       and/or poultry

(All meat should be boneless and cut into small chunks.)

1. To braise, heat 2 Tb oil in a large frying pan and brown meat in it. Add a small amount of liquid (water, broth). Cover and simmer until meat is done. Cool and grind meat fine.

2. To roast, place meat chunks in roasting pan. Bake at 350° until meat is brown and well done. Cool and grind meat fine.

3. To cook in tomato sauce:

    2   Tb olive oil
    2   Tb chopped fresh parsley
    1   stalk celery, chopped
    ½   cup chopped onion
    1   clove garlic, minced
    1   2½-oz jar mushroom
         pieces, drained
    1   8-oz can tomato sauce

Sauté parsley, celery, onion, garlic, and mushrooms in olive oil until onion is soft. Add the meat chunks and cook until meat is browned. Add tomato sauce, cover, and simmer until meat is done. Cool meat and grind fine.

    10   ozs spinach, cooked,
          drained, and chopped
     3   Tb grated
          Parmesan/Romano cheese
     2   tsp salt
     1   tsp pepper
     1   tsp freshly grated nutmeg
          or ½ tsp ground
  2 to 3 eggs

Mix above ingredients well with the ground meat. Fill the ravioli.
Cheese Filling:

- 15 ozs ricotta cheese
- 2 Tb grated Parmesan/Romano cheese
- 2 Tb minced fresh parsley
- 1 egg
- ½ tsp salt
- ¼ tsp pepper
- ½ tsp freshly grated or ground nutmeg

Mix all ingredients together. Fill the ravioli.

Risotto Milanese

(ree-zoh-toe mee-lah-na-yz)

Often served as a first course in Italy. Delicious served with chicken, chicken livers, or roasts. The real Italian method is to stir in the broth by ½ cupfuls, allowing it to be absorbed each time. Our method is simpler, and the results are as moist and creamy as can be desired.

- ¼ cup (4 Tb) butter/margarine, melted
- 1 medium onion, finely chopped
- 1 cup converted rice
- 1 tsp salt
- ¼ tsp pepper
- Pinch saffron threads, crumbled
- 1 small bay leaf
- 2 ¼ cups hot beef or chicken broth
- ¼ cup (4 Tb) butter/margarine, softened
- ¼ cup grated Parmesan/Romano cheese
- 1 2-oz can mushrooms (if desired), drained

In a 2-quart saucepan, sauté onion in melted butter/margarine until onion is soft. Add rice and continue cooking until rice turns golden. Add the salt, pepper, saffron, bay leaf and the hot broth. Cover and simmer about 25 minutes, or until rice has absorbed all the liquid. Remove from heat, stir in softened butter/margarine, grated cheese, and mushrooms if desired. 4 to 6 servings

Clam Sauce for Spaghetti

2 Tb olive oil
1 clove garlic, chopped
1 7- or 8-oz can chopped
   clams or fresh steamed
   clams
1 8-oz bottle clam juice
1 tsp fresh chopped parsley
¼ tsp salt
   Dash pepper
½ lb cooked spaghetti or
   linquini
   Grated Parmesan/Romano
   cheese

Sauté garlic in olive oil until soft but not brown. Add clams, juice, and seasonings, and simmer gently for 10 minutes. (Do not boil as clams will get tough.) Toss with cooked spaghetti. Sprinkle with grated cheese. 2 to 4 servings

For Red Clam Sauce, include an 8-ounce can tomato sauce.

Liz's Spaghetti Sauce with Meatballs

What a revelation—on our first trip to Italy, Lois kept asking for spaghetti and meatballs and not one restaurant offered it on the menu!

1 link (½ lb) mild Italian
   sausage, cut into small
   pieces
1 link (½ lb) hot Italian
   sausage, cut into small
   pieces
2 Tb chopped fresh parsley
   or 2 tsp dried flakes
1 large yellow onion
   (Bermuda, Spanish), cut up
   (about 2 cups)
4 cloves garlic, cut up
2 large stalks celery, cut up
1 medium carrot, cut up
3 Tb corn oil or bacon fat
1 28-oz can tomato puree
3 8-oz cans tomato sauce
1 bay leaf
   Dash grated fresh nutmeg
   (if desired)
1 4-oz can chopped
   mushrooms, drained, or
   sautéed fresh mushrooms

½ to ¾ lb *each*: ground beef, pork,
        and veal (usually packaged
        as "meat loaf")
1 tsp salt
½ tsp pepper
2 eggs
½ cup grated
   Parmesan/Romano cheese
1½ cups bread crumbs
   (approximately)
½ cup corn oil
½ cup red wine (Chianti)
   Spaghetti or pasta of your
   choice

Fry sausage slowly in ungreased frying pan with a small amount of water to absorb the fat. Meanwhile, put parsley, onion, garlic, celery, and carrot in blender with ¼ cup water and chop fine, or use food processor without the water.

Heat the 3 Tb corn oil (bacon fat) in a large pot and sauté ¼ of the chopped vegetables for 2 to 3 minutes. Add tomato puree, tomato sauce, 2 cups water, bay leaf, nutmeg, and mushrooms. Bring to a boil; lower heat and simmer ½ hour.

Add rest of chopped vegetables to the ground meat. Mix in salt, pepper, eggs, grated cheese, and enough bread crumbs to form unsticky meatballs. Form into 2-inch meatballs (about 2½ dozen). Brown meatballs on all sides in ½ cup corn oil. Or oven brown. Can also use Microwave oven (6 minutes per 12 meatballs). Add to the simmering tomato pot.

Add cooked sausage to tomato pot. Pour off excess sausage fat from frying pan, add Chianti wine and scrape all "brownings" in pan over heat. Pour this into the tomato pot.

Season tomato pot with small amount of salt and pepper. Allow to simmer for 1½ to 2 hours with a "cracked" lid, stirring occasionally. There will be no "foam;" little oil patches will form on top, which shows that sauce is done. Makes 2 to 2½ quarts.

Cook spaghetti or pasta of your choice per package directions. Drain and put cooked pasta back in the pot in which pasta was boiled. (Pasta absorbs sauce better this way and stays warmer for serving.) Mix in spaghetti sauce. *Buon appetito!*

Liz's Spaghetti Sauce with Meatballs offers a basic and versatile sauce. Serve it with any pasta such as fettucine, linguine, capellini, spaghettini, spaghetti, ravioli, tortellini, polenta, rigatoni, gnòcchi, giant shells, manicotti. The meatball mixture can be used for filling ravioli or macaroni shells. Use also for preparing lasagne, chicken cacciatore, and veal parmigiana.

Pesto

An Italian sauce served over hot pasta. Not only does it have the pungency of garlic, but also the fragrance of fresh basil leaves. The ingredients may be blended and pounded with a mortar and pestle, but a food processor does very well.

1	cup chopped basil leaves (must be fresh)*	3	Tb pignoli (pine) nuts
2	cloves garlic, mashed with side of a knife	½	cup grated Parmesan cheese
		½	cup olive oil
			Salt

If using a mortar, place basil, garlic, and pignoli in it and mash, pounding with a pestle until you have a coarse paste. Then alternate mixing in the cheese and oil until well blended. Salt to taste.

To use food processor, put basil, garlic, and pignoli in processor. Using metal blade, process for 3 seconds. Add the cheese. Then start motor and pour olive oil in a steady stream until sauce is of mayonnaise consistency or a little thicker. Salt to taste. 1 cup

Pesto may be refrigerated in a tightly covered container. Freezes well also.
* If fresh basil is unavailable, mix together ¼ cup dried basil and ¾ cup chopped fresh parsley.

Quick Spaghetti Sauce

All of a sudden you're hungry for a plate of spaghetti! Easy and quick!

1	lb chunk beef or ground beef	1	16-oz can tomatoes, pulp mashed
2	Tb olive oil, corn oil, or bacon fat	1	8-oz can tomato sauce
1	small onion, chopped	1	small bay leaf
2	cloves garlic, minced		Salt and pepper
1	stalk celery, chopped	1	2-oz can mushrooms, drained
1	small carrot, chopped		Pasta of your choice
2	Tb chopped fresh parsley or 2 tsp dried flakes		Grated Parmesan/Romano cheese
½	cup red dry wine (Chianti)		

Brown meat in hot oil. Add onion, garlic, celery, carrot, and parsley and sauté until onion is soft. Add the wine and tomatoes. Cook until tomato pulp is "cooked down." Add tomato sauce and 1 cup water. Season with the bay leaf; salt and pepper to taste. Add mushrooms. Let simmer until meat is fork-tender. Serve over cooked pasta of your choice, top with grated cheese. 4 servings

Tuna Fish Sauce for Spaghetti

2 Tb olive oil
1 clove garlic, chopped
1 tsp chopped fresh parsley
1 stalk celery, chopped
1 8-oz can tomato Sauce
1 7- or 8-oz can tuna fish (in olive oil best)

½ lb cooked spaghetti
Salt and pepper
Grated Parmesan/Romano cheese

Sauté garlic, parsley, celery in olive oil until garlic is soft. Add tomato sauce and tuna, and let simmer 10 minutes. Toss with cooked spaghetti. Season to taste with salt and pepper. Sprinkle with grated cheese. 2 to 3 servings

Artichoke Pie

Jean   Castello

Italian quiche. Perfect as an entrée, hors d'oeuvre, or for brunch.

1 14-oz can hearts of artichokes, packed in water, drained and chopped
8 ozs mozzarella cheese, diced or shredded
¼ cup grated Parmesan/Romano cheese

4 eggs, well beaten
1 tsp butter, softened
½ tsp garlic salt
½ tsp salt
¼ tsp pepper
1 unbaked 9-inch pie shell

In a large bowl, blend artichokes with the cheeses, eggs, butter, and seasonings. Mix well. Pour into the pie shell. Bake at 375° for 45 minutes. Remove from oven and let stand 10 minutes. Cut in wedges and serve warm. It's good cold, too!! 6 to 8 servings

Asparagus with Prosciutto

16 fresh asparagus spears
Salt
4 thin slices prosciutto or ham

¼ cup (4 Tb) butter/margarine, melted
2 Tb grated Parmesan/Romano cheese

Steam asparagus in boiling, salted water. (Use a covered frying pan with 2 inches of water in it.) Cook 5 minutes, or until just tender. Drain.

Wrap 4 spears in a slice of prosciutto (ham) and fasten with a toothpick. Put in a greased baking dish, pour melted butter/margarine over top, and sprinkle with the cheese. Heat under the broiler until bubbly. 4 servings

Eggplant Casserole Parmigiana

3 large or 6 small eggplants
  Salt
½ cup olive oil

Sauce:

1 cup chopped onion
¼ cup olive oil
3 cloves garlic, minced
2 16-oz cans tomatoes, pulp chopped
1 8-oz can tomato sauce
1 bay leaf

1 Tb chopped fresh parsley or 1 tsp dried flakes
1 tsp salt
¼ tsp pepper
1 cup shredded mozzarella cheese
½ cup grated Parmesan/Romano cheese

Peel and dice eggplants. Sprinkle with salt and let stand 30 minutes. Rinse and pat dry. Fry eggplant pieces in ½ cup olive oil until lightly browned. Drain on paper towel.

In ¼ cup olive oil, sauté onion until soft. Add garlic, tomatoes, tomato sauce, bay leaf, parsley, salt, and pepper. Simmer 20 to 30 minutes.

Cover the bottom of a 2-quart casserole with some of the sauce. Put a layer of eggplant on top. Cover eggplant with sauce and sprinkle with the cheeses. Repeat layers until eggplant is used up. Pour remainder of sauce over top. Bake at 325° for 30 minutes. 4 to 6 servings

You can use prepared spaghetti sauce. Leftover meat can be layered between eggplant layers.

Italian Sausage and Peppers

Serve as a side dish or with cooked rice. Makes delightful Hero sandwiches with crusty Italian bread. Scoop out insides of bread and fill with sausage and peppers.

1 lb mild Italian sausage
1 lb hot Italian sausage
2 to 4 green or red bell peppers, cut up
1 small onion, sliced

Salt and pepper
¼ cup dry white or red wine (if desired)
1 8-oz can tomato sauce (if desired)

Cut sausages into small pieces. Sauté slowly in ungreased pan until well done. Drain off excess fat. Add peppers and onion and continue cooking until peppers are just tender. Season to taste with salt and pepper. For more flavor after seasoning with salt and pepper, add wine and let simmer until wine evaporates, or add tomato sauce and simmer a few minutes. Use either or both. I use both. 4 to 6 servings

Torta Pasqualina

(tor-tah pah-squah-lee-nah)

Fiorella Fiorani Pergola, Italia

In Italy this is a favorite at Easter time (Pasqua). Serve as an entrée with a green salad.

2	9-inch crusts (see Mrs. Grider's recipe)	2	Tb grated Parmesan cheese
4	ozs ham	6	eggs, beaten with ¼ tsp salt
2	ozs Emmentaler cheese or Gruyère	¼	tsp nutmeg (freshly ground best)
2	ozs fontina cheese	1	Tb butter, softened
4	ozs mozzarella cheese	1	egg
1	10-oz pkg frozen spinach, asparagus, or artichoke hearts		

Cut ham and 3 cheeses into small pieces. Thaw vegetable per package directions and drain dry. Cut vegetable into small pieces. Blend ham, cheeses, and vegetable together with the grated Parmesan. Mix in the beaten eggs, nutmeg, and butter. Pour mixture into formed, unbaked pie shell. Cover with top crust, moisten and seal edges. Brush top crust all over with egg beaten with teaspoon water. Pierce crust for steam vents. Bake at 450° for 10 minutes; reduce heat to 375° and bake 30 minutes longer. Never open oven door! Serve hot, but it's delicious cold, too. 4 to 6 servings

Zucchini Napolitan

1	large or 3 small zucchini	¼	tsp thyme
2	Tb corn oil		Salt and pepper
1	small onion, chopped		Butter
1	small clove garlic, minced		Mozzarella cheese slices
4	tomatoes, peeled and diced		

Wash zucchini and slice 1 inch thick. Sauté onion and garlic in oil until soft. Add tomatoes, thyme, and salt and pepper to taste. Cook for 5 minutes. Add zucchini and cook 10 minutes. Place in a 2-quart buttered casserole. Top with mozzarella cheese. Bake at 425° for 10 minutes, or until cheese is melted and golden. 4 to 6 servings

Fish

Years ago, I remember, when Mother had her neighborhood grocery store, she would order fresh fish for the Christmas season from a supplier, Asiago Company, Chicago. The fish would arrive in a barrel packed with ice, an assortment that included eels, clams, oysters, and squid. I also remember that at Christmas time, the Scandinavians had their lutefisk and we would have our baccalà—dried codfish.

Garlic-Steamed Clams or Mussels

We enjoyed fresh garlic-steamed mussels with crusty bread and a bottle of wine, while sitting under the shade of a tree along the shores of the Adriatic Sea.

1 to 2	dz clams (cherrystone or any small clams or mussels)	2 to 4	cloves garlic, slivered
½	cup olive oil	4	sprigs chopped fresh parsley or 2 Tb dried flakes

Scrub shells thoroughly in salted water and rinse well.

In a large kettle, heat oil and garlic and sauté until garlic is soft. Add parsley and the wet clams (mussels). Cover tightly and let steam until shells crack open. Strain the juice and sop it up with chunks of crusty bread. 2 to 4 servings

Garlic-Fried Scampi

(skahm-peee)

2 lbs fresh shrimp
½ cup olive oil
2 to 4 cloves garlic, slivered
4 sprigs fresh parsley, chopped, or 2 Tb dried flakes
Lemon wedges

Remove shells and devein shrimp. Heat oil and garlic and sauté until garlic is soft but not brown. Add parsley and shrimp. Cover and cook 2 to 3 minutes. Serve with lemon wedges. Sop up juices with Italian or French bread. 4 to 6 servings

Pesce al Forno

(pay-shay all for-no)

Celso Paolucci

Cousin Celso prepared this baked fish for us at the Villa.

4 to 6   small or 1 large fresh fish (trout, haddock, red snapper, or codfish)
      Vegetable, corn, or olive oil
      Salt and pepper
3   Tb butter
1   large onion, thinly sliced
2   carrots, thinly sliced
2   stalks celery, diced

2   Tb chopped fresh parsley or 2 tsp dried flakes
1   bay leaf, crumbled
½   tsp tarragon
1   4-oz can sliced mushrooms drained
2   cups dry white wine
4   lemon slices

Rub oil all over fish and sprinkle with salt and pepper to taste. Melt butter and sauté the rest of the ingredients, except lemon slices and wine, until onion is soft. Then pour mixture into a large baking pan. Place fish on top of this bed of cooked, seasoned vegetables. Pour wine all around the fish. Arrange lemon slices on top of fish. Bake at 400° to 450° about 20 minutes. Allow 10 to 12 minutes per inch thickness of fish. A hot oven keeps fish tender and juicy. 4 to 6 servings

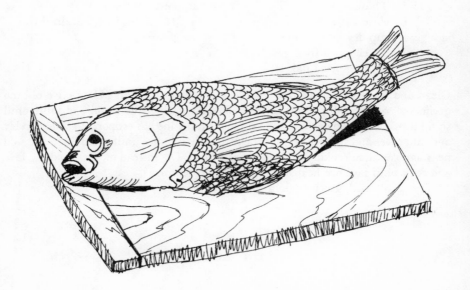

Squid

A sea mollusk with numerous tentacles, squid has a delicate flavor. In Italian it is called *calamaro* (call-ah-mah-roh) or *seppia* (sep-peey-eah), in French, *calamar*. Squid can be found in the freezer section at your fish market, usually packed three pounds to the package, and it is economically priced. It can be stuffed, added to Zuppa di Pesce or Bouillabaisse, sautéed, cooked Tempura-style, or cooked in a tomato sauce.

To clean squid: Thaw, then cut off the head just behind the eyes. Cut off tentacles just in front of eyes. Discard head and eyes and the small, hard beak in the center. Pull out and discard viscera (insides) or saclike body, including the thin, clear cartilage. Working under cold running water, with a thumbnail, loosen the thin, speckled outer skin and peel it off. Rinse sac thoroughly inside and out and rinse the tentacles.

Squid Sauté

2 to 3	lbs squid	1	tsp salt
3 to 4	Tb olive oil	2	cups cooked peas
1	clove garlic	1	16-oz can fave,* drained (if
1	cup dry white wine		desired)
2	Tb chopped fresh parsley		
	or 2 tsp dried flakes		

Clean and wash squid; cut into ¼- to ½-inch rings or strips. Heat olive oil and garlic and sauté until garlic is soft. Remove the garlic. Add squid and sauté until squid turns pink. Add dry wine and simmer until wine has evaporated. Add parsley and salt; cover and simmer over low heat 10 to 20 minutes until squid is tender. Add peas and continue cooking until peas are heated. Or, instead of peas, add the fave and cook until fave are heated through. 4 to 6 servings
*A fava is a broad, green bean, an Italian favorite.

Stuffed Squid

3	lbs squid
	Olive oil
1½	cups bread crumbs
2	Tb dry white wine
2	Tb grated
	Parmesan/Romano cheese
2	Tb chopped fresh parsley
1½	Tb chopped pine nuts (if desired)
3	cloves garlic, minced
1	egg, slightly beaten
1	tsp salt
¼	tsp pepper
	Tomato sauce (below)
	Cooked spaghetti or rice (if desired)

Clean and wash squid. Chop tentacles and sauté in olive oil for 3 minutes. Mix with all other ingredients except squid, tomato sauce, and spaghetti (rice) and stuff squid lightly (about ¾ full). Fasten end with toothpick. Lightly brown squid in 2 to 3 Tb hot olive oil; then simmer in tomato sauce of your choice, or use this recipe:

Tomato Sauce

½	cup olive oil
1	medium onion, chopped
2	cloves garlic, minced
2	Tb chopped fresh parsley
1	tsp salt
¼	tsp pepper
2	8-oz cans tomato sauce

Sauté onion and garlic in olive oil until soft. Add parsley, salt, pepper, tomato sauce, and 1 cup water. Simmer 30 minutes. Add the browned squid and simmer 30 minutes more. Serve over cooked spaghetti or rice if desired. 4 to 6 servings.

Braciòle di Manzo

(bra-zho-lay dee mahn-zoh)

8 (4x 8-inch) slices beef, pounded ⅛ inch thick
Pepper
Grated Parmesan/Romano cheese
8 half slices prosciutto or boiled ham

8 small slices mozzarella cheese (if desired)
3 Tb corn oil
2 cups spaghetti sauce

Sprinkle beef slices with pepper and grated cheese. Put a prosciutto slice (boiled ham) on each slice of beef. Then place a slice of mozzarella cheese on each. Roll up, tucking in the ends, and tie with string. Brown in the oil, turning to brown all sides. Add spaghetti sauce and simmer 1½ hours, or until meat is fork-tender, turning occasionally. Remove meat to warm platter. Remove string. Slice into thick slices, ladle sauce over. May also use sauce over cooked pasta if desired. 4 to 6 servings

In France, the stuffed slices of meat are called *paupiettes* (poh-pyet).

Fegato Romano

(fey-gah-toe)

What a delightful way to enjoy liver!

4 thick slices calf or beef liver
Salt and pepper
2 cloves garlic, finely minced

1 Tb rosemary
Grated orange peel
Bacon slices

Lightly sprinkle salt and pepper over liver slices. Sprinkle rest of ingredients, except bacon, over liver; let stand 10 minutes. Cut liver into 3- to 4-inch squares. Wrap liver in bacon slices, and skewer with a toothpick. Bake on broiler pan, so fat drips off, at 425° for 20 minutes, or until bacon is crisp. Drain on paper towel. Serve either hot or cold. Good with ice-cold beer! 4 to 6 servings

Leg of Lamb

1	3- to 4-lb leg of lamb	1	tsp salt
6	small cloves garlic	½	tsp pepper
	Rosemary	¼	cup olive oil
¼	cup dry red wine (Chianti)		

With a knife, make 6 little pockets all over the lamb. Insert a clove of garlic and a pinch of rosemary in each one. Pour wine over lamb and allow to marinate for a few hours, turning occasionally. When ready to roast, remove lamb from wine marinade and rub salt and pepper all over. Save marinade. Pour olive oil into an open roasting pan. Place roast in pan, fat side up; bake at 325° to desired doneness. While roasting, brush with the wine marinade. When done, remove lamb to a warm place. Degrease the roasting pan and pick up the "brownings" with water or more wine. Serve au jus. 4 to 6 servings

Porchetta

(por-kay-tah)

A highly seasoned, aromatic treat! In Italy, a whole pig is roasted with these seasonings. It is usually cooked for hours on a spit over hot coals until the skin is crisp and the meat is well done.

4 to 5	lbs pork loin	Fennel seed
8 to 10	garlic cloves, slivered halves	Black pepper
	Salt	

Have butcher bone and cut the pork loin so that it can be rolled and tied. Lay pork out flat. Insert garlic slivers in pockets notched into the meat. Sprinkle the whole open surface with a layer of salt. Sprinkle with fennel seed; then sprinkle whole surface heavily with black pepper. Roll loin and tie securely every 2 inches or so, like a salami. Salt and pepper outside of roll generously. Wrap in plastic wrap, then in heavy aluminum foil. Freeze at least a few days.

To serve: Thaw and remove plastic and aluminum wraps. Place in a covered roaster (no rack), fat side up. Roast at 325° until well done (about 30 minutes per pound). Serve warm or cold. Slice very thin. Make sandwiches with crusty Italian or French bread. No butter or condiments are used by Italians. Up to 10 servings

Delicious served as hors d'oeuvre; serve thin slices on tiny squares of bread or toast.

Veal Fontina Fiorella

(fohn-tee-nah fee-oh-rell-ah)

Fontina Valle d'Aosta cheese is a soft cheese, delightful as a dessert with fresh fruit. It is also a marvelous complement to veal.

6	rib or loin veal chops, cut ½ inch thick	1	tsp rosemary
2	Tb butter/margarine	½	cup dry Marsala or dry white wine
2	Tb olive oil		Thin slices prosciutto or ham
½	tsp salt		
¼	tsp pepper		Thin slices fontina or mozzarella cheese
3	cloves garlic, minced, or shallots		

In a large skillet, melt butter/margarine with olive oil until oil is hot. Brown the chops on both sides. Pour off any excess oil in skillet. Season chops with salt and pepper. Add garlic (shallots), rosemary, and wine. Cover skillet and steam the chops until wine is absorbed.* Place veal chops in a buttered baking dish in one layer. Cover chops with slices of prosciutto (ham). Top with fontina (mozzarella) slices. Bake at 400° until cheese is melted. Serve hot. 3 to 4 servings
*If desired, chops can be served at this point without the cheese and prosciutto.

Veal Parmigiana

	Sautéed veal per Veal Scallopine Lisette (below)
2	cups spaghetti sauce
6 to 8	slices mozzarella cheese

Sauté veal. Sprinkle small amount of sauce in baking pan large enough to hold veal in one layer. Place slices of veal on top. Cover with rest of tomato sauce. Top each slice with mozzarella. Bake at 350° until cheese is melted and sauce bubbly. 3 to 4 servings.

Veal Scaloppine Lisette

6 to 8	very thin (2- x 4-inch) slices boneless veal or baby beef	1	cup bread crumbs
2	eggs, beaten	2 to 4	Tb grated Parmesan/Romano cheese
½	tsp salt	¼ to ½	cup olive oil
¼	tsp pepper		Lemon wedges

Beat eggs with the salt and pepper. Mix crumbs and cheese together. Dip slices of veal into beaten egg, and then coat with crumbs and cheese mixture. Stack on platter with wax paper or foil between. Let stand 30 minutes or more (can keep refrigerated even longer). Cover bottom of frying pan with olive oil. Brown veal on both sides in medium hot oil. Fry in batches in one layer. Drain on paper towel. Serve either hot or cold with wedges of lemon. 3 to 4 servings.

Veal Scaloppine Marsala

Marsala is a wine of unique flavor founded in Marsala (Sicily), Italy. Historically, Garibaldi's troops one night, "high" on Marsala wine, attacked some Bourbon invaders, driving the foreign troops out of Italy. It was the birth of a nation!

1 to 1½	lbs veal scaloppine, cut or pounded ⅛ inch thick	¼	tsp pepper
⅓	cup flour	6	Tb butter/margarine
½	tsp salt	⅓	cup dry Marsala or dry white wine

Coat Scaloppine with flour seasoned with salt and pepper. Pat excess flour off. Let stand at least 20 minutes. Sauté in hot butter/margarine about 3 minutes on each side, or until lightly brown. Do not crowd or stack in pan. Sauté in separate batches if necessary. When all sautéed, pour off excess fat, and put scaloppine back in pan. Add the wine. Simmer for 2 to 3 minutes. Remove veal to serving platter (keep hot). Pour pan sauce over veal. 4 to 6 servings

If you are on a diet, skip the flour coating and just season with salt and pepper.

Vitèllo Saltimbocca

(vee-tell-oh salt-eem-bow-kah)

So tasty they literally "saltimbocca" (jump in your mouth).

6 to 8	very thin (2 - x 4-inch) slices boneless veal	6 to 8	thin slices prosciutto or ham
	Black pepper	6	Tb butter or combination margarine and corn oil
6 to 8	fresh sage leaves or crushed dry sage	¼	cup dry white wine

Sprinkle veal with pepper. Place 1 sage leaf (or a pinch crushed) on each slice. Cover evenly with a slice of prosciutto (ham). Roll the slices and secure with toothpick. Sauté veal in butter (combination) over medium heat until meat turns white and browns slightly. (Takes only a few minutes.) Remove veal to a hot platter. Pick up juices and "brown bits" in pan with the wine and pour over veal. 3 to 4 servings

Liz's Fried Chicken Italian

A melding of bacon, rosemary and garlic gives this chicken a unique flavor.

2	small fryers, cut up*		Salt and pepper
1	lb sliced bacon	½	cup Chianti wine
5	cloves garlic, slivered	½	lb fresh mushrooms* or 1
2	Tb rosemary		4-oz can, drained

Wash and dry chicken well (reduces sputtering). Render bacon in frying pan until crisp. Remove bacon and drain it on paper towel. In hot bacon fat, brown chicken pieces evenly, a few at a time; remove chicken from pan. Pour off all but ¼ cup bacon fat. Quickly sauté the garlic in the bacon fat until soft but not brown. Add chicken; sprinkle with rosemary, adding salt and pepper sparingly. Pour in wine, cover, and let steam a few minutes; then reduce heat and add mushrooms. Simmer until chicken is tender and wine is evaporated, stirring occasionally. Top with crumbled bacon. 4 to 6 servings

Chicken may be frozen in a casserole. To serve, thaw and heat through in 325° oven 40 to 50 minutes.

*Use choice parts. Save backs, wingtips, necks for making bouillon.

*To prepare fresh mushrooms, slice and sauté in 2 tablespoons butter/margarine quickly at high heat for a few minutes. Salt and pepper to taste.

Pollo al Forno

(poh-loh ahl for-noh)

Michelina Paulucci

1 to 2	chickens, cut up

Marinade:

¼	cup hot bacon fat	½	tsp salt
¼	cup dry Marsala (Sicilian)	¼	tsp pepper
	or Chianti wine	2 to 3	cloves garlic, minced
2	Tb rosemary	¼	tsp oregano (if desired)
1	tsp dried parsley flakes		

Mix marinade ingredients together and pour over chicken. Refrigerate overnight. When ready to serve, place chicken pieces in roasting pan, skin side down, in a single layer. Roast uncovered at 350°. When brown on top side, turn chicken pieces over and continue roasting until chicken is brown, crisp, and tender (total time about 1 hour). Use remaining marinade to pick up "brownings" from roasting pan after chicken is removed to a serving platter. Use as a sauce over chicken. 4 to 6 servings

Pollo alla Graticola

(all-ah grah-tee-co-lah)

Michael J. Paulucci

Broilers or small fryers
(½ chicken per person)

Seasoning Mix:*
>1 cup salt
>⅙ to ⅓ cup black pepper, medium
> or coarse grind
>⅓ cup garlic salt

Mix salt, pepper, and garlic salt together. Rub mixture all over the chickens. Let stand for 20 minutes or more. Grill over hot coals slowly, about 45 to 50 minutes, turning and sprinkling more mixture on chickens if desired.

*Store balance of seasoning mixture in a tightly covered jar; it's great to keep on hand for seasoning roasts, steaks, and salads.

Pollo Ragù

(ra-goo)

1 or 2 fryers, cut up
¼ cup olive oil
1 stalk celery, chopped
1 Tb minced fresh parsley or
1 tsp dried flakes
2 cloves garlic, minced
1 28-oz can Italian tomatoes, slightly chopped

1 8-oz can tomato sauce
¼ cup Chianti wine
1 tsp salt
¼ tsp pepper
Spaghetti or rice of your choice
Grated Parmesan/Romano cheese

Wash and dry chicken. Fry chicken in hot olive oil until brown. Remove and keep warm. In same oil, sauté celery, parsley, and garlic for 1 minute. Add tomatoes, tomato sauce, and wine. Season with salt and pepper. Simmer until tomato pulp is "cooked down" (about 30 minutes). Put chicken in tomato sauce, cover, and finish cooking until chicken is done. Serve sauce over spaghetti or rice with grated cheese. Or sop up sauce with chunks of crusty bread. 4 to 6 servings

Pollo di Roma

(dee roh-mah)

Angela Buratti

Makes a beautiful and delicious dish, a lovely buffet presentation.

4	chicken breasts and/or thighs, skinned and sliced
	Bread crumbs
	Flour
2	eggs, beaten with ¼ tsp salt and ¼ cup water

Olive oil
Butter/margarine
Mozzarella cheese (thick slices)
Prosciutto or ham slices
1 4-oz can mushrooms, drained and sliced
1 cup dry white wine

Flatten the chicken into thin, thin slices by pounding bread crumbs into the chicken with a heavy mallet. (Angela gave me a heavy metal mallet which looks like an inverted mushroom—it really flattens.) Then work flour into the slices to coat heavily. Dip slices in the egg mixture, and brown in hot olive oil.

Place browned chicken in a large casserole in one layer. Dot with butter/margarine. Lay slices of mozzarella over the chicken, then the prosciutto (ham). Cover with the mushrooms. Again dot with butter/margarine. Pour wine into the pan to completely cover the bottom. Bake at 425° until cheese is melted and wine is absorbed. 4 servings

Meat Stuffing for Fowl

Michelina Paulucci

Enough to stuff a 3- to 5-pound chicken.

1	lb ground beef
1	lb ground pork
1 to 2	eggs
1	stalk celery, diced
3	sprigs fresh parsley, minced, or 1 tsp dried flakes
1	2- to 4-oz can mushrooms, drained
1	Tb margarine, softened

1 clove garlic, minced
1 small onion, chopped
1½ tsp salt
¼ tsp pepper
¼ tsp oregano
⅛ tsp basil
¼ cup grated Parmesan/Romano cheese
1 cup bread crumbs

Place meat in a large bowl. Blend all other ingredients except cheese and bread crumbs in a blender. Add to the meat. Mix in the cheese. Add enough bread crumbs to make dressing hold together. Stuff chicken. Serve cooked dressing sliced. Makes delectable sandwiches!

Delicious for quail, squab, pheasant, partridge, and Cornish hens, too!

Meat Stuffing for Turkey

Michelina Paulucci

A delicious entrée in itself. Enough to stuff an 18-pound turkey.

2½	lbs ground beef*	3	cloves garlic, chopped
½	lb ground pork*	1	large onion, chopped
8	eggs	2	Tb salt
3	stalks celery, diced	1	tsp pepper
10	sprigs fresh parsley, chopped	2	tsp oregano
1	fresh tomato, chopped	1	tsp basil
1	4-oz can mushrooms, drained	¼	cups grated Parmesan/Romano cheese
¼	cup (4 Tb) margarine, softened	3	cups bread crumbs

Place meat in a large bowl. Blend all other ingredients except cheese and bread crumbs in a blender. Add to the meat. Mix in the cheese. Add enough bread crumbs to make dressing hold together. Stuff turkey. Serve cooked dressing sliced. Makes delectable sandwiches!

*You can substitute, in any combination, 3 lbs of beef, pork, and veal.

Blend ingredients in two batches if too much for one blend. Meat stuffing can be prepared ahead and frozen until needed.

Salads

Salad greens must be washed thoroughly, drained, and crispened. If your tap water is not very cold, add ice cubes to wash greens. To really dry them, I find my vegetable spin-drier does the best job. Of course, my French friend Jackie tells me that as a child it was her job to dry the lettuce—by shaking a wire basketful out on the back porch, no matter what the weather!

Greens can be stored in an airtight container in the refrigerator for a couple of days. When preparing your salad, fill a salad bowl with an assortment of greens and whatever other vegetables you wish. Cover with a damp paper towel and refrigerate until ready to toss with dressing. I prefer to serve salad on flat salad plates, rather than in bowls.

Italian Broccoli Salad

1	bunch broccoli	Lemon juice
	Olive oil	Salt and pepper

Wash and peel broccoli. Steam in 2 inches salted boiling water, covered, for 5 minutes (will be crunchy). Drain. Place on a platter and while still hot, drizzle with olive oil and lemon juice. Season to taste with salt and pepper. Refrigerate covered.
4 to 6 servings
For a Provençale touch, also sprinkle broccoli with minced garlic.

Cabbage Salad

Coleslaw Italian Style

4   cups shredded cabbage
    (green or purple)
2   green onions and tops or 1
    small onion, chopped

1   carrot, grated (if desired)
    Oil and Vinegar Salad
    Dressing (see recipe)

Toss all ingredients together. Keep refrigerated until serving time. 4 to 6 servings

Caesar Salad Junia

An Italian, Giacomo Junia, invented this salad and named it after Julius Caesar.

Cos lettuce, known to us as romaine, originated in Italy. It was usually cooked, and never used alone in a salad. In Junia's recipe it was mixed with leaf or head lettuce. Since Junia was never successful in making a good mayonnaise, he just took the ingredients and blended them separately into the salad! He used no anchovies, and used grated Swiss cheese instead of Parmesan/Romano.

Assorted lettuce
4   slices bacon, fried crisp and
    crumbled
½   tsp salt
¼   tsp pepper
¼   tsp dry mustard
1   clove garlic, minced
½   cup grated Swiss cheese

Dressing:
6   Tb olive oil
4   Tb lemon juice
½   tsp Worcestershire sauce
2   raw eggs (lemon juice will
    "cook" eggs)

Croutons, if desired

In a large salad bowl, tear lettuce into small pieces. Add crumbled bacon and sprinkle remaining ingredients, except croutons and dressing, over all.

Mix dressing ingredients together in a separate small bowl. Pour over lettuce and bacon. Lightly toss together. Croutons, made from fresh bread, cubed and fried in beef suet or vegetable oil, can be added. 4 to 6 servings. Junia also used fried lettuce leaves to top individual salad servings.

Dandelion

Springtime on the Iron Range was dandelion time. We had patches of them growing wild in our own backyards, or we would pick them in open fields.

Coming from the Italian "Dente Di Leone" (den-tay dee lee-oh-nay), meaning Lion's tooth, the dark green plant has jagged leaves and yellow flowers which mature into "puff balls" that we used to blow into the air. Dandelions are greens of a distinct flavor, rich in vitamins and so delicious! We called it chicoria (chee-kor-ee-ah).

Today dandelions are a commercial fresh crop in Vineland, New Jersey, and processed in cans in Maine. If you are fortunate enough to find fresh dandelions, enjoy them in a salad with an oil and vinegar dressing. Or try wilted dandelion salad, using the "headed" vinegar and bacon dressing as for fresh spinach salad (see recipe). Use the small, tender leaves for salads.
Chicoria Cotto

(chee-kor-ee-ah koh-toh)

When older dandelions were about to flower, the leaves would get tough. So these we cooked. We would steam them in salted boiling water until just tender, drain well, and then sauté in hot olive oil and garlic cloves. Salt and pepper to taste.

Dandelions make the best wine, too!

Oil and Vinegar Salad Dressing

This is still a favorite dressing for green salads. Lower in calories, too. Wine vinegar and a good grade of olive oil (Bertolli) are essential. Wine vinegar made in your own franjoh-working vinegar barrel provides you with a lifetime of the best vinegar. Just keep adding wine to "Mother" in the barrel. Olive oil for salads should be light.

Use a proportion of about ⅓ wine vinegar to ⅔ olive oil
Salt and pepper
Garlic salt

Sprinkle salt and pepper to taste and garlic salt on greens. Add the olive oil and toss lightly so oil coats greens. Then add the vinegar and toss. Adjust seasonings.

String Beans Italiano

1 to 2	lbs fresh pole or string beans		1	ripe tomato, chopped (if desired)
4	slices bacon, cut into pieces			Salt and pepper
1	cup thinly sliced onion			

Snap and wash beans. If beans are extra long, snap into pieces. Steam beans in 2 cups boiling salted water for just 5 minutes. Drain well and run under cold water to stop further cooking. Render bacon pieces. Add onion and tomato and sauté until onion is soft. Add the green beans, cover and let steam and meld through. Season to taste with salt and pepper. Beans will be of crunchy texture. 4 to 8 servings

Savoy Cabbage

This is the dark green, curly variety.

1 large savoy cabbage, quartered	½ tsp salt
¼ cup olive oil	¼ tsp pepper
1 small onion, chopped	1 Tb rosemary

Parboil cabbage in a large covered pan in 3 cups salted boiling water with 2 Tb salt for 5 minutes. Drain thoroughly; then chop cabbage into small pieces. Sauté onion in hot olive oil until soft; add cabbage, sprinkle with salt, pepper, and rosemary. Cover and simmer 5 or more minutes. 4 to 6 servings

Potatoes al Forno

An Italian favorite.

Wash and wipe dry peeled potatoes. Cut them in chunks. Dip in vegetable, olive, or corn oil to cover completely. Bake at 450° for 40 to 50 minutes, or until golden brown and tender. Salt to taste. As good as French fries, with half the trouble and probably less calories.

Italian Spinach Lisette

2 lbs fresh spinach	2 to 4 cloves garlic, slivered
¼ cup olive oil	Salt and pepper

Wash spinach carefully. In a big kettle, heat oil and garlic and sauté until garlic is soft but not brown. Add spinach gradually, stirring to mix with hot olive oil. Cook, uncovered, 5 minutes. Salt and pepper to taste. 4 to 6 servings

Fried Zucchini

4 zucchini	1 tsp salt
1 egg, beaten with 1 tsp water	¼ tsp pepper
½ cup flour	¼ to ½ cup olive oil

Wash and dry zucchini and cut into ¼-inch slices. Dip in egg mixture and then in flour seasoned with salt and pepper. Fry in hot olive oil until golden and crisp. Drain on paper towel. Season to taste with salt. 4 to 6 servings

Use this same recipe for fresh okra. Italians fry the zucchini blossoms, too.

Italian Cheese Bread

2	packets dry yeast or 2 cakes fresh yeast	1	cup grated Parmesan/Romano cheese
2½ to 3	cups sifted flour	3	eggs, beaten
1	tsp salt	2	Tb olive oil
½	tsp pepper		

Dissolve yeast in ⅓ cup warm water, stirring gently. Put 1 of the 3 cups flour, salt, and pepper in a large bowl. Add cheese, eggs, olive oil, and dissolved yeast, and beat until smooth. Add enough additional flour to make a stiff dough. Remove dough to a lightly floured board and knead until smooth and elastic. Form into a ball. Place in oiled bowl and turn dough to oil all over. Cover. Let rise in warm place 2 to 2½ hours. Punch dough down and let rise again until double in size (1½ hours).* Shape into round ball, place in oiled round cake pan. Cover and let rise about 1 hour. Brush top of dough with additional olive oil and bake at 350° approximately 40 minutes. Remove from pan and cool on wire rack. 1 loaf

*Minimum total rising time, 4 hours; maximum, 5 hours. Tip: let dough rise with pan of hot water underneath it in unheated oven.

Crescia

(kray-sheah)

Antonia Fiore

In our visits to Italy, we were treated to crescia, a colloquial version of pizza. Our relatives in Bellisio Solfare serve it with roasted meats. And, whenever Mother used to bake bread, she would set aside some of the dough to make crescia.

Basic Dough:

1	oz (4 packets) yeast
1	tsp salt
3	Tb olive oil
2	eggs, at room temperature, slightly beaten
5 to 6	cups flour

Dissolve yeast in 2 cups lukewarm water. Blend with salt, olive oil, and eggs. Make a medium stiff dough by adding flour, 1 cup at a time. Then use balance of (or more) flour to knead dough on a floured board until smooth, elastic, and not sticky. Oil all sides with olive oil and let rise in bowl covered with towel in a warm place until double in size (30 to 50 minutes).* Cut dough into 3 pieces and stretch dough to cover bottoms of 3 oiled 8-inch square or round cake pans. Proceed with either variation below.

*Tip: Place in unheated oven with pan of hot water underneath.

Marchigiana:
(mar-key-john-ah)
>Olive oil
>Sliced onions
>Salt and pepper
>Rosemary

Brush dough in pans with olive oil. Press sliced onions into dough. Sprinkle with salt, pepper, and rosemary. Let dough rise until half again its size. Bake at 425°for 20 to 30 minutes, or until crusty and lightly browned.

Romana:
>Olive oil
>Garlic salt
>Oregano

First let dough rise again in pans with half again its size. Bake at 425° for 20 to 30 minutes. Remove from oven and immediately brush with olive oil and sprinkle with garlic salt and oregano.

Crescia is delicious served with cooked greens. Can be served either hot or cold, and it freezes beautifully—just thaw and reheat.

Pizza

Pizza—at one time it belonged only to the southern Italians—now it belongs to the world! Hamburgers, fried chicken, and hot dogs move over!

The name pizza originated from the Greek *pitta*, meaning "thin bread;" and Greek-founded Naples (Neopolis, "new city") became famous as home of the pizza.

Pizza, either thin and crispy or thick and soft dough, is basically topped with tomatoes, cheeses, olive oil, and spices, along with such extras as anchovies, sausages, mushrooms, green pepper. In France, pizza is topped with an egg (à cheval—on horseback); in Japan, with squid and bamboo shoots. In other countries, even fruits, beans, and kosher innovations are added.

Frozen pizza is big business and the best frozen pizza in the business is JENO'S, world's largest packer of pizza products.

Zucchini Bread Norina

In New Orleans, I heard about Zucchini Bread from a New Englander. Restaurants are serving it in Florida. Mother thinks it's delicious. Here is her dear friend's recipe from Hibbing.

3	cups flour	3	tsp vanilla extract
¼	tsp baking powder	1	cup vegetable oil
1	tsp salt	2	cups shredded raw zucchini
1	tsp baking soda		(unpeeled)
1½	tsp cinnamon	1	cup chopped nuts (try
1½	tsp nutmeg		unsalted peanuts)
3	eggs, well beaten		
2½	cups sugar (part brown sugar if desired)		

Sift together flour, baking powder, salt, baking soda, cinnamon, and nutmeg. In another bowl, beat eggs until light and fluffy. Add sugar to eggs, beating continuously. Add vanilla, and continue beating until you can't feel sugar granules. Add oil and dry ingredients alternately to the egg mixture. Add zucchini and beat until well mixed and blended. Add nuts, mixing well by hand. Pour into two 9- x 5-inch greased and floured loaf pans. Bake at ˜50° for 1 hour, or until toothpick inserted in center comes out dry. Cool on wire rac₊.s in pan until thoroughly cool. Then remove from pans. 2 loaves

The loaves must be kept in plastic bag in refrigerator; they freeze well, wrapped in heavy aluminum foil.

Biscotti

Michelina Paulucci

This is a dunking favorite—especially if dunked in wine!

1	cup (2 sticks) butter/margarine, softened		Grated peel of 1 lemon
1½	cups sugar	6	cups flour
1	Tb anise seed (if desired)	¼	tsp salt
6	eggs, beaten	3	tsp baking powder
		¼	tsp cinnamon or nutmeg
		2	cups milk

Cream butter/margarine and sugar. Add anise seed. Beat in eggs and lemon peel. Combine flour, salt, baking powder, and cinnamon (nutmeg). Add to egg mixture, alternating with the milk. Beat until smooth. Dough should be fairly soft. Roll dough on a floured surface into an oblong loaf (4 x 9 inches, approximately). Place on greased cookie sheet. Bake at 350° for 20 minutes until golden. Remove from oven. Cool slightly. Cut loaf into 1-inch slices. Replace on cookie sheet, with a cut side down, and toast slices at 425° just 3 to 4 minutes until lightly brown. Watch carefully not to burn. 36 biscotti

Biscottini

Michelina Paulucci

A sweet biscuit fried like castagnoli

3	eggs, beaten	1	tsp salt
1	cup milk	1	tsp anise seed or extract
½	cup corn oil	1	oz whiskey or 1 Tb lemon
3 to 4	cups flour		juice
2	tsp baking powder		Corn oil
2	tsp sugar	1	cup honey

Mix all ingredients together, except corn oil and honey, to form a soft dough. Pull dough into strips. Form strips into twists or rings. Drop into hot oil. When they come to the surface, turn them over. Drain on paper towel. Heat honey in a saucepan. Dip each biscottino in warm honey. 12 biscottini

Castagnoli

(kah-stah-neey-oh-lee)

Michelina Paulucci

1	packet dry yeast	¼	tsp salt
3	eggs	2½ to 3	cups flour
¼	tsp vanilla extract		Olive oil
1	tsp brandy or blended		Corn oil
	Canadian whiskey		Granulated sugar or honey
½	tsp sugar		

Dissolve yeast in ¼ cup lukewarm water and blend with eggs, vanilla, liquor, sugar, and salt. Add ½ cup flour at a time to form soft dough. Turn dough onto a floured surface and knead until smooth. Put dough into a bowl, brush with olive oil, and keep in a warm place until double in size. Roll out dough to pie-crust thickness. Cut into strips or different shapes. Fry in hot corn oil. Sprinkle with granulated sugar or warm honey. 24 castagnoli

Dough may be refrigerated in a plastic bag up to 2 weeks. Allow to come to room temperature before frying.

Cannoli

Michelina Paulucci

These are hand-rolled pastry shells filled Italian-style with ricòtta cheese and fruits; they can also be filled with pudding, ice cream, whipped cream, custard cream—even fruit yogurt. Cannoli shells are difficult to make. Ready-made shells can be found in Italian and specialty shops packed six to a package.

Pizza, p. 190

Egg Rolls, p. 231

Cherry Pie, p. 47; Rowena's Cola-Fudge Cake, p. 279;
Krum Kaka, p. 75

1½ cups ricòtta cheese
½ cup confectioners sugar
2 Tb grated bittersweet
chocolate
½ tsp vanilla extract
Dash freshly grated nutmeg
or ground cinnamon

6 ozs candied fruit or candied
maraschino cherries,
chopped
Chopped nuts (if desired)
6 cannoli shells

Combine all ingredients except shells. Mix well and chill in refrigerator. When ready to serve, fill cannoli shells. 6 servings

Pizzelle

(pee-zay-lay)

Jill Campanozzi

Lacy, paper-thin cookies with imprinted designs. Remindful of the Scandinavian Krum Kaka. Can be rolled when warm and then filled with different sweets, or they can be left flat and crisp. This is a rare recipe from Foggia, Italy. Forerunner of our ice cream cone?

1½ cups sugar
6 eggs, beaten
1 cup (2 sticks) margarine,*
melted and cooled
2 Tb vanilla extract or anise
seed

3½ cups flour (approximately)
4 tsp baking powder
¼ tsp salt (if desired)
1 cup finely chopped walnuts
or pecans (if desired)

Beat sugar gradually into eggs until smooth. Stir in cooled margarine and flavoring. Sift flour, baking powder, and salt together and add to egg mixture. Add nuts if desired. Drop a spoonful of the batter in the center of heated Pizzelle iron. Lower the top plate and cook for 1 minute or per iron directions. Remove from iron with a fork. While still warm, roll up into a cylinder or let cool flat. Stack and store in airtight container on shelf or place in refrigerator. 6 to 7 dozen
*Do not use vegetable oil.

Chocolate Pizzelle:
To the ingredients above add:

½ cup cocoa
½ cup additional sugar
½ tsp additional baking
powder

Sift together with the flour and beat into the egg mixture.

Similar to the Krum Kaka iron, a Pizzelle iron has two patterned plates hinged together and is used directly on electric or gas burner. Electric irons are also available now.

Kiwifruit Cassata

Kiwifruit is a brown, egg-sized fruit of a subtropical vine. It has a sweet green pulp having a strawberry flavor. This attractive and succulent fruit is a New Zealand import. Cassata is a cream tart or cake of Sicilian origin.

1	13½-oz container non-dairy whipped topping	½	cup coarsely chopped candied red cherries
1	oz dry sherry		Dash grated fresh ginger (if desired)
4	kiwifruit,* peeled and sliced	1	2-qt block vanilla ice cream
¼	cup slivered almonds	2	ozs semi-sweet chocolate morsels
½	cup coarsely chopped candied green cherries		

Mix one half whipped topping with wine, kiwifruit, almonds, cherries, and ginger. Cut ice cream in half lengthwise. Spread cream mixture between the 2 layers. Frost with remaining whipped topping and top with chocolate morsels. Wrap in aluminum foil or plastic wrap and return to freezer until serving time. 10 to 12 servings
*Fresh or frozen strawberries can be substituted.

Cassata Siciliana

(kah-sah-tah see-chee-lee-ah-nah)

This is a very rich Italian dessert.

1	loaf pound cake	½	cup coarsely chopped candied green cherries
2	cups ricòtta cheese	¼	cup slivered almonds or chopped pecans
4	sqs semi-sweet chocolate, grated		Non-dairy whipped topping or 2 cups chocolate frosting
1	oz Curaçao (orange liqueur)		
½	cup coarsely chopped candied red cherries		

Slice cake lengthwise into 3 layers. Beat ricòtta cheese until smooth and creamy. Mix together the next 5 ingredients. On each of the 2 middle layers, spread half of the ricòtta and then half of the fruit mixture. Top with the third layer of cake. Frost with whipped topping (chocolate frosting). Garnish with additional chocolate or cherries. Cover with aluminum foil or plastic wrap and refrigerate overnight. 10 to 12 servings

Instead of using candied cherries, try 1½ cups strawberry or seedless raspberry jam!

Crèma–Zuppa Inglese

(kra-mah zoo-pah een-glay-say)

Nina Borbiconi

This is a rich, festive dessert. Fluffy, light, and creamy, the liqueurs enhance the flavor. Maraschino cherry juice can be used, however, instead of the spirits.

One chiffon, angel food, or sponge cake, sliced ¼ to ½ inch thick
Rum, Brandy, or Rosolio (a red Italian liqueur)

	Full Recipe	Half a Recipe
Egg yolks	12 yolks	6 yolks
Sugar	12 Tb	6 Tb
Flour	8 Tb	4 Tb
Milk	1 Qt	1 Pt
Whipping Cream	1 Pt	½ Pt
Stick Cinnamon	1 stick	½ stick
Lemon Peel	1 whole, pared off in a thick piece	½ lemon

Arrange cake slices on a large platter (use smaller platter for ½ recipe). Sprinkle generously with 1 or more of the liquors or liqueur. Refrigerate. In electric mixer or blender, beat egg yolks until lemon yellow in color. Add sugar and flour, and continue beating up to 30 minutes. Heat milk and cream to lukewarm in a heavy pan. Gradually stir in the egg mixture; add the cinnamon and lemon peel. *Important*: During the whole process, *stir in one direction only* to prevent curdling. Cook over low heat, stirring constantly, until *custard* is thick (thickly coats spoon), 30 minutes or more. Remove cinnamon and lemon peel. Let custard cool. Pour custard over cake slices and refrigerate for 1 hour covered with wax paper.

Macedònia

Angela Buratti

Fresh fruit, drained canned fruit, or thawed frozen fruit such as:
    Strawberries and pineapple chunks
    Raspberries and pineapple chunks
    Peach slices and raspberries
    Raspberries and strawberries

    Liqueur
    Whipped cream

Combine fruit and macerate in Cognac, kirsch, Cointreau, or Grand Marnier (1½ ozs liqueur to each cup of fruit) for 1 hour. To serve, put fruit in champagne glasses or use fruit plates. Spoon some of the liqueur over fruit and top with whippped cream.

Tortoni di Torrone

Torrone is an Italian nougat candy which originated in Cremona in 1441 at a famous wedding celebration. Ornamenting the buffe table was a new sweet made of almonds, honey, and egg whites in the shape of the famous Torrione Tower of Cremona.

Torrone are tiny "nuggets" (.49 ounce), coated with an edible flaky white wafer and packaged in picturesque boxes. They come in flavors from lemon to chocolate.

Confetti (sugared almonds) and Torrone are traditional Italian wedding celebration confections.

4 eggs, at room temperature, separated	7 ozs Torrone or chocolate candy bars,* chopped
¾ cup sugar	Oil
3 Tb rum, brandy, or Amaretto	2 ozs semi-sweet chocolate, cut into small pieces (if
2 cups heavy cream	desired)

Beat egg yolks with the sugar until thick and lemon color. Add the rum (brandy, Amaretto). In a separate bowl, beat the cream until stiff. Refrigerate. Beat egg whites until stiff but not dry. Fold the whipped cream into the egg whites. Fold this mixture into the egg yolks. Sprinkle ⅓ of the Torrone (chocolate bars) over bottom of a loaf pan, oiled and lined with plastic wrap or wax paper. Add half the cream mixture. Top with another ⅓ of the Torrone. Add remaining half of the cream mixture. Top with remaining ⅓ Torrone. Cover and freeze for at least 4 hours. When ready to serve, remove from freezer and unmold. Decorate with chocolate pieces and serve at once. Mint leaves or crystallized violets are lovely decorations. 12 servings
*Candy bars: Chocolate-covered English toffee; chocolate-covered carmel, peanuts, and nougat bars.
Tortoni can be prepared in a glass mold or Bundt pan. Do not oil. Begin with the cream mixture and make two layers each of cream mixture and nougat. Freeze. Unmold onto a platter by covering mold with a hot towel to loosen, or dipping mold in warm water. Individual servings can be made by using custard cups or aluminum cupcake molds.

Zabalone

(zah-bah-loan-ay)

A Piamontese sweet sauce made with egg yolks, sugar, and laced with Marsala wine or brandy, served over cake and ice cream. I remember grownups used to beat the mixture, add a little milk, and drink it as raw egg grog. Good for what ailed you!

1 qt ice cream, any flavor, softened	4 egg yolks
	4 Tb confectioners sugar
1 sponge or angel food cake cut into 3 layers	6 Tb Marsala wine or brandy

Spread softened ice cream between layers of cake. Store in freezer until serving time. To make sauce, beat egg yolks with sugar in round-bottomed bowl until eggs are fluffy and pale yellow. Place bowl over hot, but not boiling, water and continue beating with whisk or egg beater, gradually adding the Marsala (brandy). Keep beating until sauce is of the consistency of thin pancake batter. Let cool. To serve, cut cake into serving pieces and pour sauce over. 10 to 12 servings

This sauce can also be served over fresh strawberries or raspberries.

Bellini Cocktail

Bartenders in Italy pride themselves on winning recognition for concocting new drinks in mixologist contests. It then becomes the "house" drink.

A specialty at Harry's Bar is a cocktail lovingly named after the Master Painter Bellini, famous for his sunny pastels. Created by Cipriani, it is a blend of fresh peach juice and a sparkling Italian wine, Prosecco. Here is our adaptation.
For 1 cocktail:

1	oz freshly squeezed peach juice or canned apricot juice	2	drops lemon juice
		2 to 4	ozs dry champagne

Since fresh peaches are seasonal, we use canned apricot juice. Pour the juice into a stemmed cocktail glass. Add lemon juice and gently stir in the champagne. Serve well chilled.

Excelsior Piano Bar Special

Rome, Italy

For 1 cocktail:

1	bunch fresh mint leaves, crushed	1	"squirt" lemon juice
5	tsp confectioners sugar	8	ozs bourbon

Muddle ingredients together. Strain and serve over ice. Garnish with cherries if desired.

Coffee Royal

Just as many Italians, our family did not especially like milk products. Mother tried preparing morning coffee for us with hot milk (Italian and French style: Café au Lait), which we hated. So, instead, we would have a nip of wine in our coffee for breakfast—Coffee Royal.

Father, Ettore, always carried Coffee Royal in his lunch pail when he worked in the open pit iron ore mines—until one day when the foreman checked out his thermos of coffee. Father was suspended from work for a few days. Even at $4.20 per day wages, that was terrible punishment. No more Coffee Royal on the job.

Cold Buttered Rum Coffee

An after-dinner drink.
For 1 drink:

⅓ oz apricot brandy
⅓ oz Crême de Noya (almond)
⅓ oz light rum
1½ scoops butter pecan ice cream
⅓ cup coffee
Whipped cream

Put all ingredients except whipped cream in blender and blend well. Serve in Irish coffee cup and top with whipped cream.

EASTERN EUROPEAN

Pat Mestek of Hibbing, who's Irish and married to a Slovenian, says, "Since each little area in Yugoslavia speaks its own language variation, it's difficult to get any two to agree on pronunciation or on anything else for that matter!" This is not difficult to understand when one realizes that there are six republics (not provinces) in Yugoslavia: Slovenia, Croatia, Bosnia-Hercegovina, Montenegro, Macedonia, and Serbia. Then, to top this, "Slavic" is defined as the language of the Slavs of northeast and southeast Europe, which encompasses countries such as Russia, Bulgaria, Czechoslovakia, and Yugoslavia!

The first Slavs to work in iron ore mines were a few Slovenians and Slovaks from East Czechoslovakia, who joined the Cornish, Finns, and Irish in Upper Peninsula Michigan.

When the word got around that there was a labor shortage on the Mesabi Range due to an iron ore "rush," they migrated there. But labor of the open-pit type was not that attractive to these Slavs, so many turned to lumber and farming.

In 1900 the mining companies began recruiting labor directly from southeast Europe. Croatians arrived. On the Mesabi Range the Croatians and Slovenians became known as "Austrians." Then followed hundreds of Bulgarians, Bohemians (West Czechoslovakia), and Serbians. To these immigrants, America was the Land of Opportunity; for many the goal was to make lots of money and then retire in style back in the Old Country. In 1907 the Montenegrins were imported as strike breakers.

On the Mesabi Range by 1910 there was a total of 9,660 Croatians, Montenegrins, and Slovenians. The Slovaks, Bohemians, Bulgarians, and Serbians added another 2, 135 to the population.

Names typical of the Slavs ranged from Adamich to Chrep, Huzak, Hydukovich, Milinkovic, Musich, Prosnick, Satovich, Koslowski, Radakovich, Bachnik, and Chanak.

I remember that in 1936, when we had a Mesabi Iron Range basketball championship team, every player on the team had a name that ended in ich (itch).

When you think of the music of Slavic people, you think of Tamburitza or Button Box Accordion music. Favorite tunes on the Range were and still are "Cujes Mala Cép Cép," "Jadoda Polka," "Marijana" (Mary Anna), and "Zaplet Kola" as recorded by the Range's Tony and Paul Crnkovich.

And when you think of Slavic food, you think of strudel, potica, stuffed cabbage, meat dumplings (*piroshki*), and especially sausages: *cavapcici* (chevap chichi), a mixture of beef, veal, and mutton; garlic sausage (*cesnek klobása.*); and blood sausage (*krev klobása*). This hearty food still prevails everywhere. In Yugoslavia, although roast suckling pig, lamb, and veal cutlets are now served in restaurants, sausages, especially cevapcici, are still the most savored.

Attempts have been made over the years in the capital of Belgrade to set up restaurants serving foreign dishes, such as French, and just recently Chinese. Any success? "Ne, ne,"—no way! But pizza is great in Bulgaria!

On our recent visit to Yugoslavia, we walked through cobblestone streets and climbed steep steps of rock in the old section of Dubrovnik. Interesting was the design of the homes there. The kitchen was always located on the top floor. This kept the pungent odors of cooking foods from permeating the other floors, and it was supposed to be a safety feature. If a fire started in the kitchen, the downstairs would be saved from burning!

We also saw an ancient order of nuns in their habits of black for winter and white for summer: full length dirndl with vest, pleated apron, and a sunbonnet-like headdress of white.

Green Pepper Soup

Ann Chrep

This Croatian creation was handed down from Mother Chrep to daughter Goldie Brunner. Mrs. Chrep made Klobása and marinated her own version of pickled cabbage.

1½	lbs ground beef	¼	tsp pepper
1	cup chopped onion	6 to 8	green peppers (good size for stuffing)
½	cup chopped celery		
2 to 3	Tb minced fresh parsley	1	16-oz can tomatoes
¾	cup uncooked rice	1	8-oz can tomato sauce
1	tsp salt	3	large carrots, sliced

Mix together beef, onion, celery, parsley, rice, salt, and pepper. Cut tops off green peppers, remove seeds. Stuff with the meat mixture about ⅔ full. Place peppers in a large kettle. Completely cover the peppers with water. Add tomatoes, tomato sauce, and carrots. Bring to a boil, then gently simmer for 1½ to 2 hours. Serve with crusty chunks of bread. *Dober apetit!* 6 to 8 servings

Austrian Goulash

Anna Chanak

2	lbs boneless beef, cut into 1-inch cubes	¼	tsp pepper
4	cups sliced onions	¼	tsp marjoram
¼ cup	butter/margarine or 4 Tb corn oil	4	slices bacon, diced
		2	ozs wide egg noodles
1½	Tb paprika	1	Tb butter/margarine
½	cup chicken broth	4	wieners
1	Tb vinegar		Chopped Parsley
1	Tb tomato sauce		Lemon peel, thinly sliced
½	tsp salt		(soak in hot water before slicing)

Sauté onions in the 4 Tb butter/margarine (corn oil) until soft. Stir paprika into the onions. Add beef to onions, sauté, but do not brown; cover and simmer slowly for 1 hour until meat is tender.

Then add the next 6 ingredients. Fry bacon until crisp, drain on paper towel and add to the goulash.

Cook noodles with the wieners and 1 tablespoon butter/margarine in boiling salted water. Drain. When ready to serve, pour goulash into a large bowl. Sprinkle drained noodles on top. Top with the wieners. Garnish with parsley and lemon peel. 4 to 6 servings

Melva's Noodle Kugal

1 lb egg noodles (medium width)	8 oz sour cream
	4 eggs, beaten
8 oz cottage cheese	Butter

Partially cook noodles in boiling salted water. Drain. Mix cottage cheese and sour cream with the eggs. Beat well. Toss with the noodles. Put in a buttered casserole and bake at 350° until golden brown. 4 to 6 servings

Serbian Sarma

Members of my family so enjoyed this stuffed cabbage dish in Yugoslavia a few months ago, that Jeno wrote to the hotel hostess and asked for the recipe. The reply came back that she and the chef would be very happy to come to Minnesota (expenses paid) to teach Lois how to prepare it! And all the while I had this recipe from Melva Mason in Hibbing, Minnesota, from years back! Both Lois and Jeno agree that this is more delicious than what they had tasted in Europe!

Melva Mason

1	lb ground beef	1	cup chopped onion
½	lb ground pork	1	tsp salt
½	lb ground ham	¼	tsp pepper
1	cup cooked rice	¼	tsp garlic salt
2	large eggs	1	large head cabbage
¾	cup chopped green pepper	1	8-oz can tomato sauce

Combine meat, rice, eggs, green pepper, onion, and seasonings. Remove core from cabbage and steam cabbage in hot salted water until leaves begin to wilt. Separate leaves and wrap (roll) meat mixture in the individual leaves, tucking in the ends so the meat won't fall out. Place in kettle (bottom of kettle may be lined with cut-up cabbage). Pour can of tomato sauce over sarma rolls. Add water to cover. Simmer covered for about 1½ to 2 hours. Any meat mixture left over can be used to stuff green peppers. 8 to 10 servings

Haluski Capüsta

Jean and Lee Vann

This recipe was handed down by Grandmother Anna Sabol from Prague, Czechoslovakia, to Lee's mother.

¾ to 1 lb bacon, diced
    2 Tb butter/margarine
    1 medium head cabbage, chopped
    4 large potatoes, peeled and cut into small pieces

1 egg
   Flour
   Salt and pepper

Fry bacon until crisp; remove from frying pan. Drain all but 1 tablespoon fat from the pan and melt butter/margarine with the remaining bacon fat. Sauté cabbage until soft but still firm. Set cabbage aside and keep warm. Grate potatoes by placing them in a blender with the egg. Empty potato-egg mixture into a bowl. Add enough flour to make a soft dough. (Test dough by dropping a teaspoonful into boiling salted water; if it breaks up, dough needs more flour.) Drop dough by the teaspoonful into boiling salted water; cover and cook dumplings for 2 to 3 minutes (grandmother's cooking time was described as "3 rolling boils"). In order not to crowd the pot, cook dumplings in 2 or 3 batches. When dumplings are cooked, remove with slotted spoon, and mix them with the cabbage and bacon. Season to taste with salt and pepper and serve. 4 to 6 servings

London Broil Rouladen Sophia

A delicious steak in a Slovenian flavored marinade.

2½ lbs London broil (beef top round steak) 1½ to 2 inches thick

Marinade:

½ cup oil
½ cup dill pickle juice
¼ cup chopped dill pickle
¼ cup minced onion
1 clove garlic, minced

1 clove shallot, minced (if desired)
1 tsp prepared mustard
½ tsp salt
¼ tsp pepper

Use your blender to chop, mince, and mix the marinade ingredients. When well blended, pour over meat.

Marinate meat for several hours, covered, in the refrigerator. Turn meat in marinade once or twice. Remove from refrigerator a short time before broiling in oven or on outdoor grill. Cook to desired doneness (about 15 to 20 minutes on each side) while basting with the marinade. To serve, slice thin diagonally and across the grain. 6 to 8 servings

Chicken Kiev

A European favorite, supposedly of Russian origin, that is enjoyed in diverse versions, such as: Princess Galitzine's method of wrapping frozen butter chunks in the flattened chicken breasts, securing with chicken bones, covering them in egg and bread crumb batter and deep frying in hot vegetable oil. The first cut into the hot chicken breast—melted butter just spills or squirts out!

8 to 12	single chicken breasts, boned and skinned (or use sliced turkey breast)	½	tsp pepper
		½	tsp rosemary
½	cup (8 Tb) butter, softened	1	egg
1	clove garlic, crushed and minced		Flour
		¾	cup bread crumbs
1½	tsp salt	¾	cup cornflake crumbs
			Corn or peanut oil

Cream butter with garlic, salt, pepper, and rosemary until smooth. Chill until firm. Place each piece of chicken between two sheets of wax paper and pound thin. Place 1 teaspoon butter mixture on each breast. Tuck in ends and roll tight. Secure with toothpick.

Beat egg with ¼ cup water. Press each roll first in flour: tap off excess flour. Let stand 10 to 20 minutes. Then dip into egg mixture, then into combination of bread and cornflake crumbs and let stand 10 to 20 minutes. Heat oil to depth of ¼ inch in frying pan until bread cube browns immediately. Use tongs to place rolls in oil and remove them, and fry each roll until delicately browned. Discard toothpicks. (Rolls can be frozen at this point.)

When ready to serve, finish cooking by baking rolls in a single row in baking pans (thawed, if frozen), uncovered, at 325° for 30 minutes. If desired, serve with frilled toothpick in center of each. 8 to 10 servings

These are so juicy inside that Lenka of Jugoslavia cautions one to first pierce the delicacy gently with a fork so the hot butter mixture doesn't squirt out!

Potica

(poh-tee-tzah)

Mary Anderson

Mary Anderson is mayor and holder of the first passport issued for the "Republic of Kinney." Kinney, Minnesota, has threatened to secede from the union and fight if necessary to win against government bureaucracy and red tape in order to get the town a new $183,000 water system. And Mary's Bar, on "the Avenue of Giants" in downtown Kinney, is also known to serve the best potica this side of secession. The correct name, says the mayor, is povitica, but everyone says potica for this Balkan delicacy.

Dough:

2	packets dry yeast
1½	cups milk
1	tsp salt
¾	cup sugar
½	cup (8 Tb) butter, softened
4½	cups flour (more or less)
2	eggs, well beaten

Filling:

⅔	cup heavy cream
½	cup (8 Tb) butter, softened
2	cups sugar
1	tsp vanilla extract
½	tsp salt
2	lbs walnuts, ground

Scald milk; cool to lukewarm; add yeast and let dissolve. Add salt, sugar, butter, and ½ the flour. Beat until smooth. Add beaten eggs and mix well. Add rest of the flour. Knead lightly for soft dough (not a stiff dough). Place in greased bowl. Grease top of dough. Let rise in a warm place until double in bulk.

While dough is rising, prepare the filling. Heat cream with butter until butter is melted. Mix in rest of the ingredients. Set aside.

Place dough on a large floured cloth on top of a round table. Pull dough from center to edge until you have dough all stretched out. Spread filling evenly all over dough. Roll up as for a jellyroll. Place in a greased 12- x 13-inch pan, either three strips cut to the length of the pan and laid side by side, or the entire roll placed in the pan in an "S" shape. Bake at 350° for 1 hour, turning oven down to 325° for the last 20 minutes. Remove from oven, brush top with melted butter. Cool in pan on a rack. May be frozen. 12 or more servings

Serbian Cheese Cake

Mary Anderson

Mayor Anderson of the "Republic of Kinney" (Minnesota) also sent me this cheese cake (presnatz) recipe that her mother used to make.

Crust:

2½	cups flour
2	Tb sugar
½	tsp salt
1	cup shortening or lard
2	eggs, beaten
¼	cup ice water (approximately)

Filling:

1	12-oz container small-curd cottage cheese
4	eggs, beaten
½	cup sugar
½	cup grated mild Wisconsin brick cheese or Monterey Jack
¼	cup (4 Tb) butter, melted
1	Tb yellow cornmeal

Combine crust ingredients to make 2 9-inch pie crusts. Form bottom shell.

Mix first 4 filling ingredients together. Put in unbaked pie shell. Cover with top crust. Seal edges well, but do not perforate top crust. Bake at 350° for 50 minutes. Brush top with butter and sprinkle with cornmeal. Serve either hot or cold. Can be warmed up to serve the next day *if any is left*. 6 to 8 servings

Serbian Potica

Melva Mason

No festivity is complete for Serbians and Slovenians without this rich sweet bread.

Dough:

2	packets dry yeast
1	cup milk
1½	tsp salt
¼	cup sugar
½	cup (8 Tb) butter, softened
4	eggs, well beaten
6	cups flour

Walnut Filling:

½	cup heavy cream
1	lb walnuts, ground
1	cup honey
3	eggs, unbeaten
½	cup sugar
½	cup (8 Tb) butter, softened

Soften yeast in ¼ cup lukewarm water. Scald milk and add salt, sugar, and butter, and set aside to cool. Then add eggs, softened yeast, and 3 cups flour to milk mixture. Beat well; add rest of flour and beat vigorously until dough is satiny. Place in greased bowl and let rise until double in bulk (about 2 hours).

For walnut filling, scald cream in heavy saucepan over low heat. Add nuts and let mixture come to a boil, stirring constantly, as mixture burns easily. Add rest of the ingredients except butter and cook for about 5 minutes. Then add butter and let cool.

Place dough upside down on lightly floured cloth (cotton dishtowel or tablecloth), which completely covers a large table. Roll dough gently until it covers table (about 36 x 48 inches oval or 36 inches round). The dough may be paper-thin in spots. Cut off all dough that hangs over the table so you won't have any thick spots of dough in the potica. Spread filling on dough, evenly and thinly. Roll like a jellyroll by lifting end of cloth to get it started. Place dough in greased 14- x 10- x 2-inch pan, forming an "S." Cover and let rise for about an hour. Bake at 350° for 1 hour. Invert on rack to cool. 12 or more servings

Potiza

Ann Chrep

Mother's very dear friend taught her to make this delicious Croatian version of potica. Proceed with Mary Anderson's recipe, but using this different filling.

Filling:

2	cups sugar
½	cup (8 Tb) butter, softened
3	eggs, slightly beaten
1	tsp vanilla extract
1	tsp cinnamon
¼	tsp nutmeg (freshly ground best)

1	cup raisins, dark or light
1	cup chopped nuts
1	6- to 8-oz maraschino cherries, drained and chopped

Mix all ingredients together in a bowl and spread evenly over dough.

GREEK

The first Greek Colony in the New World was founded in 1768 on the Florida coast at a place known today as New Smyrna Beach. These Greeks had emigrated 1,400 strong with a British nobleman to Florida with promises of rich land and a new life. However, only about half of the group survived the perils of disease and reptiles. By 1778 they had migrated north to St. Augustine (the oldest city in America). Some ended up forming a Greek community in Tarpon Springs on the west coast of Florida, diving for sponges being their main industry.

Today there is a shrine honoring the memory of these first Greeks. Dedicated to the Greek patriarch St. Photios, it is located in a 200-year-old house in St. Augustine.

To this day a commemorative ritual is performed everywhere by the Greek Orthodox on Epiphany. Worshipers gather at a shore where the water is blessed by the reverend. A cross is tossed into the water and youths dive in to recover it, symbolizing the baptism of Jesus.

It was when open-pit mining operations increased after 1905 that the Greeks joined the southeastern Europeans to work in track gangs on the Mesabi. They first came from the Aegean region of Macedonia. Later they came from the Grecian mainland and worked on the railroads running to the area. Some worked on farms, some worked as lumberjacks, and a few opened restaurants. In Hibbing, Canelake's Cafe was a favorite spot where classmates would gather after football and basketball games to enjoy special fountain treats like Two Step, French Hash, Chop Suey, Yankee Special, and Hot Butterscotch Sundaes, priced from 25¢ to 50¢.

Originally there were never more than thirty to forty Greek families in Hibbing; today about twenty remain on the Mesabi Range, mostly in Hibbing and Virginia.

Many of the original Greek immigrants returned to their homeland for military service during the Balkan Wars and World War I. Others retired to Greece after saving up a so-called "pot of gold."

Typical Greek foods include cheese such as Feta (feh-tah), Kasseri, and Kefaloteri (like Italian Parmesan); olives from Calamata, also shriveled black and cracked green—all found in Greek and sometimes Italian stores. Oregano is the most often-used herb. Pilafs (served instead of potatoes) are made with pignolia seeds and bulguri (cracked wheat kernels). And we have all heard of stuffed grapevine leaves and salonika peppers. Turkish coffee is brewed to make a strong taverna and after-dinner Greek drink served with a glass of Cognac. A popular apéritif is a high-proof liquor, Ouzo, made from raisins, fennel, and anise seeds.

We were fascinated by Greek lettering. Some Greek letters of the alphabet correspond to some English letters, but mostly they are symbols Π Λ Θ are equivalent to letters P, L, and Th, and are pronounced Pi Lambda Theta (the name of my college's honorary women's sorority). But we gave up trying to read their language as it was—you'll pardon the expression—"all Greek to us"!

On a recent Mediterranean cruise, we enjoyed the hospitality of an all-Greek crew aboard the *M/S Stella Maris II*.

The crews' names ranged from Captain Stavros Dandouras and Steward St. Paraskevopoulos to Purser G. Kopsinis and Bartender Paschos Spiros. Such impeccable, handsome, versatile, and talented men.

The night of the Greek Taverna Dinner (a taverna is a typical small restaurant in Greece, often with music and dancing), we savored Amphissa Olives, Taramosalata (Fish Roe Mousse), Dolmadakia (Stuffed Grape Leaves), Bourekakia (Cheese Pies), Keftedakia (Oregano Meatballs)—and that was just the hors d'oeuvre course. Then we were served Shrimp Turkolimano and Souvlakia with green peppers and zucchini, Horeatikee Salata (salad of the islands), and Spanakopitta.

We ended this delicious dinner with the classic Greek dessert Baklava, which is traditionally served for all festivities. Wines served were Retsina Camba, Santa Helena, Minos Rosé, and Chevalier de Rhodes.

And, to our delight, members of the crew performed the native dance of Greece to the music of the bouzoukia (mandolin). They were dressed in traditional costume—white body stockings, white shirts tucked into pleated white ballet-type skirts, ornate blue vests, and red tasseled toques. In a row, with arms entwined at the shoulders (they looked like a string of paper dolls), they danced an intricate step with many knee bends and much foot stomping. It is a strenuous dance, as we later found out at dancing class!

Dolmadkia Stella Maris

Grapevine leaves resemble maple leaves in shape, having five points and a stem. They are used either fresh or preserved in brine. Most nationality stores and delicatessens and some supermarkets carry them.

1	16- to 18-oz jar grapevine leaves or 50 fresh	1	tsp salt
		1/4	tsp pepper
1/2	cup olive oil	2	Tb pignoli (pine nuts)
1 1/2	cups chopped onions	2	Tb lemon juice
3/4	cup uncooked converted rice	1/2	cup olive oil
2	Tb dried mint or dill weed		

In 1/2 cup olive oil, sauté onions until they are soft. Add the rice and sauté until golden. Add herbs, seasonings, pignoli nuts, and 1 cup hot water. Simmer five minutes. Set aside. Rinse grapevine leaves in cold water and pat dry. If fresh grapevine leaves are used, put them in boiling water for 3 minutes; pat dry.

Cover bottom of a saucepan with leaves. Place a spoonful of rice mixture on each leaf close to the stem. Tuck in the sides and roll up into a cylinder. Place seam side down in saucepan, side by side in layers. Sprinkle with lemon juice, 1/2 cup olive oil, and 1 1/2 cups hot water. Place a heavy plate on top to weigh down the domaldakia so they don't open up. Cover saucepan with lid and simmer gently about an hour (rice should be done). Let cool in the saucepan. Serve with yogurt or with Taramosalata (recipe below).

These delicacies are known as dolmas when made with ground beef and tomato sauce. Add 1 pound raw ground beef and 1/2 cup tomato sauce to the mixture.

Taramosalata Stella Maris

Serve with Dolmadakia when used as an appetizer. Tarama is fish roe, red caviar. Can also be served with crackers or crudités.

2	slices bread	3	Tb lemon juice
4 or 5	ozs fish roe	1/2	cup olive oil
1/4	cup minced or grated onion		

Soak bread in water and then squeeze out the water. Combine bread, roe, onion, and lemon juice in a blender. Blend at medium speed until smooth. Continue beating and gradually pour in the olive oil. Chill.

Pickled Octopus Fotopolus

Pickled octopus is served as an appetizer. It can be found in specialty food stores.
Arrange octopus on a lettuce leaf. Garnish with:

Chopped onion   Lemon wedge

Tomato wedges

Serve with a hot cocktail sauce.

Avgolemono

Georgio Papatheodorou

Avgolemono, the best known Greek soup, is chicken broth with rice-shaped macaroni (orzo). What makes this soup unique is the adding of eggs and lemon to make it frothy and piquant.

6	cups chicken broth	2	eggs, separated
1	cup uncooked orzo or rice	4	Tb lemon juice

Add orzo (rice) to boiling chicken broth. Cover and cook from 10 to 20 minutes, until orzo (rice) is done.

Beat egg whites until stiff. Beat in the egg yolks. Gently blend in the lemon juice. Spoon a ladle of hot chicken soup into the egg mixture; then pour this mixture back into the pot of chicken soup. 6 to 8 servings

Use as a soup course or enjoy as a main course with crusty bread and a green salad.

Spanakopitta

Arlis Greiling

In Italy, it's Torta Pasqualina, in France, Quiche Lorraine—a cheese and greens pie.

1	pkg filo dough* (1 lb, about 20 sheets)	6	eggs, beaten with ½ tsp salt, ¼ tsp pepper
2	lbs fresh spinach or 3 10-oz pkgs frozen	1	lb Feta cheese,* crumbled
1	Tb salt	1 ¼	tsp dill weed
1	lb butter, melted, or 1 cup olive oil (approximately)	¼	tsp nutmeg (freshly grated best)
1 ½	cups chopped onions	⅛	tsp oregano
		¼	tsp dried parsley flakes

Thaw filo per package instructions. Wash and dry fresh spinach and chop it fine. Add salt to fresh spinach and rub spinach with your hands. Let stand for an hour. Then squeeze out all the juice exuded. If using frozen spinach, thaw and drain thoroughly. Spinach must be very dry.

In 3 tablespoons of the butter/oil, sauté onions until yellow and soft. Combine with the spinach, eggs, Feta cheese, and herb seasonings. Set aside.

Butter a baking pan (approximately 9½ x 13½ inches) generously—bottom, sides, and rim. Place first filo sheet in pan, allowing it to come up the sides of the pan. Brush liberally with butter/oil. Repeat this procedure with 6 more filo sheets, buttering each one well (can use up to 10 sheets if desired). Spread spinach mixture evenly over filo. Then cover with more filo sheets (6 to 8 more), buttering each one as you layer them. Butter/oil the top sheet. Trim edges around the pan. Sprinkle

water over top filo sheet and moisten the edges so they won't curl up. Bake at 350°
for 45 to 50 minutes. Cut into squares and serve either hot or cold as an entreé (10 to
12 servings) or cut into tiny squares for hors d' oeuvres.

*Filo (fee-low) or phyllo is a very, very thin dough used in most Greek pies and
pastries. It takes an expert to make it. Can be bought in Greek or gourmet shops
or in some supermarkets in the frozen-food department.

*Feta cheese is a soft, salted white cheese made either from ewe's milk or goat's
milk. Found in Greek and Italian shops.

Aubergine Moussaka Patrice

Eggplant Casserole

Pat Southward

¼ cup uncooked rice	¼ cup fresh mint or 1 tsp
¼ cup olive oil	dried mint
1 large eggplant, peeled and	½ cup raisins (if desired)
chopped	½ cup slivered almonds
¾ cup minced onion	1½ cups canned tomatoes or 2
½ cup minced green pepper	cups fresh tomatoes
1 clove garlic, minced	Salt and pepper
½ cup chopped fresh parsley	

Boil rice in 1½ cups boiling water salted with ½ teaspoon salt for about 15 minutes.
Heat olive oil; add eggplant, onion, green pepper, and garlic. Cook until tender.
Add parsley, mint, raisins, nuts, and tomatoes. Combine with rice: salt and pepper
to taste. Bake in greased 2-quart casserole at 375° for 40 to 60 minutes. 4 to 6
servings

Skewered Cookery

Its origin is ancient Assyrian, *shish kabob*. Italians call it *allo spiedino*; French, *en
brochette*; Russians, *shashlik*; and Greeks call it *souvlakia*. It's the method of
cooking meat, fish, or fowl on skewers—either grilled on the outdoor grill or broiled
or roasted indoors.

Usually vegetables such as small onions, cherry tomatoes, and green pepper pieces
are skewered alternately with the meat, fish, or fowl, but due to cooking time
differences, vegetables are better skewered and cooked separately. Skewers should
be long and flat rather than round for easier turning of the food. Wooden skewers
soaked in water for a few minutes are ideal when entertaining a large group.

Meat should be of the highest quality to insure tenderness. It should be cut in 1½-
to 2-inch cubes to control even cooking and proper marinating. When chicken is
used, either breasts or thighs are best—separate, never cooked together. Fish, such
as halibut, swordfish, and scallops, should be fresh and sweet smelling. Serve kebabs
with cooked rice and a green salad. A glass of wine is delightful, too.

Fish Souvlakia

2 lbs halibut or swordfish,
cut into small pieces, or
scallops
1 tsp lemon juice
¼ tsp salt
Black pepper

Flour
Bay leaf
2 Tb butter/margarine,
melted
Bread crumbs

Sprinkle lemon juice, salt, and pepper to taste over fish. Just before assembling, roll fish in flour; shake off excess. Skewer fish with a small piece of bay leaf between every two pieces of fish. Brush with melted butter/margarine and then roll skewered fish in bread crumbs. Just 2 to 3 minutes of cooking time on each side is sufficient. Will be springy to the touch. 4 to 6 servings

Lamb Kebabs

Leg of lamb, cut into 1½-inch cubes (½ lb per person)
Slab of bacon, cut into 1-inch chunks
Marinade:

2 Tb olive oil
1. Tb lemon juice
1 tsp rosemary
1 tsp salt
¼ tsp pepper (freshly ground
best)

1 clove garlic, minced
Lemon peel from 1 lemon,
minced

Mix marinade ingredients together. Marinate lamb pieces for 20 to 30 minutes. Meanwhile, blanch the bacon by simmering gently in hot water for 10 minutes. Drain. Assemble on skewers by alternating a chunk of bacon first, then lamb (5 to 6 pieces per skewer). Cook 8 to 9 minutes on each side. Lamb should be a pale pink inside to be just right and not overcooked.

Serve with pita, the flat round bread of Greece, Bulgaria, and Syria. Just slip skewer into the hollow center of pita and pull off the kebabs.

Middle East Hamburgers

1	lb ground beef (chuck or top round)	1	green pepper, finely chopped
2	Tb vegetable or corn oil	½	tsp salt
1	bunch green onions and tops, finely sliced	¼	tsp pepper
		3	Tb catsup or chili sauce
¾ to 1	cup pimiento-stuffed olives, sliced	1	Tb coriander*
		4	small rounds pita bread
1	clove garlic, crushed and minced		

Sauté meat in hot oil until lightly browned; add green onions, olives, garlic, green pepper, salt, and pepper; sauté for 5 minutes, stirring well. Stir in catsup (chili sauce) and coriander. Cut pita bread open at top (use kitchen shears); stuff with hamburger mixture. 4 servings
*A favorite Mediterranean spice.

Greek Salad Pappas

This is a famous salad. Many order it in a Greek restaurant over any other salad. The pièce de résistance is the potato salad at the very bottom of the bowl. So, we will begin from the bottom and progress to the top.

For each serving:

	Lettuce cup (1 or 2 leaves head lettuce)	2	chunks Feta cheese
½	cup potato salad (your favorite)	1	sliced green pepper ring
		1	whole green onion
	Shredded lettuce	1	beet slice
3	Greek peppers, pickled in vinegar	2	shrimp
		3	anchovies
1	radish		Watercress or rugala (if available)
1	slice cucumber		Oil and vinegar or lemon dressing
2	Greek black olives		
2	tomato wedges		

In an individual salad bowl of good size, form a lettuce "cup" at the bottom of the bowl. Then add the potato salad. As you add the other ingredients, sprinkle a little shredded lettuce in with them. Arrange the ingredients in the order listed. Top with a few sprigs watercress or rugala (similar to watercress). Drizzle oil and vinegar or lemon dressing on top. Vinegar can be either white or cider. Use a light olive oil or vegetable oil.

Feta is uniquely Greek. It is white, rather soft cheese, refrigerated in brine.

Baklava

(bahk-luh-vah)

Mara Drivas

A dessert so rich, it is served in tiny 1½-inch diamond-shaped servings. It is a Turkish delight as well as Greek. The pastry is made with filo (fee-low) or phyllo, a paper-thin buttery dough which can be bought in Greek and Lebanese stores or sometimes in supermarkets in the frozen-food department.

4	cups finely chopped walnuts*	1	pkg filo dough (1 lb, about 20 sheets)*
⅛	tsp nutmeg (freshly grated best)	1	cup (2 sticks) butter/margarine, melted
1½	tsp ground cinnamon	1	12-oz jar honey, heated
⅛	tsp ground cloves		
½	cup sugar, light brown or granulated		

Mix nuts, spices, and sugar together. Butter a baking pan (approximately 9½ x 13 ½ inches) generously. Place 1 filo sheet in pan; trim to fit or can allow to extend up the sides of pan. Brush with melted butter/margarine. Add 4 more sheets, brushing each one with melted butter/margarine. Spread 1 cup of nut mixture over the 5 buttered sheets. Repeat this process 3 more times (using 3 sheets each time, well buttered and spread with 1 cup nut mixture). Top with the remaining 5 filo sheets, each sheet brushed with butter/margarine. Trim sheets evenly around sides of baking pan, so they do not extend over edges of pan.

With a sharp knife, mark off—and cut halfway through—diamond-shaped guidelines (24 to 36 servings). Bake at 300° for 1½ hours, or until golden brown. Pour heated honey over hot baklava. Cool on wire rack. Finish cutting baklava into diamond-shaped pieces. Store in the pan.

*Can also use part pistachio and toasted blanched almonds.

*Start with 5 sheets for bottom layer; then 3 sheets, then 3 sheets, then 3 sheets; end with 5 sheets for top layer; total: 19 sheets.

Baklava Syrup

For a richer syrup topping. Prepare before making the baklava.

4	whole cloves		Peel from 1 lemon, finely grated
½	stick cinnamon		
	Peel from 1 orange, finely grated	2¼	cups sugar
		1	cup honey

Bring spices, grated peels, sugar and 1½ cups water to a boil. Simmer, uncovered, for 5 minutes to thicken. Remove cloves and cinnamon. Stir in the honey. Cool mixture to room temperature. Pour over hot baklava. Let stand for several hours before serving. 2 to 3 cups syrup

JEWISH

With the arrival in New Amsterdam (New York) in 1654, of twenty-three Jewish refugees from Brazil, the history of the Jews in America began.

Descendants of an ancient people, the Jews scattered in exile to all parts of the world. With this migration into different geographical environments, the Jews became racially diversified: there are Italian Jews, German Jews, Russian, Polish, French, even Chinese Jews. Those who emigrated to the Mesabi Range around the 1890s were mostly Lithuanian Jews.

Jews who emigrated to America found themselves in the melting pot and they eventually emerged as American Jews. But they kept their cultural and religious heritage through a strong sense of kinship for Jews all over the world.

In Hibbing we grew up with Jewish families named Sachs, Hallock, Friedman, Stone, Nides, Milkes, and Sapero. We got to know the rabbi in his black accoutrements, wearing his skullcap–the rabbi, who officiated at religious and legal rituals in their synagogue and who, in accordance with their dietary laws, supervised the slaughtering of livestock.

We marked their holidays with all their traditions: Passover (the Exodus); Rosh Hashana (New Year), Yom Kippur (Day of Atonement), Hannukkah. We sampled their foods. We watched with interest how they practiced the rituals, such as using a special set of dishes but once a year on Passover and then packing them away until next year's holiday. We knew of the Shabbat and of their symbolic Star of David. We were aware that we were the Gentiles and that mixed marriages were not tolerated, although this strict tradition has seemingly eased up. Orthodox Jews were regulated to eat only kosher foods, but we sure did sell a lot of Italian salami, pork, and ham.

Most Jews were merchants on the Mesabi Range. They owned Lippman's Department Store, Shapiro's Drugstore, Zimmerman's Hardware, and specialty men's and women's shops.

Such interesting and delicious food—bagels, knishes, chicken soup (Mama Goldberg's cure-all for sickness), chopped liver, challah, and lox.

Gefilte Fish

Joan Feher

2 to 4	lbs white fish or pike	4 to 5	onions, sliced
1	cup minced onion		Bones and skin of fish
3	eggs		Sliced carrots
½	tsp sugar		
	Salt and pepper to taste		

Grind first 5 ingredients together until it is like a batter that can be handled, shiny and fairly smooth.

Layer sliced onions and fish bones and skin in a Dutch oven. Cover with boiling water. With wet hands, form the ground mixture into fish balls and place in Dutch oven to make one layer. Then place a layer of sliced carrots over fish balls and make alternate layers. Simmer gently for 2½ hours. Add more water if needed. Remove fish balls with slotted spoon. 1 to 2 dozen fish balls

Chopped Liver

Ruth Baum Carlton

The Jewish menu always includes an appetizer. Most popular are gefilte fish, herring, and chopped liver.

1½	lbs chicken livers	3	extra-large or large eggs,
¼	cup (4 Tb) oil		hard boiled
¼	cup (4 Tb)	1	tsp salt (or to taste)
	butter/margarine	¼	tsp pepper
5 to 6	medium-sized onions,	½	tsp garlic powder
	chopped		

Sauté onions in oil and butter/margarine until soft. Add chicken livers and cook covered until done, turning occasionally (about 10 to 15 minutes).

Chop livers with hard-boiled eggs (using a hand food chopper or knife). Also use all the oil that the livers and onions were cooked in. When smooth in consistency, add salt, pepper, and garlic powder. Store overnight, covered, in refrigerator. Spread on crackers. 1½ cups

Matzo Balls

Knaidlach

Mary Ann and Nate Fox

At Passover Time, the most symbolic food is matzo, the unleavened bread. Traditional, too, is Matzo Balls, made from matzo meal and served in chicken broth.

3	eggs	3	Tb schmaltz (rendered
1/4	tsp cinnamon (if desired)		chicken fat)
1	tsp salt	1 1/4	cups matzo meal
1/4	tsp pepper (white preferred)	6	cups chicken broth

Beat eggs. Add 1/2 cup water, cinnamon, salt, and pepper. Mix in chicken fat and matzo meal. Cover and let rest for an hour. First wet hands in cold water and then form mixture into small balls. Drop balls into boiling salted water. Cover and cook from 20 to 40 minutes, depending on size of balls. The knaidlach (matzo balls) will first sink to the bottom of the pot, then rise to the top. Remove with slotted spoon and place matzo balls in hot chicken broth. Can also be served with butter as a side dish. 6 to 8 servings

Some recipes even call for ground almonds and minced mushrooms.

Mother's Tuna Loaf

John Feher

2	7-oz cans tuna, drained	2	eggs, beaten
2	Tb butter/margarine	4	Tb sour cream
1	cup chopped onion	2	Tb butter/margarine,
1	cup chopped celery		melted
1	green pepper, chopped	1	Tb lemon juice
2	Tb minced fresh parsley	1	tsp baking powder
1	cup matzo meal		Salt and pepper to taste
			Buttered bread crumbs

Sauté onion in 2 tablespoons butter/margarine until soft. Add celery and green pepper and cook until tender. Add parsley. Set aside.

Mix tuna with all remaining ingredients except bread crumbs. Add to the vegetable mix. Pour into a well-buttered loaf pan. Sprinkle with buttered bread crumbs. Bake at 350° for 45 minutes. 6 to 8 servings

Knishes

We enjoyed hot knishes on the boardwalk at Coney Island many years ago. They were sold from stands much like hot dog stands. Delicious with mustard or catsup. Knishes are traditional for Jewish weddings and Bar Mitzvahs.

4	cups boiled or baked potatoes	½	tsp salt
1	Tb butter/margarine	¼	tsp pepper
½	cup chopped onion or scallions	1	package pie-crust mix (2 crusts) or own recipe
2	Tb butter/margarine or corn oil	1	egg, beaten
		2	tsp vegetable or corn oil

Mash potatoes with 1 tablespoon butter/margarine. Sauté onion (scallions) in the 2 tablespoons butter/margarine (oil) until onion is soft. Add to mashed potatoes. Season with salt and pepper and beat well with electric mixer until smooth.

Prepare pie-crust dough. Roll dough thin (⅛ inch). Cut crust into 4-inch squares. Place a heaping tablespoon of potato mixture in center of each square; bring corners up over filling and seal. Place seam side down on an ungreased cookie sheet. Brush with mixture of beaten egg and oil. Bake at 350° for 40 to 45 minutes. 8 to 10 knishes

Knishes can also be made with egg pasta dough (see Ravioli recipe). Fillings can be chopped liver (see recipe in this section) or ground beef sautéed with chopped onion and seasoned with salt and pepper.

Bagels

Bagels—that doughnut-shaped roll, fresh from the oven, in several flavors: plain, poppyseed, pumpernickel, onion—are a universal delight. They are spread with butter and cream cheese and served with lox (kosher salmon) for breakfast.

Bagels split in half hold the best stuffings for a good sandwich. Stuff them generously with kosher delicatessen salami, pastrami, corned beef, or chopped liver, spread with mustard. Serve kosher pickles on the side.

Good for any time of the day—but be sure they are fresh—nothing palatable about an old bagel!

Elegant Cheese Cake

Jean Kleffman Clauser

Crust:

1¼ cups graham cracker
    crumbs
¼ cup (4 Tb) butter, melted
1 Tb sugar

To make crust, mix crumbs, melted butter, and sugar. Press into bottom and up sides of greased 9-inch round springform pan.

Filling:

3 8-oz packages cream cheese,
    softened
1 pt sour cream
4 eggs
1¼ cups sugar
4 Tb heavy cream
2 tsp vanilla extract
1 Tb lemon juice
1 tsp grated lemon peel

Blend together all filling ingredients with electric beater. Beat until light and fluffy. Pour into crust. Bake at 350° for 35 to 40 minutes.

Topping:

1 pt sour cream
1 Tb sugar
1 Tb lemon juice
1 tsp vanilla extract
¼ cup graham cracker crumbs

Blend together first 4 ingredients of topping near end of baking time. Remove cake from oven. Spread sour cream topping over the top. Sprinkle with crumbs and return cake to oven for 5 minutes. Gently remove cake from oven, cool in pan, then refrigerate overnight to mellow. 6 to 8 servings

LATIN AMERICAN

Would you believe that in a pictorial booklet entitled "North Hibbing, Reminiscences of a Ghost Town," there is a photograph of a street peddler with his three-wheel contraption, a sort of covered bin, peddling tortillas! This was in the early 1900s, when peddlers were a common sight, especially around the numerous saloons. But where the peddler got his Mexican tortillas is not known, according to the old-timers.

During Chun King days, we had Mexican migrant help at the celery farms in Zim, Minnesota. Old city buses were converted into comfortable living quarters for the workers there on the farmlands. These people were excellent workers and the women kept a neat house.

We would watch the women make tortillas, their "staff of life." Mexican tortillas are made of cornmeal, whereas Spanish tortillas (omelet) are made with eggs, potatoes, rice, or a variety of vegetables.

Limes, avocado, frijoles (black beans), hot peppers, oregano, saffron, tomatoes, green plantain for French-fried chips and ripe plantains fried as a side dish, chorizos (highly seasoned sausage), empanadas (sweet pies or meat pies), wines, sangría, and cafe con leche (half coffee, half milk) are Mexican and Spanish ingredients and fare.

Guacamole Dip

Bob Heimbach

2 large ripe avocados, peeled and mashed
3 Tb minced onion
1 clove garlic, minced
½ tsp chili powder
½ tsp salt
⅓ cup mayonnaise
8 to 10 slices bacon, fried crisp and crumbled

Combine mashed avocado, onion, garlic, and seasonings in small bowl and spread top with mayonnaise, sealing all edges to prevent discoloration. At serving time, stir in mayonnaise and bacon. For a colorful presentation, scoop out pulp from large tomatoes and fill with guacamole. Serve with tortilla chips (corn, nacho, or taco flavors). 1½ cups

To make above dip hot, add ½ to 1 (depending how hot) 4-ounce can chopped chilies, drained—or a few dashes of hot pepper sauce will do it!

Chilled Gazpacho

Originally a Spanish or Mexican dish, gazpacho is a cold, colorful, spicy soup. It is now very popular in northern Europe and in the United States. In New Orleans it was prepared in a blender and served as a "juice" for breakfast and as a pre-dinner appetizer. For a novel Bloody Mary, serve in goblets with a celery stick to stir in the vodka!

4 to 5 medium tomatoes, peeled, de-seeded, and diced
2 large cucumbers, peeled, de-seeded, and diced
2 green peppers, diced
1 medium onion, diced
1 small clove garlic, finely minced
1 stalk celery, diced
2 (12 oz) cans tomato juice or 1 26-oz jar of combined 8 vegetable juices
½ cup white dry wine
⅓ cup wine vinegar
2 Tb olive oil
1 to 2 tsp Worcestershire sauce
2 to 3 tsp salt
½ tsp pepper
6 drops hot pepper sauce

Dice all vegetables same size. Peel tomatoes by piercing them with long fork and immersing in boiling water for just 4 seconds (count "21–22–23–24"). Peel, cut in half, squeeze out seeds, and dice. De-seed cucumbers by cutting lengthwise and scraping out seeds with a spoon. Then dice.

Mix all ingredients together; refrigerate until icy cold. Serve as a side dish or in place of a salad. 4 to 6 servings

To serve as breakfast juice or pre-dinner appetizer, mix all ingredients in a blender.

222

Chili con Carne

Originally chili con carne meant just that, chili (peppers) with meat. The adding of other ingredients like tomatoes and beans were later variations. The Italians of southern origin made it this way, too, only using hot round cherry peppers. I remember seeing some of our paisanos just pop these peppers into their mouths without a wince! Caldo caldo!

1	lb round or flank steak
2	Tb oil
1 or 2	hot chili peppers, canned or fresh

In hot oil, fry steak until brown and to preferred doneness. Add cut up chili peppers. Peppers will help tenderize the meat—like a "blowtorch!" *Muy caliente!* 2 to 4 servings

Chili con Carne Roberto

Bob Heimbach

4	lbs ground beef
3 to 4	cups chopped onions
1	cup chopped green pepper
3	Tb vegetable or corn oil
4 to 5	cups canned stewed tomatoes, drained
4	Tb vinegar
4	Tb chili powder (or less)
2	cloves garlic, minced
2	Tb Worcestershire sauce
4	drops hot pepper sauce
2	6-oz cans tomato paste
	Salt and pepper
2	14- or 15-oz cans red kidney beans

Sauté meat, onions, and green pepper in hot oil until meat is browned. Add stewed tomatoes and bring to a boil. Stir in vinegar, chili powder, garlic, Worcestershire sauce, hot pepper sauce, and tomato paste, and bring to a boil. Let simmer gently for about 1 hour. Season highly with salt and pepper to taste. Add the kidney beans with their juice. Bring to a boil and then simmer, covered, for 30 minutes more, stirring occasionally. *Muy bueno!* 10 to 12 servings

Chili con Frijoles

Dorothy McWhorter

2 lbs lean ground beef
2 Tb vegetable or corn oil
2 medium onions, chopped
1 clove garlic, minced, or ⅛ tsp garlic powder
2 Tb chili powder
1 Tb Worcestershire sauce
½ Tb ground cumin (comino)

1 tsp sugar (if desired)
½ tsp ground oregano
1 15-oz can whole tomatoes
2 8-oz cans tomato sauce
1 6-oz can tomato paste
Salt
2 15-oz cans Mexican-style chili beans

In large skillet, sauté onions in hot oil until soft. Add meat and garlic and stir until well separated and all pink color is gone from the meat. Add all the spices to meat mixture and mix well. Blend tomatoes, tomato sauce and paste in blender and add to meat mixture. Salt to taste. Bring to simmer over low heat. Simmer, covered, for 1½ hours. Stir occasionally to prevent sticking. If any grease has accumulated, remove with spoon. Add chili beans with their juice, stir; simmer, covered, 20 to 30 minutes more, stirring occasionally to prevent sticking. Seasonings should be adjusted to taste. Cut down amounts if too spicy; add more if you like your chili highly seasoned. 10 to 12 servings

For variation, try adding 1 teaspoon paprika or a dash of hot pepper sauce.

Tostadas or Tacos

(Tohs-tah-dahs) (tah-kohs)

Tostadas and tacos are virtually the same thing. They are both tortillas (tor-tee-yahs) made from stone-ground corn mixed with spices and deep-fried to a crisp, golden color. Tostadas are flat, tacos are folded tortillas.

This is a delightful way to entertain. Prepare everything ahead—keep hot things hot, cold things cold. Serve buffet style and invite guests to make their own from all the condiments arranged on the table. But look out for those green chilies and jalapeños (hah-lah-pey-nose). Hotsy-totsy!

Tostadas or Tacos

Dorothy McWhorter

1½ lbs ground beef	½ tsp basil or thyme
1 cup chopped onion	1 tsp salt
1 clove garlic, minced	¼ tsp black or cayenne pepper
1 green pepper, chopped	½ cup dry white or red wine
1 Tb ground cumin (comino)	or water
1 Tb chili powder	Tortillas*

In an ungreased pan, sauté ground beef, onion, garlic, and green pepper, starting out on low heat and then increasing heat until beef is browned. Add the spices and seasonings, plus wine (water). Cook gently, covered, 15 to 20 minutes, stirring occasionally. Keep hot.

Prepare tortillas by following directions on the package. Keep warm. To serve tostadas or tacos, layer tortillas with meat, then top with as many of these condiments as you like:

Shredded sharp cheddar cheese
Heated refried beans or chili con carne
Chopped canned jalapeño peppers
Sliced pimiento-stuffed olives
Shredded lettuce
Chopped tomatoes
Chopped green onions

Sliced Spanish onions
Chopped pickled chilies
Sliced pitted black olives
Chopped hard-cooked eggs
Sliced avocados, sprinkled
with lemon juice
Taco Sauce (recipes below)

Before topping with other ingredients, you may place tortillas on a cookie sheet, top with meat and cheese and heat at 350° until cheese melts. 8 to 10 servings

*Either from freezer section, refrigerated department, or from your grocery shelf.

Mary Schmitt serves tortilla chips instead.

Taco Sauce

1 cup chili sauce or 1 8-oz can tomato sauce	1 or 2 pickled chilies jalapeños, chopped (more for hotter sauce)
½ cup chopped onion	
¼ cup wine vinegar	1 tsp salt
2 Tb diced green pepper	¼ tsp garlic powder or 1 clove garlic, minced
1 to 2 Tb fresh green chilies or 1 4-oz can, drained and minced	¼ tsp ground cumin (comino)
	¼ tsp basil

Mix all ingredients together and refrigerate for at least one hour. Will keep for weeks refrigerated in tightly covered jar. 1½ to 2 cups

Taco Sauce Caliente

Bob Heimbach

1   16-oz can tomatoes, chopped
2   4-oz cans green chilies, drained and chopped
1   large white onion, chopped

2   cloves garlic, pressed or mashed, then minced
1   (6-oz) can jalapeño green peppers, drained and chopped

Put all ingredients into blender and whirl until smooth. Keep refrigerated in a tightly sealed jar. Use for tacos or tostados. 3½ cups

Boliche Hazado Ramirez

(boh-lee-chay ah-zah-doh)

*There is a Spanish adage that beef without marinating (*sin adobar*) is like potatoes without salt.*

3 to 4   lbs eye round roast
½   lb pre-cooked ham
4   cloves garlic, slivered
1   cup chopped onion

⅛   tsp grated fresh nutmeg
1   cup dry white or red wine
1   cup oil

Roast should marinate overnight before cooking. Cut a tunnel through the middle of the boliche (roast). Insert a piece of ham through it, end to end. Press garlic cloves into pockets notched into the surface of the meat. Combine onion and nutmeg with the wine. Pour over boliche and marinate in a covered bowl, turning occasionally.

In a deep pan, brown meat in hot oil on all sides just until golden. Use tongs to turn. Pour marinade over and let simmer gently on top of stove for about 2 hours, or until beef is done. Turn and baste occasionally.

Instead of cooking on top of the stove, you can roast boliche in an open roasting pan in the oven. Roast at 450° until beef is golden brown, then turn over down to 325° to finish roasting. Keep basting with the marinade. Serve sliced either hot or cold. *Muy delicioso!* 6 to 8 servings

Arroz con Pollo

(ah-rose kone poy-oh)

Chicken with Rice

Cira Borgard

My good Spanish friend Cira says that the art of good Spanish cooking is in the use of saffron (an old-world flowering plant), not only for color (deep yellow orange) but, more important, for distinct flavor. It is expensive (about ¼₀ ounce costs $1.15) but worth it. The English and Scandinavians use saffron also, mainly in baking breads.

2	fryers, choice parts	2	Tb chopped fresh parsley
4	Tb olive oil	1	tsp salt
1	large (1 lb) Spanish onion, chopped	½	tsp pepper
		½	tsp oregano
1	medium green pepper, sliced into strips	1	8-oz can tomato sauce
		1	cup dry white or red wine
4	cloves garlic, crushed and minced	1	tsp crushed saffron
		2	cups uncooked rice
2	bay leaves	2	tsp salt

Sauté vegetables and seasonings in olive oil until onion is soft. Add tomato sauce. Add chicken pieces and mix everything together well. Add wine, bring to a boil, and simmer 5 to 10 minutes. Add saffron and enough water to fully cover chicken (about 2½ cups); let boil gently, uncovered, until chicken is half done (about 20 minutes). Add rice with 2 teaspoons salt and cook on high heat, stirring constantly, until it comes to a boil (about 5 minutes), then turn to medium low heat and cover with wax paper between pot and lid (for better steaming). After 10 minutes, stir and then cover again for 10 minutes. Chicken will be done when rice is cooked, though there will still be plenty of juice.*

Serve on a deep platter surrounded by buttered baby green peas, pimiento strips, and pimiento-stuffed olives. Or serve in a bowl with pimiento strips, olives, and peas served on the side. Tossed salad, buttered string beans, French-fried plantains,* and a sweet potato casserole round out a sumptuous meal. 8 to 10 servings

*If boiled down too far, add some hot chicken broth.

*Plantains are an Antilles bananalike fruit. Slice diagonally ½ inch thick and French-fry. Be sure they are ripe!

Arroz con Pollo leftover? Wrap in aluminum foil. Reheat at 350° for 45 minutes.

Velvet Hammer

For 1 serving:

½ pt vanilla ice cream	½ oz Triple Sec
1½ ozs Tia Maria	½ oz Crême de Cacao

Mix all ingredients together and serve as an after-dinner drink and/or dessert. Mighty smooth, delicious, pow————er-ful!! *Salud!*

FAR EASTERN

Of the 50,000 population count on the Mesabi Iron Range in 1910, only about 100 were Chinese. The only Chinese I remember were a few families who set up Chinese restaurants. And, Japanese, they came much, much later, perhaps from the California area after the war.

The Chinese throughout their history were reluctant, due to their social philosophy, to leave their ancestral homes. However, political and economic strife over the years prompted some emigration. With the growth of railways in this country in the 1860s and 1870s, Chinese laborers were brought in to build the railroads, including the first intercontinental, which was completed in 1869.

In San Francisco, Chinatown became the largest Chinese settlement outside of the Orient, and still is to this day. Although Americanized, they cling to their ancestral traditions. Each year they celebrate, as usual, their Chinese New Year with parades of golden dragons and fireworks. But they have done some migrating to other parts of the country.

Despite Japan's strong indigenous characteristics, Chinese influence in language, government, culture and the art of gardening dates back to the seventh century. The first Europeans to discover the sacred soil of Japan were the Portuguese and the Italians who sent Jesuits there in the 1540s. Later came other Europeans and finally the United States, arranging trade treaties with the Japanese in the nineteenth century.

Proverb; "East is East and West is West and ne'er the twain shall meet"—never more.

Teahouses, silk kimonos, sake, temples, sushi, tempura, sukiyaki, teriyaki—all signify Japanese. And we have all heard of The Great Wall, Chinese arts and crafts in ivory, jade, and cloisonné, and the Dynasties.

The pleasure of good food has been represented through poetry and folklore as a work of art, so important is the joy of eating to the Oriental. Unique is the timing of the preparation of Oriental food; maximum time for preparing and lining up the ingredients, mimimum time for cooking.

Ingredients from meat to vegetables are cleaned, peeled, sliced, chopped, diced, minced, marinated. Meats are cooked tender, vegetables crunchy.

Essential ingredients are soy sauce, bean sprouts, onions, cilantro (parsley), Chinese cabbage (baak-choy), ginger root, mushrooms, bamboo shoots, water chestnuts, plus a whole collection of sauces, spices, and herbs. Dry sherry and sake are used as cooking wines.

Chinese cook in a wok; Japanese have their hibachi.

Rice is the staple food and all other dishes are the accompaniments. A Chinese place setting usually includes chopsticks, a medium plate, a saucer, a bowl for soup and rice, a porcelain spoon, and a tiny tea cup.

Chinese cookery is distinguished by regions and dialects, such as Cantonese, Hunan, Szechuen, and Mandarin. And then there is Chun King Oriental-American as originated by that Italian in Scandinavian Minnesota—brother Jeno!

Egg Rolls

Chinese appetizers are known as deem sum, *which means "touch the heart." They are served whenever the heart craves them.*

Filling

1-1/2 cups chopped cooked chicken, pork, beef, or shrimp (or a combination)
2 Tb peanut or vegetable oil
1 Tb soy sauce
1 Tb dry sherry wine
1 tsp grated or minced fresh ginger
2 chopped green onions, including tops
1/2 cup chopped celery

1 cup fresh bean sprouts or canned, drained
1/2 clove minced garlic (if desired)
1/2 cup chopped baak-choy (if desired)
Salt and pepper
Egg Roll wrappers*
Sweet and sour sauce
Hot mustard sauce

Saute chicken, meat and/or shrimp in 2 Tb hot oil for 2 minutes. Add soy sauce, sherry wine and ginger. Stir in green onions, celery, bean sprouts, garlic and baak-choy. Saute for 2 to 3 minutes. Salt and pepper to taste. Drain off any excess fat and let mixture cool. Place 1 Tb mixture on bottom half of egg roll wrapper and roll, tucking in the ends. Moisten edge and seal. Deep fry in hot oil. Drain. Serve with sauces. 36 egg rolls.

* Prepared egg roll wrappers can be purchased in most supermarkets or in Oriental food shops. Or use recipe egg pasta for ravioli, rolled and cut into 6 inch squares.

Oriental Ribs

Puu Puus

3½ to 4 lbs lean baby spareribs, cut into 2- or single-rib pieces

Marinade

½ cup soy sauce
⅓ cup brown sugar
2 tb dry sherry or sake
1 clove garlic, minced
1 Tb grated or minced fresh ginger
Pinch grated fresh nutmeg (if desired)

1 tsp salt
Pinch cayenne pepper or dash of hot pepper sauce (for hotness)

Sweet and sour sauce and/or hot mustard

Blend all marinade ingredients together; pour over ribs and marinate for 1 hour. Place ribs on broiler pans lined with foil or use foil broiler pans. Roast at 325° for 1 hour. After first 30 minutes, turn ribs over and baste with remaining sauce. Serve hot with sweet and sour sauce and/or hot mustard.

Ribs may be prepared ahead and reheated by placing in 275° oven (uncovered) for 10 minutes. May be frozen and reheated after thawing.

Cocktail Quantities:

Double recipe for 35 people.
Triple recipe for 50 people.
Quadruple recipe for 70 people.

Rumaki

Puu Puus

12	slices of bacon, cut in half	*Marinade:*	
6	chicken livers (about ½ lb), quartered	3	Tb soy sauce
		1½	tsp sugar
12	whole water chestnuts, sliced in half	¼	tsp grated fresh ginger
		¼	tsp monosodium glutamate (if desired)

Blend all marinade ingredients together; pour over chicken livers and marinate for at least 20 minutes. Fry bacon halves until partially cooked but soft. Wrap chicken livers and water chestnuts in bacon strips and skewer in place with toothpicks. Arrange on broiler pans (or foil broiler pans). Bake at 450° for 10 to 15 minutes, or until bacon is crisp. 24 rumaki

Rumaki can be prepared ahead and refrigerated until time to serve. To reheat, place in 450° oven (uncovered) for 5 minutes. Can be frozen also, and reheated after thawing.

To make 144 rumaki, you'll need 4 to 5 lbs bacon, 2¼ lbs chicken livers, 5 cans water chestnuts, 1 cup soy sauce, 3 Tb sugar, 1½ tsp each of ginger and monosodium glutamate.

Tips:

1 lb bacon averages about 14 strips or 28 halves (depends on thickness).
1 can water chestnuts averages 16 whole or 32 halves.
Save bacon grease for Liz's Fried Chicken Italian.

Sweet and Sour Rumaki

Winifred MacPherson

1	8-oz can whole water chestnuts	12	slices bacon, cut in half
½	cup cider vinegar		Light brown sugar

Drain water chestnuts and mix the liquid in a bowl with vinegar. Place water chestnuts into marinade for approximately 1 hour. Spread each bacon half with light brown sugar and place a water chestnut at the end of strip. Roll up and secure with a toothpick. Place in baking pan or on cookie sheet and bake at 350° for approximately 30 minutes. Serve at once. 20 to 24 rumaki

Teriyaki Chicken Wings from Nellie

2½ lbs chicken wings (14 to 20 count)

Marinade:

¼	cup soy sauce	¼	tsp ginger (fresh grated best)
1	Tb oil		
¾	tsp dry mustard	⅛	tsp pepper
		1	clove garlic, minced

Blend all marinade ingredients together; pour over chicken and marinate for at least 30 minutes (best overnight). Bake on cookie sheet at 350° for 1 hour.

Chinese Cucumber Tong

6	cups chicken broth or bouillon	¼	tsp grated fresh ginger
¾	cup diced cooked lean ham	1	tsp soy sauce
2	cucumbers, peeled, de-seeded, and cut into julienne strips.		Pinch monosodium glutamate (if desired)
		2	eggs, beaten

Bring broth (bouillon) to simmering and add ham. Cook 5 minutes. Add cucumber and simmer 1 minute more. Add ginger, soy sauce, and monosodium glutamate. Beat eggs into the soup. Serve hot. 6 to 8 servings

Befera's Lobster Tail Cantonese

Frank Befera

1	cooked lobster tail, cut up (12 to 14 ozs)	1	tsp oyster sauce* or clam juice
3	Tb corn or peanut oil	1	cup chicken broth or bouillon
1	lb ground pork	¼	cup dry sherry or sake
2	cloves garlic, crushed and minced	1	egg, beaten
2	Tb fermented (salted) black beans*	½	cup chopped green onions and tops
1	tsp grated fresh ginger	4	tsp cornstarch
6	drops sesame oil*		Cooked rice

In a preheated (to medium) wok or frying pan, combine oil, pork, garlic, and black beans, and stir-fry until pork is well done. Pour off any excess fat. Add ginger, sesame oil, oyster sauce, chicken broth, (bouillon) sherry, (sake), and lobster, stirring constantly. Cook for 5 minutes. Add egg and green onions, stirring constantly for 2 minutes. If gravy is too thin, add cornstarch blended with 4 tablespoons water. Or, thin gravy with broth, if needed. Serve with cooked rice. 8 to 10 servings
*Black beans, sesame oil, and oyster sauce can be found in Gourmet or Oriental Food Shops.

Befera's Teriyaki

Frank Befera

1¼	lbs flank steak or London broil, cut crosswise ⅛ inch thick	½	cup chicken broth or bouillon
½	cup soy sauce	¼	tsp grated fresh ginger root
2	cloves garlic, crushed and minced	1	green pepper, cut into chunks
2	Tb cornstarch	2	cups onions, (cut lengthwise 1 inch thick)
1	tsp monosodium glutamate (if desired)	4	tsp cornstarch
¼	cup corn or peanut oil		Cooked rice or chow mein noodles

In a bowl, mix thoroughly soy sauce, garlic, cornstarch, and monosodium glutamate. Add meat and stir well. In a preheated (to medium) wok or frying pan, combine oil and meat mixture. Stir-fry until meat is done, about 5 minutes. Add broth (bouillon), ginger root, green pepper, and onions. Stir-fry until gravy thickens and vegetables are bubbling hot but crisp. Add additional broth if gravy is too thick or cornstarch blended with 4 tablespoons water if gravy is too thin. Serve over rice or chow mein noodles. 4 to 6 servings

Teriyaki Imperial

Assemble ingredients ahead. Then cook about 30 minutes before serving time. Vegetables will be crisp and crunchy.

1½ to 2 lbs sirloin, flank steak, or London broil
½ tsp salt
¼ tsp pepper
3 Tb corn or peanut oil
1 bunch green onions and tops, chopped
1 clove garlic, minced
⅛ tsp grated or minced fresh ginger root
2 green peppers, sliced into rings

4 stalks celery diagonally cut into 2-inch lengths
1 can beef bouillon or 1 cup beef broth
4 tsp cornstarch
¼ cup soy sauce
1 can bean sprouts, drained (if desired)
Steamed rice and/or chow mein noodles

Slice meat into thin strips. Sprinkle with salt and pepper. Brown meat in heated oil. Stir in green onions, garlic, ginger root, green peppers, and celery. Cook 2 minutes, stirring constantly. Add the bouillon (broth), stir; simmer over low heat 5 minutes. Stir in cornstarch blended with soy sauce; bring to a boil, stirring constantly. Lower heat; simmer 3 minutes. Add bean sprouts; stir to heat through. Serve with steamed rice and/or chow mein noodles. Fresh sautéed mushrooms add a sumptuous touch! 8 to 10 servings

Oriental Marinade

Naoe Amemiya, Tokyo

1 slice London broil* (2 to 3 lbs, 2 to 3 inches thick)

Marinade:

1 Tb peanut or sesame oil
2 Tb soy sauce
¼ tsp salt
¼ tsp pepper

¼ tsp garlic powder
1 Tb grated fresh ginger
¼ tsp cayenne pepper (if "hot" desired)

Blend all marinade ingredients together; pour over beef and marinate for several hours. Either broil or grill meat. Serve sliced thin. 4 to 6 servings
*Also known as beef round top or round steak first-cut.

Ghuy Hunan

Chicken is a favorite in the Chinese diet and Hunan cooking is on the hot side.

3 chicken breasts, boned, skinned, and cut into thin strips (12 ozs)

1/4 cup vegetable, corn, or peanut oil

Marinade Sauce:

1/3 cup soy sauce
2 Tb dry sherry
2 cloves garlic, mashed and minced
1 tsp sugar
1 tsp cornstarch
3/4 tsp minced or grated fresh ginger root

1/2 tsp hot pepper sauce

2 cups carrots (cut into julienne strips)
1/2 cup snow peas or tiny green peas
Cooked rice

Blend all marinade sauce ingredients together; set aside.

In hot oil, sauté chicken until it turns white. Add the sauce mixture and carrots. Fry 3 minutes. Add peas and fry 2 minutes more. Serve over cooked rice. 2 to 3 servings

Instead of all carrots, try a combination of carrots, celery, Chinese cabbage, even bean sprouts, and a few mushrooms to equal 2 cups. Thin strips of beef or pork, or strips of turkey breast instead of chicken are very good, too. Serve hot pepper sauce on the side for extra hotness. For a gourmet touch, add cashews!

Naoe's Teriyaki Chicken

1 or 2 chickens, cut up

Marinade:

1/4 cup soy sauce
1/4 cup dry sherry or sake
2 Tb sugar
1 clove garlic, minced

1 Tb minced or shredded fresh ginger
1/2 tsp monosodium glutamate (if desired)

Heat soy sauce, sherry (sake), and sugar until sugar is dissolved. Mix in garlic, ginger and monosodium glutamate. Pour over chicken and marinate for 1 hour or more, turning occasionally. Either broil in oven or charcoal broil. 4 to 8 servings

This marinade can also be used for steak.

My Japanese maid was recommended to me by a "heavy duty" housecleaning service. She looked like Carol Burnett's TV maid, pail in hand filled with cleaning supplies, bandana on her head, and dust mop slung over her shoulder. I wondered about the dust mop, since floors were carpeted. I found out—she used it to wipe down the plaster ceilings. That solved the puzzlement of the grit settling on the furniture. She was such a meticulous cleaner, scrubbing on her hands and knees, using a toothbrush in the corners. The grit on my French Provincial furniture was scrubbed with hot water and strong detergent.

She sure did a beautiful job of teaching me Japanese cooking.

Gyoza

(gee-oh-zah)

Gyoza are wrappers (made of flour, water, and eggs, rolled very thin, and cut into rounds about 3 inches in diameter) filled with a vegetable-meat mixture. Wrappers are available at Oriental Food Shops in the frozen-food department.

Filling:

½ to ¾	lb ground beef	½	tsp salt
1 to 2	Tb peanut or vegetable oil	¼	tsp pepper
2	Tb chopped green pepper	¼	tsp monsodium glutamate
1	Tb chopped fresh ginger		(if desired)
	(scrape skin off)	1	cup chopped cabbage
2	Tb chopped onion or green		Gyoza wrappers
	onion		Beef or chicken broth
2	Tb chopped carrot		*or*
			Sauce Dip (below)

Brown ground beef in hot oil. Add green pepper, ginger, onion, and carrot. Season with salt, pepper, and monosodium glutamate. Stir and cook 2 minutes. Add cabbage; stir and cook until cabbage is transparent. Remove from heat; pour off any excess fat. Set aside to cool

Wet rim of wrappers with water. Place 1 teaspoon mixture on each wrapper. Fold over to form half-moon shape. Crimp around edge to seal tightly. Makes about 60 gyoza.

Gyoza may be served two ways:

As a soup: Cook filled gyoza in boiling beef or chicken broth.

Steam-fried: Fry gyoza in small amount of hot oil until brown on both sides. Add 2 tablespoons water. Cover, cut off heat, and let steam for 1 minute. Remove to serving platter. Serve with Sauce Dip.

Sauce Dip:

2	Tb soy sauce	1	tsp lemon juice
1	tsp horseradish	¼	tsp hot mustard

Combine all ingredients in small bowl. 1 serving

Oriental-Style Rice

1   cup rice (not long grain)
    Watermaid (Oriental type)

Wash rice in pan 2 to 3 times, pouring off water and adding more until water runs clear. Fill pan with cold water to cover rice by about 1 inch over top. Let soak at least 30 minutes.

Then cover pan and let come to a boil over medium heat; turn to low heat and continue cooking until water is absorbed. Remove from heat. Rice can be served cold as well as hot. Rice will stick together for easy handling with chopsticks. Makes 3 to 4 cups cooked rice.

Japanese Fried Rice

½   cup diced leftover meat
    and/or chicken, ham,
    shrimp
1   Tb peanut or vegetable oil
½   cup thinly sliced canned
    green beans
½   cup cooked and crumbled
    bacon
½   cup chopped canned
    bamboo shoots

⅓   cup chopped green onions
    or regular onion
1   tsp monosodium glutamate
    (if desired)
    Salt and pepper
2   eggs, unbeaten
2   cups cooked rice
    Soy sauce

In hot oil, sauté meat, chicken, ham, or shrimp. Stir in green beans. Add bacon, bamboo shoots, and green onions. Add monosodium glutamate; continue to sauté. Season to taste with salt and pepper. Stir in the whole eggs. Turn to high heat and continue cooking until eggs are done as for scrambled. Remove egg mixture from pan to a bowl. Put pan back on high heat and reheat cooked rice in it. Then mix rice into the egg mixture. To serve, sprinkle with soy sauce. 4 to 6 servings

Sukiyaki

Any kind of meat, thinly sliced	1 tsp sugar
Corn oil	½ tsp salt
1 small bunch celery cabbage	¼ tsp pepper
¼ whole cabbage	2 ozs soy sauce
1 stalk celery	½ oz sake
2 small carrots	4 ozs bean threads*
1 medium onion	2 small bunches green onions or 2 large leeks, chopped
½ lb fresh mushrooms, sliced	Eggs
1 (6-oz) can giant bamboo shoots	Soy sauce
	Cooked rice

Cut both cabbages, celery, carrots, and onion in large chunks. Cover bottom of deep, large kettle with corn oil and sauté meat a few minutes, then push to one side in kettle. Add celery cabbage and celery and sauté; push to one side. Add mushrooms and other cabbage; keep separated in kettle. Add carrots and bamboo shoots. Put onion pieces on top of carrots. Sprinkle with sugar, salt, pepper, soy sauce, sake and 2 oz water. Let come to a boil, then cover and let steam over medium heat.

Meanwhile, wash bean threads in cold water and then soak in more water. Make a well in the middle of the steaming vegetables in kettle and add drained bean threads. Put green onions (leeks) on top of carrots and onion pieces. Steam a few minutes more.

To serve: In each individual bowl slightly beat 1 egg and add a few drops of soy sauce. Spoon Sukiyaki into bowls. Serve rice on the side. 4 to 6 servings
*Purchase at Oriental Food Shop.

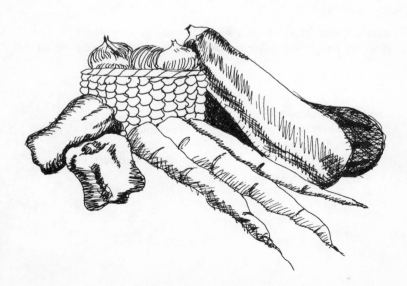

Vegetable Tempura

Shojin Age

Tempura is a simple, diversified type of cooking. So delicious! Sauté any number of vegetables, dipped in batter, to a delectable crispness.

½	cup flour
1	tsp salt
¼	tsp pepper
¼	tsp monosodium glutamate (if desired)
1	egg white
½ to 1	cup corn or sesame oil*
	Assortment of vegetables, cut into julienne strips:

>   Carrots
>   Spinach
>   Green beans
>   Eggplant, peeled
>   Zucchini
>   Green pepper
>   Potatoes
>   Squash
>   Mushrooms
>   Onion rings

Mix first 5 ingredients together with enough water to make a thin, smooth batter. With tongs or chopsticks, dip vegetable strips into batter. Pick up 4 to 6 strips at a time and fry quickly in hot oil in a deep-fry pan until golden brown on all sides. Drain vegetables on paper towel. Arrange on a large platter. Keep in warm oven until ready to serve.

Try Tempura Batter Mix, which is found in most grocery stores.
*Keep oil at hot temperature. See footnote in following recipe on hot oil.

Tempura

For chicken, fish, or seafood.

Fish fillets, small
Chicken, cut into small chunks
Squid, cut into rings
Shrimp, shelled and deveined

Tempura batter (see recipe above)*
½ to 1 cup corn or seasame oil

Dip fish, poultry, or seafood into batter and fry in hot oil† until crisp and brown on all sides. Drain on paper towel. If more crispness is desired, first dredge food in flour and then dip in batter. Cook a few pieces at a time in order to maintain constant hot oil temperature.

*Tempura batter should be thicker than for vegetables. Use less water or try beer instead! Try Tempura Batter Mix, which is found in most grocery stores.

†Oil is hot when: it reaches 320° to 350°; a drop of dough splashes in the oil; a cube of bread browns in seconds.

Squid Tempura

2	lbs squid, cleaned and washed	1	Tb salt
2	Tb lemon juice	1	Tb paprika
1	12-oz can beer		Oil
2¼	cups flour		Lemon wedges

Leave squid tentacles whole and slice squid into ¼-inch rings. Place squid in a small bowl and toss with the lemon juice. Pour the beer into a medium-sized mixing bowl and sift 1 cup of the flour, the salt, and the paprika over it; stir and then beat with a fork or wire whisk to make a smooth batter. Pour oil into a deep, medium-sized saucepan or deep-fry pan to depth of about 2 inches and heat over moderately high heat until cube of bread browns quickly. While oil is heating, place remaining flour in a bag, add about a third of the squid and shake to coat. Remove squid and repeat with remaining squid. Take a two-pronged fork, arrange 6 floured squid rings along each tine, and dip into the batter. Allow excess batter to drip back into the bowl and then, with a knife, push one ring at a time off the fork into the hot oil. Cook rings until golden brown. Remove with a slotted spoon and drain on paper towels. To keep hot and crisp, heat oven to 200°. Turn off heat. Place squid, uncovered, in oven. Continue dipping and frying remaining squid. Serve squid with salt to taste and lemon wedges. 4 to 6 servings

Curry

Debbie Sherrill

A dish consisting of meats, fish, and rice, cooked in a pungent sauce of Indian origin, highly seasoned with spices and condiments. Curry powder is prepared with dried leaves of an Indian plant together with other pungent spices. Chinese use it for curried chicken. Chutney is a Hindu word meaning "an appetizer," and is used as a condiment or garniture. It is made with mangoes, raisins, and ginger. Raisin sauce is a condiment made of raisins, vinegar, and pineapple.

3	cups cut up pork, lamb, veal, chicken, or turkey	3	cups chicken broth
6	Tb margarine	2	Tb margarine
½	cup chopped onion	4	tsp cornstarch
6	Tb flour		Salt and pepper
3	tsp curry powder		Saffron rice (below) or cooked white rice
¼	tsp garlic salt		Condiments (below)

In a large pot, sauté onion in 6 tablespoons margarine until yellow and soft. Blend in flour until smooth. Mix in curry powder and garlic salt. Blend in chicken broth and stir until smooth; simmer gently.

Melt the 2 tablespoons margarine in a frying pan. Brown the meat or poultry, then add to the curry sauce, and let simmer together gently about 1 hour (uncovered). Stir occasionally. If thicker sauce is desired, blend cornstarch with 4 tablespoons water and add to mixture. Season to taste with salt and pepper. Serve over saffron or plain white rice topped with a choice of condiments. 10 to 12 servings

Saffron Rice:

1	cup converted rice	½	tsp crumbled saffron threads
1	Tb margarine/butter		
1	tsp salt		

Bring 2½ cups water to boil. Add rest of ingredients. Cover tightly and simmer about 20 minutes until all water is absorbed. Keep hot.

Condiments:

Serve a choice or all of these ingredients (1 to 1½ cups each):

Chopped green onions and tops	Chopped tomato
Crumbled crisp bacon	Chopped hard-boiled egg
Chopped cucumber	Fresh diced pineapple or canned crushed, drained

Sliced banana
Chopped cashews or
peanuts
Spanish peanuts
Grated fresh coconut or
canned

Salted sunflower seeds
Chopped green pepper
Chutney
Raisin sauce
Fresh lime wedges

Shrimp curry

Use basic Curry Recipe except:

Instead of 3 cups chicken broth for the sauce, use 2 cups clam juice mixed with 1 cup chicken broth.

Instead of meat or fowl, use 2 lbs fresh shrimp, cleaned and deveined and added to sauce the last 10 minutes of cooking.

Chutney Balls

LuRene Ball

Combine equal amounts of cream cheese and chopped chutney. Form into balls. Roll in coconut. Refrigerate until serving time.

Delightful to serve with your curry dinner.

Melon Basket

An exquisite Chinese Festival dish.

  1   small round watermelon
      (about 12 lbs)
  2   cups watermelon balls
  2   cups cantaloupe balls
  2   cups honeydew melon balls
      lemon wedges (if desired)

Cut thin slice of rind from one end of watermelon so that it will stand upright on cut end.

Mark center top of melon. Then measure ¾ inch on each side, to make a 1½-inch-wide handle. Cut out melon wedge on each side of handles ⅓ of the way down. Then carefully cut fruit away from rind at top, to form handle.

Now make and cut a rickrack edge with a small, sharp knife around cut edge. Or use a tablespoon or small saucer as pattern to make a scallop design.

Cut balls from melon and scoop out rest of fruit to hollow out for a basket. Fill basket with watermelon, honeydew, and cantaloupe balls; mound high. Tie a bow to handle. Refrigerate until ready to use. Place on table as a centerpiece. Let guests serve themselves at dessert time. Serve with lemon wedges, if desired. 10 to 12 servings.

May use oval-shaped watermelon. Lay it lengthwise, cut thin slice from bottom so it will stand upright. Design the top third ot it.

U.S. - US

Yes, the Mesabi Iron Range was a microcosm—a miniature universe—the epitome of culture and customs of the world brewed together in a Melting Pot. What emerged was a conglomerate from all those nationalities—our own identity. We became our own nation of baseball and football, jazz and country music, corn on the cob and pumpkin pie, chow mein and chop suey and Jeno's pizza, hoedowns and barbecues, cake mixes and corn flakes, square dancing and rodeos, colas and hamburgers, popcorn and hot dogs.

That's the U.S. That's Us!

Cheese Puffs

Bee Lee

1   loaf unsliced sandwich bread (Pullman)*

1   cup (2 sticks) butter, softened

1   5-oz jar American cheese spread, softened

½   tsp dry mustard

⅓   tsp salt

¼   tsp paprika

1   egg yolk

1   egg white, beaten

Remove all crusts from loaf. Cut bread into 1-inch-thick slices. Cut each slice into 3 sticks. Cream butter with the cheese. Add mustard, salt, paprika, and egg yolk. Fold in the beaten egg white. Spread three sides of each stick with cheese mixture. Place sticks (unspread side down) on cookie sheet covered with wax paper. Bake at 350° for 15 minutes. Can be refrigerated until ready to bake. Or they may be kept in freezer until ready to serve, thawed and baked. 36 puffs
*Pullman bread can be specially ordered.

Chipped-Beef Spread

Cindy Soderstrom

1   8-oz pkg cream cheese

½   cup sour cream with chives and onion*

1   3-oz pkg chipped beef, chopped*

½   cup chopped pimiento-stuffed olives

¼   cup finely chopped onion

Combine all ingredients. Serve with cocktail rye bread. 2½ cups
*If sour cream with chives and onion is not available, add 1 tablespoon chopped chives and/or onion to plain sour cream. You may use corned beef instead of chipped beef.

Cocktail Meatballs

Lois Paulucci

Meatballs:

¾   lb ground beef

½   lb ground veal

¼   lb ground pork

1½   cups soft bread crumbs

½   cup beef bouillon or water

½   cup finely chopped onion

¼   cup dried parsley flakes or minced fresh parsley

¼   tsp ground ginger or grated fresh ginger

¼   tsp pepper

Sauce:

1   cup catsup

1   cup canned tomato soup

2   Tb Worcestershire sauce

    Dash hot pepper sauce

½   cup finely chopped onion

½   cup brown sugar

1   Tb lemon juice

1   Tb salt

1   Tb chili powder

Combine all meatball ingredients in electric mixer or food processor. Roll into 1-inch meatballs. Place in a wide-bottom casserole. Bake at 350° for 30 minutes. Turn meatballs once while baking. Fifty to sixty meatballs

Combine all sauce ingredients and bring to a boil. Then simmer for 5 to 7 minutes. Pour sauce over hot meatballs. About 3½ cups sauce

Sauce may be frozen, thawed, and reheated at 350° for 30 minutes. Any left over is a delicious topping for stuffed green peppers.

Dip for Vegetables

Jane Cardiff

1 cup real mayonnaise	1 Tb dill weed
1 cup sour cream	1 Tb minced onion
1 Tb seasoned salt	

Blend thoroughly. Serve in individual tiny plates with assortment of crisp, raw vegetables.

Dip Delite

Joyce Van Meer

8 ozs cream cheese, Neufchâtel cheese, or cottage cheese	1 green onion and top, chopped
8 ozs sour cream	1 Tb Worcestershire sauce
12 large pimiento-stuffed olives, chopped	1 tsp garlic salt
	2 to 4 dashes hot pepper sauce

Blend all ingredients together. Serve with raw vegetables (have you tried sliced zucchini?) or assorted crackers. About 2½ cups

To make this dip "Mexican hot," add two chopped jalapeño (hah-lah-peyno) peppers (they come in a small can, are peeled and roasted). Serve with tortilla chips in nacho, taco, or corn flavors.

Munch 'n Crunch Party Mix

1 3-oz can chow mein noodles	1 Tb sesame seeds (optional)
½ cup chopped pecans	½ tsp chili powder
2 Tb butter, melted	¼ tsp garlic salt
1 Tb soy sauce	¼ tsp dry mustard

Combine all ingredients and toss to mix well. Heat in shallow pan at 350° for 10 to 15 minutes, stirring occasionally. Place mixture on paper towels to absorb excess fat and to cool. About 2½ cups

Party Rye

1 loaf cocktail rye bread
8 ozs cream cheese or
  Neufchâtel cheese

Pimiento-stuffed olives,
medium to large size, sliced

Spread cream cheese on bread slices. Decorate with olives. Cut bread slices in half. Serve as soon as possible or refrigerate, covered with plastic wrap.

Pickled Okra-Cauliflower Delite

Juliet Baraban

1 12-oz jar pickled okra,
  either mild or hot crisp
1 head cauliflower, cut into
  florets from base
2 cloves garlic, mashed
1 bay leaf (broken in half)

1 Tb lemon juice
½ cup white vinegar
¼ tsp sugar (if desired)
½ cup dry Chablis wine
¼ tsp oregano (if desired, to
  "Italianize")

Drain okra and reserve vinegar liquid. Place cauliflower in water to cover and add garlic, bay leaf, and lemon juice. Bring to a boil and steam cauliflower for 5 minutes. Drain.

Heat white vinegar with sugar, wine, and oregano; set aside. In a quart jar, layer the okra and florets alternately. Pour in the reserved okra vinegar. Then fill the jar with the white vinegar mixture. Tighten lid. Turn jar upside down and marinate for 48 hours. Delicious with a pre-dinner cocktail.

Sausage Cheese Balls

Ruth Pooser

2 cups biscuit baking mix
10 ozs cheddar cheese, grated

1 lb bulk sausage

Mix ingredients together with hands and roll into bite-size balls. Freeze on cookie sheets; store in plastic bags until needed. When needed, thaw first. Bake at 400° for 15 minutes, or until brown. About 70 cheese balls

Extra sharp cheddar and Italian sausage, ½ mild, ½ hot (casings removed), really spices up these treats!

Toast Round Puffs

Ruth Pooser

	Sandwich bread	1	medium small onion, grated
1	qt mayonnaise*		
1	cup grated		
	Parmesan/Romano cheese		

With small round biscuit cutter, cut bread slices into rounds. On ungreased cookie sheet bake at 200° for 1½ to 2 hours. (Do not brown, just dry out.)

Mix other ingredients well. Place 1 heaping teaspoon on each toast round and bake at 375° for about 7 minutes, or until puffed and tinged with brown. About 80 puffs

Variations:

Trim crust of sandwich bread and cut each slice in half.

For a smaller batch, use 1 cup mayonnaise, ¼ cup grated Parmesan/Romano cheese, 1 tablespoon grated onion, and white melba toast rounds.

*Be sure you use a mayonnaise that uses more eggs.

Boston Baked Beans

This used to be a New England traditional Saturday night supper, served with hot brown bread.

4	cups dried navy or pea beans	1	Tb salt
1	tsp salt	1	tsp pepper
½	cup dark brown sugar, firmly packed	½	lb salt pork, thickly sliced, or bacon
⅔	cup dark molasses	2	medium onions, sliced
1	Tb dry mustard	½	cup catsup (if desired)

Rather than soak beans overnight, bring 2½ to 3 qts water to a boil; add the beans and boil for 2 or 3 minutes. Set aside and let beans soak for 1 hour. Add salt and bring to a boil again and then simmer gently for 1 hour, partially covered. Drain beans and reserve the liquid.

In a large bowl, mix sugar, molasses, seasonings, and ½ cup bean liquid. In a large 4- to 5-quart casserole, layer beans, salt pork (bacon), and onions alternately. Pour the molasses mixture over the beans. Add just enough more bean liquid or water to cover. Cover casserole with lid. Bake at 250° to 300° for 7 hours. Remove lid, add more liquid if needed and the catsup. Bake for 1 hour more. Makes about 4 quarts.

Enough for a large party!

Broccoli Casserole

Dorothy McReynolds

1	10-oz pkg frozen broccoli spears	4	ozs processed American cheese slices
½	cup broken crispy round crackers	½	cup (8 Tb) butter/margarine, melted

Prepare broccoli according to package directions. Drain well. Line bottom of a small buttered casserole with ½ the broccoli. Add a layer of crackers and top with cheese slices. Repeat layers. Pour melted butter/margarine over top. Cover and bake at 325° for 20 to 30 minutes until cheese melts. *Yummy and not too rich!* 4 servings

Hamburger Pot Pie

Florence Trepanier

Crust:

2	cups flour	¾	cup shortening
1	tsp onion salt		

Filling:

1	lb ground beef	1	tsp salt
½	cup chopped onion	1	tsp sugar (if desired)
1	Tb vegetable or corn oil	¼	tsp pepper
1	15-oz can green beans, drained	⅛	tsp oregano
		1	10¾-oz can tomato soup

Mix flour with onion salt. With pastry blender or 2 knives, cut shortening into the flour. Sprinkle with ¼ cup cold water and mix lightly with fork. Roll into 2 crusts.

Brown meat and onion in hot oil. Stir in green beans, seasonings, and soup. Pour into formed pie shell. Place top crust over. Slit top to vent. Bake at 400° for 25 minutes. 4 to 6 servings

Hog Jowls and Black-Eyed Peas

Georgianna Allen and Elizabeth Martin

Down South there is a traditional dish which, if consumed on New Year's Day, will bring you happiness (hog jowls), good luck (black-eyed peas), and money (Southern greens).

3	cups black-eyed peas	2	Tb oil or bacon fat
2½	lbs hog jowls or smoked ham hocks, cut up	2	cups chopped onions
		1	tsp salt

Wash beans. In a saucepan, cover black-eyed peas with water (1 quart or more). Bring to a rolling boil; turn off heat and let stand. In large kettle, sauté jowls (ham hocks) in hot oil (bacon fat) until golden. Add onions and sauté until onions are soft. Drain black-eyed peas and add to the kettle along with salt. Add water (about 3 qts) to cover peas and jowls. Bring to a boil; cover and simmer until meat and peas are tender (1½ to 2 hours). 6 to 8 servings

Elizabeth sometimes adds 2 tablespoons butter/margarine to enrich the gravy. Serve with golden corn bread and Southern Greens (see recipes).

Potato Casserole

Hazel DeSanto

2 lb bag frozen hash brown potatoes (chunk style)	½ cup chopped onion
1 10¾ oz can cream of chicken soup	¼ cup (4 Tb) butter/margarine, melted
1 pint sour cream	1 tsp salt
2 cups shredded cheddar cheese	½ tsp pepper
	2 cups coarsely crumbled corn flakes

Mix together soup, sour cream, shredded cheese, onion, butter/margarine, salt, and pepper. Add frozen potatoes. Pour into 13- x 9-inch greased baking dish and top with crumbled corn flakes. Bake at 350° for 45 minutes. If reheated, cover with aluminum foil. This dish can be prepared ahead, even frozen, and baked at serving time. 10 to 12 servings

Tuna Casserole

1 7- or 8-oz can chunk tuna, drained and shredded	1 11-oz bag potato chips
1 2-oz jar pimiento olives, sliced	1 10¾-oz can cream of mushroom soup mixed with 1 can water
2 hard boiled eggs, sliced	

Layer a buttered casserole with tuna, olives, eggs, potato chips, alternately. Pour mushroom soup over. Top with more potato chips. Cover and bake at 350° 30 to 40 minutes. 4 servings

Wild Rice Dish

Lori Paulucci

1	cup uncooked wild rice	1	10¾ oz can cream of
1	lb ground beef		mushroom soup
4	slices bacon, diced	1	2-oz can mushroom pieces,
½	cup diced celery		drained
½	cup diced onion		Salt and pepper

Wash rice and soak for 1 hour in hot water to cover, then bring to a boil and cook for 30 minutes (careful not to boil water away). Drain, if necessary.

Brown together beef, bacon, celery, and onion; stir in soup, mushroom pieces, and salt and pepper to taste. Bake in a 2-quart covered casserole at 350° for 1 hour. 4 to 6 servings

Zucchini au Gratin

Anna Draghicchio

3 to 4	zucchini (2 lbs), unpared	½	lb processed American
1½	lbs ground beef, chuck, or		cheese, cubed
	round steak	1	10¾ oz can cream of
1	medium onion, chopped		mushroom soup
1	tsp salt		Buttered bread crumbs
½	tsp pepper		

Wash zucchini and slice thin. Brown ground beef with onion slowly. Add salt and pepper and cubed cheese. Layer beef and raw zucchini in a 2-quart buttered casserole, starting with the meat. Cover with the soup and top with layer of buttered bread crumbs. Bake, uncovered, at 350° for 45 minutes. 4 to 6 servings

Hobo Eggs

Capt. Norman A. Helfrich, Ret. USN

2 to 3	Tb butter/margarine	Eggs
	Sandwich bread	Salt and pepper to taste

Melt butter/margarine in frying pan, Place one slice of thin sandwich bread, which has had the center removed by use of a small glass, in pan.

Fry bread until golden brown, then turn over. Break egg into the hole and cook until done. Season with salt and pepper. As a dividend fry the round center of bread while egg is cooking.

Crab Cakes

1 lb crab meat	2 slices bread, crusts
1 Tb baking powder	removed, broken into pieces
1 Tb mayonnaise	and moistened with milk
1 Tb Worcestershire sauce	1 egg, beaten
1 Tb chopped fresh parsley	¼ cup vegetable or corn oil
1 tsp dry seafood seasoning	Lemon wedges
¼ tsp salt	

Combine all ingredients except oil and lemon wedges and shape into cakes. Fry quickly in hot oil until brown, about 3 to 4 minutes, turning once. Serve with lemon wedges. 4 servings

Fish Fry Batter at the Outpost Camp

Tom Stevenson

Mix together:

2 cups Pancake mix	1 tsp garlic salt
(Buttermilk or plain)	¼ tsp pepper
1 12-oz can beer	1 tsp vanilla extract

Keep batter on the thin side. Makes a puffy, flavorsome coating. Batter will keep refrigerated in a tightly covered jar. 3 cups

Salmon Loaf

Jane Moore

1 15½-oz can salmon, drained	¼ cup green pepper and/or celery, chopped
1 10¾-oz can cream of mushroom soup, undiluted	1 Tb lemon juice
½ cup mayonnaise	1 tsp salt
1 Tb fresh parsley, minced or 1 tsp shredded	¼ tsp pepper
½ cup onion, chopped	1 cup bread crumbs
	1 8½-oz can peas, drained and added last

Mix all ingredients together. Pour into a greased loaf pan. Bake at 350° for 1 hour. 1 loaf

Ham Loaf

Pearl Souers

1	lb lean ham, ground	2	cups milk
1	lb lean pork, ground	1	Tb Worcestershire sauce
1	lb lean veal, ground	1	10¾-oz can tomato soup or
3	eggs beaten		Ham Glaze (see recipe)
1	cup cracker crumbs		

Roll crackers fine and add the milk and beaten eggs to cracker crumbs. Mix and add meat and Worcestershire sauce. Place in well greased loaf pan and cover with the tomato soup. Bake 1½ hours at 325°. 1 loaf

Ham Glaze

1	cup light brown sugar	1½	Tb dry mustard
½	cup cider vinegar		

Prepare glaze while ham loaf is baking. Combine ingredients in a saucepan. Mix well, bring to a boil and boil for 2 minutes.

In the last hour of baking, pour half the sauce over the loaf. Let cook for 30 minutes. Then pour remaining sauce over for the last 30 minutes of baking.

Chuck Steak in Onion Gravy

Dorothy McReynolds

A tangy sauce, like barbecue. Very tasty!

3	lbs chuck steak, 1½ inches thick	2	Tb corn oil
¼	cup flour	1	8-oz bottle Russian dressing
⅛	tsp freshly ground black pepper	1	envelope dry onion soup mix

Combine flour and pepper; use to dredge the chuck steak. Sear steak in a skillet over high heat until the meat is browned on all sides, using about 2 Tb corn oil to keep it from sticking. Meanwhile, combine dressing and soup mix. Pour over the steak. Reduce heat, cover, and simmer gently for about 1½ hours, or until meat is fork-tender. Remove to heated platter. Serve with sauce remaining in pan. 4 servings

Champagne-Glazed Ham

Jerri Kirk

One day our neighbor knocked on our door with this to say, "Remember in the old days when you used to borrow a cup of sugar from your neighbors? Well, we're sure living 'high off the hog' nowadays, neighbor, because I've come to borrow a bottle of champagne to glaze our ham!"

1	whole smoked ham (15 to 16 lbs)		Whole cloves
1	egg	¾	cup champagne
1	cup brown sugar (or more)	¾	cup pineapple juice

Bake ham according to packer's directions. One hour before ham is thoroughly cooked, remove from oven. Cut away skin, leaving thin layer of fat. Score fat in diamond shapes. Brush with unbeaten egg. Pat with brown sugar and stud with cloves. Bake ham for 1 hour more at 300° to 350° in an aluminum foil-lined pan. Baste frequently with mixture of champagne and pineapple juice. 10 to 12 servings

Meat Loaf

Bertha Mims

2	lbs ground beef or combination of beef, pork, and veal	1	tsp seasoned salt or onion salt
2	eggs	½	tsp salt
1½	cups bread crumbs	¼	tsp pepper
½	cup catsup		Dash Pickapeppa, steak sauce or hot pepper sauce
¼	cup chili sauce or taco sauce		Gravy of your choice*
2	Tb grated Parmesan/Romano cheese		

Mix all ingredients except gravy together and mold into a greased loaf pan. Top with gravy. Bake at 350° for 1 hour. 4 to 6 servings

*For gravy, use any of the packaged gravy mixes, prepared per package directions.

Great Meat Loaf

Mary Helfrich

1½	lbs ground beef (chuck)	2	slices bread torn in pieces
½	lb hot sausage, ground or chopped	1	egg, beaten with ¼ cup milk or water
1	Tb onion, minced	2	slices bacon

Soak bread in egg mixture and add to meat and onion. Mix well and mold into a greased loaf pan. Top with bacon. Bake at 350° for 1 hour. 4 to 6 servings

"Giving a Party?" Burgundy Stew

So popular that my dear fried Eleanor Adamic says, "No credits, please. This recipe has been widely passed around the Range. I got it from Rite Barry, who got it from Betty Rich, who got it from Mrs. Devan, and on and on!"

5	lbs beef stew meat	1	cup dry red wine
2	10¾-oz cans golden		(Burgundy, or Chianti)
	mushroom soup	1	3-oz can sliced mushrooms
2	10¾-oz cans onion soup		Cooked rice, egg noodles,
	with beef broth		potatoes

Cut beef into uniform bite sized pieces; put into a covered Dutch oven together with soups and wine. Cook covered in a 315°oven for 4 hours. Remove cover near end of cooking time to allow gravy to thicken. Add mushrooms. Serve over wild rice, long grain rice, egg noodles, or creamy au gratin potatoes. 14 to 16 servings

This is party size. After a party, freeze any remaining stew, or you may cut recipe in half.

"Those Were the Days" Stew

Students during the Depression at the University of Minnesota prepared this dish as their favorite Sunday dinner, for it could be "stretched" with additional potatoes to include a guest at their table.

1½	lbs round steak or flank steak, cut into serving pieces	3 to 4	stalks celery, cut into 2-inch-long strips.
2	Tb corn oil	2	or more potatoes, peeled and cut into chunks
	Salt and pepper	1	10¾-oz can tomato soup,
1	large onion, sliced		diluted with 1 can water
3 to 4	carrots, sliced		

Brown meat in pan with hot oil. Season to taste with salt and pepper. Mix in onion, carrots, celery, and potatoes. Pour diluted soup over all. Bring to a boil, cover, and put in oven. (Transfer to a covered baking dish if pan is not ovenproof). Bake at 325° for 1½ hours. Serve with chunks of bread for dunking. 4 servings

Chicken Divine

Lois Paulucci

4 to 5	whole chicken breasts, skinned
1	10-oz pkg frozen broccoli

Sauce:

1	10¾-oz can cream of mushroom soup	1	Tb dry sherry
½	cup mayonnaise	¾	cup shredded cheddar cheese
½	tsp curry powder	½	cup bread crumbs
1	tsp lemon juice	1	Tb butter, melted

Bring chicken to a boil in salted water to cover. Skim off foam. Simmer for 45 to 60 minutes. Drain and debone. Prepare broccoli according to package directions. Place broccoli on bottom of a 2-quart casserole. Layer chicken breasts on top of broccoli.

For sauce, mix together soup, mayonnaise, curry, lemon juice, and sherry; pour over chicken breasts and broccoli. Sprinkle with cheddar cheese and the bread crumbs combined with melted butter. Cover and bake at 350° for about ½ hour. 4 to 6 servings

Southern Fried Chicken

Elizabeth Martin

Elizabeth, my housekeeper, was born in Jasper, Hampton County, Florida, and was reared on a farm owned by her family for two generations. They grew corn, cotton, tobacco, peanuts, and watermelon. They raised hogs and chickens. Elizabeth really knows good soul-food cooking.

2	fryers (less than 2 lbs each if available)	½	tsp pepper
1	cup flour		Dash paprika or seasoned salt
1	tsp salt	1 to 2	cups corn oil or lard

Cut chicken into serving pieces, reserving backs and necks for chicken stock. Remove skin if desired. Wash chicken and pat dry with paper towel. Mix flour and seasonings together. Either coat chicken parts with flour mixture by shaking in a paper bag or dredge chicken by pressing flour mixture into the chicken with your fingers. Pat excess flour off and allow chicken to stand for at least 20 minutes.

Heat oil (lard) in a large frying pan. Oil has to be hot and kept hot (a cube of bread should turn golden in seconds), and there should be enough oil to immerse chicken at least halfway so that you need to turn chicken only once to completely cook. Fry chicken, skin side down, until golden brown, then turn over and fry until other side is brown. Fry a few pieces at a time. Remove to paper towels. Let chicken drain for a few minutes, then sprinkle with salt. To keep hot and crisp until serving time, heat oven to 200°, turn heat off, and keep chicken uncovered in closed oven. 4 to 6 servings

Allow frying pan to cool so that flour and brown bits will separate from the oil and settle to the bottom of the pan. Pour cooled oil into a jar, cover tightly, and keep refrigerated. Oil gives even more flavor to chicken when reused.

Barbecue Sauce

Jerri Kirk

A homely family favorite.

½	cup catsup		Dash onion juice or 1 green onion, chopped
1	tsp prepared mustard		
1	Tb lemon or lime juice		Dash garlic juice or 1 clove garlic, minced
½	tsp salt		
¼	tsp pepper	2	Tb butter/margarine or oil, if used on chicken
1	Tb Worcestershire sauce		
½	tsp chili powder	1	Tb brown sugar

Mix ingredients together.

Brush on ribs, steak, pork chops, or on chicken the last 30 minutes of cooking.

Raisin Sauce

A perennial favorite served with baked ham

2	Tb butter/margarine, melted	2	cups apple cider
2	Tb flour	½	cup raisins

Blend together the butter/margarine and flour in a pan. Blend in the cider and raisins slowly. Put over heat and bring to boiling, stirring constantly. Cook 1 more minute. Serve hot.

Avocado Fruit Squares

Marsiella Greenfield

1	large ripe avocado (a tropical fruit)	1	cup well-drained canned peaches, grapefruit, or pears
2	Tb lemon juice		
1	3-oz package cream cheese, softened	¼	cup well-drained chopped maraschino cherries
2	Tb sugar	½	cup heavy cream, whipped
¼	cup mayonnaise		
¼	tsp salt		

Cut avocado in half, remove seed. Peel and dice into a bowl. Sprinkle with 1 tablespoon of the lemon juice. Blend cheese, remaining lemon juice, sugar, mayonnaise, and salt. Add fruit, fold in whipped cream. Pour in pan. Freeze until firm. 10 to 12 servings

Chicken Salad

Jean Kleffman Clauser

¾ lb cooked chicken diced coarsely	⅓ cup flaked coconut
½ cup mayonnaise	¾ cup sliced ripe bananas
⅓ cup raisins	Salt and pepper to taste
⅓ cup salted peanuts	Lettuce leaves

Mix together mayonnaise, raisins, peanuts, and coconut. Toss with chicken. Combine gently with bananas. Season with salt and papper and mound on lettuce leaves in bowl or on individual plates. If desired, add ⅓ cup sliced stuffed olives; you will find that it adds a little something to the flavor, if you like olives. 4 to 6 servings

Corned Beef Salad

Martha Yancey

1 12-oz can corned beef	1 cup mayonnaise
1 pkg lemon gelatin	2 Tb chopped onion
¼ cup vinegar	2 hard cooked eggs, chopped
2 cups diced celery	

Dissolve gelatin in ¾ cup hot water; add vinegar. Refrigerate until thickened. Break corned beef into bite sized pieces; add gelatin and remaining ingredients, folding in eggs last. Pour into a 9- x 13-inch pan. Chill until set. 10 to 12 servings

Frozen Fruit Salad

Pearl Souers

1 pt heavy cream	3 bananas, peeled
½ cup mild salad dressing	½ lb seedless green grapes
⅓ cup sugar	½ cup dates
1 14-oz can sliced pineapple, drained	½ cup figs (if desired)
1 17-oz jar white cherries, drained	1 cup miniature marshmallows
1 6-oz jar maraschino cherries, drained	½ cup slivered almonds

Beat cream stiff. Fold in salad dressing and sugar. Dice all fruits (except grapes) and add to the cream mixture. Stir in marshmallows and almonds. Pour into a large mold. Freeze. Serve frozen. Will keep a month or longer in freezer. 10 to 12 servings

Gelatin Desserts

Years ago Aunt Francesca was the first to try making gelatin dessert. Every Sunday she would serve a big bowlful of shimmering raspberry, cherry, or strawberry gelatin.

My brother and I would beg to have Sunday dinner at her house with our cousins and a number of boarders. We would watch round-eyed as Zia spooned the quivering treat into sauce dishes and topped it with a dollop of whipped cream. Not so one of her boarders who had been carousing the night before and had the shakes. No dessert for him!

Lime Gelatin Treat

Marsiella Greenfield

A popular "salad dessert."

1	pkg lime gelatin	1	17-oz can fruit cocktail or
10	large marshmallows, cut		fruits for salad, drained
	up, or 1 cup miniature	½	pt heavy cream, whipped,
1	8-oz pkg cream cheese, cut		or 12 ozs non-dairy
	up		whipped topping

In 1 pt hot water, dissolve gelatin, marshmallows, and cream cheese (the latter will not dissolve completely). Add the canned fruit. Chill. When partially set, fold in the whipped cream. Chill until firm. 10 to 12 servings

Small pieces of ripe avocado add a delicious taste. For a festive touch, decorate with drained maraschino cherries cut in half.

Orange Salvador Salad

Marsiella Greenfield

2	pkgs orange gelatin dissolved in 1 cup boiling water	2	11-oz cans mandarin orange segments, drained
		1	pt orange sherbet

Add drained liquid from both cans of mandarin oranges to dissolved gelatin. Stir orange sherbet into liquid. Mix until smooth. Add orange segments. Pour into mold rinsed with cold water. Refrigerate until firm. Push orange segments down until gelatin sets. 10 to 12 servings

Party Salad

Lori Paulucci

1   20-oz can crushed
    pineapple
1   3-oz pkg lime gelatin
⅓   cup chopped pimiento
6   ozs cream cheese, softened

½   pt heavy cream, whipped,
    or 12 ozs non-dairy
    whipped topping
1   cup diced celery
1   cup chopped walnuts

Heat pineapple with juices to boiling. Add gelatin. Chill until partially set (2 to 2½ hours).

Mix pimiento with the cream cheese. When gelatin is partially set, add cheese mixture. Fold in the cream. Add celery and walnuts. Put in a 1½ quart mold. For larger mold, double the recipe. 6 to 8 servings

Frozen Party Salad

Marsiella Greenfield

1   cup salad dressing
1   8-oz pkg cream cheese,
    softened
1   13½-oz can pineapple
    tidbits, drained
1   16-oz can chopped apricots,
    drained

½   cup drained maraschino
    cherries
2   Tb confectioners sugar
5   drops red food coloring
2   cups miniature
    marshmallows
½   pint heavy cream, whipped

Gradually add salad dressing to cream cheese; mix until blended. Stir in fruit, sugar, and coloring. Fold in marshmallows and whipped cream. Freeze in a pan or in paper cups in muffin tins. 10 to 12 servings

Pistachio-Pineapple Salad

Ruth Pooser

1   20-oz can crushed
    pineapple
1   4½-oz pkg instant pistachio
    pudding
1   cup miniature
    marshmallows

½   cup chopped pecans or
    walnuts
1   9-oz container non-dairy
    whipped topping
    Maraschino cherries

Drain pineapple and reserve juice. Empty pudding mix into bowl; add 4 tablespoons of the pineapple juice and stir. Add pineapple, marshmallows, nuts, and whipped topping. Mix well. Chill. Especially pretty with a cherry on top of each serving. 10 to 12 servings

Shrimp Tomato Mousse

Mary Helfrich

1½ cups drained canned
    shrimp (tiny or small)
2 Tb gelatin
1 10¾-oz can tomato soup
1 8-oz pkg cream cheese,
    softened
1 cup mayonnaise

¾ cup diced celery
¾ cup diced green pepper
1 Tb minced onion
1 Tb chopped pimientos
1 Tb Worchestershire sauce
¼ tsp salt

Dissolve gelatin in 1 cup cold water. Cream together soup and cream cheese; then heat it. Add gelatin. Mix in the rest of the ingredients. Refrigerate until firm in either a mold or a tin, then cut into squares. 10 to 12 servings

Three or Four Bean Salad

Goldie Brunner

An old standby. Really flavorful if made a day ahead.

Vegetables:

1 16-oz can French green
    beans
1 16-oz can yellow wax beans
1 15½-oz can kidney beans
1 20-oz can chick peas (if
    desired)
1 14-oz can bean sprouts (if
    desired)
¼ cup chopped green pepper
¼ cup chopped green onions
    and tops

Dressing:

½ cup cider vinegar
½ cup sugar
½ cup vegetable oil
1 tsp salt
½ tsp pepper
⅛ tsp garlic salt

Drain all the vegetables together in a large colander and let sit for at least 1 hour. Place in a large bowl. Make dressing and mix into the bean mixture. Cover tightly and refrigerate for several hours to marinate. 6 to 8 servings

Tomato Aspic

Marian Manly

4 cups canned combined 8
    vegetable juices
½ cup chopped onion
¼ cup chopped celery leaves
2 Tb brown sugar

1 tsp salt
2 bay leaves
2½ envelopes unflavored
    gelantine

3	Tb lemon juice	6	green onions, chopped
1	cup chopped celery	1	lb whole shrimp, shelled,
1	avocado, cut into small		deveined, and boiled
	pieces		Sour Cream Sauce (below)
½	green pepper, chopped		

Combine first 6 ingredients and simmer for about 5 minutes; then strain. Soften gelatine in ¼ cup cold water and add to the still hot strained juice. Stir until dissolved. Add lemon juice. Chill until partially set. Add rest of the ingredients. Chill in 1 very large mold or in 2 smaller ones.

To serve, unmold and garnish with more shrimp. Serve with Sour Cream Sauce in separate bowl. 10 to 12 servings

Sour Cream Sauce:

> 2 cups sour creám
> ½ cup mayonnaise
> 2 Tb horseradish
> 2 green onions, minced
> Salt to taste

Mix all ingredients together and chill. About 2½ cups

Cousin Filiberto Buratti, who lives in Rome, Italy, spent Thanksgiving with us one year not so long ago. My menu included:

> *Roast Turkey Stuffed with Bread Dressing*
> *Kernel Corn in Butter Sauce*
> *Twenty-Four-hour Salad*
> *Glazed Sweet Potatoes with Marshmallows*
> *Mashed Potatoes and Gravy*
> *Cranberry Sauce*
> *Praline Pumpkin Pie*

The only item on the menu that Filiberto had ever eaten before in Italy was the turkey! (tachino—tah-kee-noh)

Twenty-Four-Hour Salad

Mary Trepanier

1 egg
2 Tb lemon juice
2 Tb sugar
⅛ tsp salt
½ cup heavy cream, whipped
12 marshmallows, quartered
  (or equivalent in miniature
  marshmallows)
1 cup diced canned pineapple

1 cup Queen Anne cherries
  (halved and pitted)
1 cup sliced banana
1 cup diced orange
8 maraschino cherries,
  quartered
½ cup chopped or slivered
  almonds
  Salad greens

Beat egg well and combine with lemon juice, sugar, and salt. Cook and stir over hot water about 5 minutes until mixture thickens. Remove from heat and cool. Fold in whipped cream, marshmallows, and fruits. Cover bowl and chill overnight. Just before serving, fold in almonds. Serve on crisp salad greens. 8 to 10 servings

Green Beans Southern

Gladys Trepanier

3 lbs green pole beans
3 to 4 medium-size ham hocks
2 to 3 slices salt pork (¼ inch
  thick)

2 tsp salt
  Black pepper to taste
1 tsp sugar (if desired)

Wash and snap green beans. Set aside. Remove rind from ham hocks. Cook ham hocks and salt pork with 3 cups water in a tightly covered pan for 30 minutes. Add the beans and seasonings. Cover and simmer over medium heat for 30 minutes. Uncover and stir the beans and meat. Cover and cook on low heat an additional 30 minutes until liquid is nearly all evaporated. 4 to 6 servings

Southern Greens

Elizabeth Martin

From the Deep South. Corn Bread is traditional with this dish.

3 lbs greens (collard, turnip,
  mustard, or mixed)
½ lb smoked ham hock

¼ lb salt pork, cut into pieces
1 Tb salt
½ tsp pepper

Simmer ham hock and salt pork with 5 cups water in a large covered kettle for 1 hour. Meanwhile, clean and wash greens thoroughly and chop in big pieces. Add salt and pepper to the kettle. Gradually add the greens, stirring, until all greens have been added. Cook greens, covered, just until tender, about 30 minutes. Sliced raw onion is good with this. 4 to 6 servings

You will be "in the money" if you include Southern Greens with Hog Jowls and Black-Eyed Peas (see recipe) on your New Year's Day menu.

Hush Puppies

Bertha Mims

In the South, Indian corn became a part of a Southern traditional dish: fish and hush puppies! The story goes that while Southern mammies were busy preparing dinner for their plantation folk, their hunting dogs would be howling for food at the back door. Mammy would toss them some of this cornbread with the admonition, "Hush, puppy!"

2½	cups self-rising cornmeal	
½	cup flour	
2	eggs, slightly beaten	
1	cup milk, beer, or canned tomatoes, mashed	

1	cup minced onion
1	tsp dried parsley flakes
½	tsp salt
½	tsp baking powder
	Vegetable Oil

Mix all ingredients except oil together until well blended. Shape into small balls (walnut-size). Dough will be sticky. Deep fry until golden. Drain on paper towel. 24 hush puppies

Molasses-Bran Brown Bread

Pearl Souers

1	cup bran cereal
½	cup seedless raisins
½	cup molasses
¼	cup sugar
2	Tb shortening
1	egg, beaten

1	cup flour
1	tsp salt
¾	tsp baking soda
½	tsp baking powder
½	tsp cinnamon

Place cereal, raisins, molasses, sugar, and shortening in bowl. Add ¾ cup boiling water; cool a bit, and add egg; mix well. Add the rest of dry ingredients. Stir only until combined. Place in well-greased loaf pan. Bake at 350° for approximately 45 minutes, or until done. 1 loaf

Sourdough Rolls

Bill (Winifred) Gielow

Sourdough is fermented dough saved from one baking to the next. Prospectors and early settlers of the western United States and Canada, especially those living alone, were known as Sourdoughs, as their staple food was sourdough bread. Bill got her Sourdough Starter ten years ago, and it has been passed around from one to another until someone in each state and even in Canada has received a cup of Starter from her perennial batch!

1	packet dry yeast		A throw of salt (½ tsp
1	cup Sourdough Starter (see		approximately)
	below)	2	cups self-rising flour
2	Tb sugar		Butter/margarine, melted
2	Tb oil		(4 Tb per pan)

In a bowl, dissolve yeast in ½ cup lukewarm water. Add next 4 ingredients and mix well. Then mix in the flour (add more if needed until mixture leaves the spoon). Cover with a towel and let rise 2 to 3 hours.

Knead dough on a lightly floured board. Pinch a small amount of dough and roll in your hands into small rolls (walnut-size). Place in baking pans (2 large or 3 small) in which butter/margarine has been melted. Cover and let rise again, 2 to 3 hours. Bake at 325° for 15 to 20 minutes. 24 rolls

Sourdough Starter

Mary Schmitt

1	packet yeast	1	Tb sugar
1½	cups plain white flour		

Dissolve yeast in 1½ cups lukewarm (80° F) water. With a wooden spoon, mix in the flour and sugar. Allow mixture to sit in a warm place in a large, lightly covered glass bowl or jar for 4 to 7 days. Stir it 2 or 3 times each day. Temperature will determine how long it takes for souring to occur. When the starter is bubbly and has developed an acidic, tart odor, you can refrigerate it in a covered container.

Sourdough Starter Feeder

Dorothy Karns

Starter must be replenished and active. After each baking or at least every 3 weeks if not used, feed the Starter.

1	cup milk	1	cup plain white flour
¼	cup sugar		

Mix the ingredients and blend well together either by hand or in blender. Pour into Starter mixture.

Keep Starter in a wide-mouth gallon-size container, tightly covered and refriger-ated.

Should you go traveling, ask your neighbors to feed your Starter while you are away! Reward them with a cup of your Starter!

Banana Split

Gerri Patnode

Crust:

1½	cups crushed graham crackers	½	cup (1 stick) margarine, melted

Filling:

2	eggs	1	tsp vanilla extract
4	cups sifted confectioners sugar	4 or 5	bananas, peeled
1	cup (2 sticks) margarine, softened	1	20-oz can crushed pineapple, drained

Topping:

1	8-oz container non-dairy whipped topping	1	cup drained and chopped maraschino cherries
1	cup chopped walnuts		

Mix ingredients for crust together and press into a 9- x 13-inch cake pan.

Beat eggs with sugar, margarine, and vanilla until well blended (5 minutes). Spread over crust to form second layer. Slice bananas over this filling, then spread crushed pineapple on top. Spread whipped topping over bananas and pineapple. Sprinkle with walnuts and cherries. Refrigerate overnight. 10 to 12 servings

Chocolate Balls

Mary Helfrich

This is a delightful buffet-style dessert.

2 Tb cocoa
1 cup confectioners sugar
3 ozs bourbon, Cognac, or
   Kahlúa liqueur
1 Tb light corn syrup
½ cup finely chopped pecans,
   walnuts, or unsalted
   peanuts

1½ cups finely crushed vanilla
    wafers (about 50)
2 egg whites
3 to 4 ozs chocolate sprinkles or
    shredded coconut

Sift cocoa and sugar together and set aside. Mix bourbon (or other) with corn syrup in a bowl. Add cocoa mixture, nuts, and crushed wafers. Roll mixture into small 1-inch (walnut-size) balls. Then roll in confectioners sugar, or first dip in egg whites and then roll in chocolate sprinkles (shredded coconut). Refrigerate in covered container. These freeze beautifully. About 25 chocolate balls

Chocolate Chip Bars

½ tsp salt
½ cup sugar
1 tsp vanilla extract
2 eggs, at room temperature,
   beaten
½ cup Fleischmann's
   margarine (no substitute)

2 sqs unsweetened baking
   chocolate
½ cup flour
½ cup black or English
   walnuts (pieces or halves)
8 to 12 ozs semi-sweet chocolate
   morsels

Beat salt, sugar, and vanilla into the eggs. Melt margarine and chocolate together over low heat. Add gradually to the egg mixture. Mix in the flour. Pour batter into 8- x 8-inch greased baking pan. Layer batter with walnuts and then top with a layer of chocolate morsels. Bake at 350° for 20 to 25 minutes. Cool and cut into squares. 16 bars

Chocolate Honey-Graham Pie

Crust:

20 graham crackers, rolled fine
¼ cup sugar
¼ cup (4 Tb)
   butter/margarine, softened

Filling:

1 11½-oz chocolate almond
  bar
½ pt heavy cream, whipped

Blend together graham crackers, sugar, and butter/margarine. Press firmly into a pie plate. Bake at 375° for 8 minutes. Cool.

Melt chocolate bar over hot water. Cool. Stir whipped cream gently into the cooled chocolate. Pour into pie shell. Chill in refrigerator for several hours. Garnish with additional whipped cream if desired. 6 to 8 servings

Coconut Pie

Jackie Eldredge

2	7-oz pkgs frozen coconut, thawed	¼	tsp salt
		3	Tb sugar
1	frozen deep-dish pie shell	1	cup milk
6	egg yolks	1	tsp vanilla extract

Bake pie shell per package instructions—but only until half cooked. Beat together eggs, sugar, milk, vanilla, and salt. Mix in the coconut. Bake in pie shell at 350° oven about 45 minutes (until knife inserted in middle comes out clean). 6 to 8 servings

Amazing Coconut Pie

Mary Schmitt

1	cup coconut, shredded or flaked	½	cup baking biscuit mix
2	cups milk	4	eggs
½ to ¾	cup sugar	¼	cup (4 Tb) butter
		1½	tsp vanilla extract

Blend all ingredients except coconut in blender on low speed for 3 minutes. Pour into 9- or 10-inch greased pie pan. Let rest for about 5 minutes, then sprinkle with coconut. Bake at 350° for 40 minutes. Serve either hot or cold. 4 to 6 servings

Amazing—makes its own pie crust!

Cream Cheese Pie

Jackie Forget Eldredge

16	ozs cream cheese	1	pkg instant lemon pudding
16	ozs sour cream	1	prepared graham cracker crust
1	13½-oz tub non-dairy whipped topping		

Blend and mix with electric beater the first 4 ingredients until smooth and very fluffy. Pour into graham cracker crust. Chill until firm. 6 to 8 servings

Date and Orange-Slice Bars

Marsiella Greenfield

½ lb dates, chopped	⅛ tsp salt
½ cup sugar	1 tsp vanilla extract
2 Tb flour	¾ cup flour
¾ cup shortening	½ cup chopped nuts
1 cup light brown sugar	1 16-oz pkg orange slice
2 eggs	candy, cut lengthwise into
1 tsp baking soda	thirds

Boil the first 3 ingredients with 1 cup water until thick. Cool.

Cream shortening and sugar together. Mix in eggs. Add baking soda blended with 2 tablespoons hot water, salt, and vanilla. Blend in the flour and mix until batter is smooth. Stir in the chopped nuts.

Grease a 9- x 12-inch baking pan. Spread half of batter in bottom of pan. Cover with orange slices. Spread date mixture over orange slices. Top with remaining batter. Bake at 350° for 40 minutes. Cool before cutting into squares. 24 bars

Ede's Doughnuts

Ede and Eddie Muccilli

2 eggs	1 cup buttermilk
1 cup sugar	2½ cups flour
½ tsp salt	½ tsp nutmeg
1 tsp vanilla extract	¼ tsp cinnamon
4 tsp vegetable or corn oil	1 tsp baking powder
1 tsp baking soda	1 lb shortening or lard

Beat eggs. Add sugar, salt, vanilla, and oil. Mix baking soda with the buttermilk. Mix flour with nutmeg, cinnamon, and baking powder. Add buttermilk mixture to the egg mixture alternately with the flour mixture. Handle dough as little as possible. Roll out dough on lightly floured board to ½-inch thickness and cut with doughnut cutter. Fry in hot shortening in a kettle, 4 at a time. As soon as doughnuts rise to the top, flip over to avoid ridge, and then back again. Drain on paper towel. 12 doughnuts

Karen's Old-Fashioned Fudge

Karen Everett

Years ago an evening's entertainment was gathering around the stove to make fudge—being careful not to let it "sugar."

1 cup milk (not skim)	2 Tb butter
2 sqs unsweetened baking chocolate	1 tsp vanilla extract
2 cups sugar	½ to 1 cup chopped walnuts

Put milk and chocolate in pan. Stir over medium heat until chocolate is melted. Add sugar. Stir until candy starts to boil, and then occasionally until it forms a soft ball in cold water. Remove from heat and add the butter without stirring. Cool thoroughly (bottom of pan will feel lukewarm). Add vanilla and beat until candy loses its glossiness. Quickly stir in walnuts. Pour into a greased 8- x 8-inch pan. When cold, cut into pieces.

Girdle Buster Barbizon

Coffee Frozen-Fudge Pie

Crust:

1	cup crumbled graham crackers
¼	cup (4 Tb) butter/margarine, softened
¼	cup sugar

Filling:

1	qt coffee ice cream
1	24-oz jar fudge syrup
	Pecan halves

Remove ice cream from freezer to refrigerator 1 hour before using.

Mix crackers, butter/margarine, and sugar together until like meal. Line 9-inch pie plate with crumb mixture, mashing it down smoothly and evenly. Bake at 350° for 8 minutes.

After crust is completely cool, fill with ice cream. Spread chocolate syrup thickly over ice cream. Arrange pecan halves over top. Place in freezer until frozen solid. 6 to 8 servings

Grasshopper Pie

Marsiella Greenfield

Crust:

24	cream-filled chocolate cookies, crushed	7	Tb butter/margarine, melted

Filling:

24	marshmallows	4	Tb green Crême de Menthe
⅔	cup milk		Grated sweet or semi-sweet chocolate (if desired)
½	pt heavy cream, whipped		
2	Tb white Crême de Cacao		

Mix crushed cookies with butter/margarine. Press into a greased pie plate. Melt marshmallows in milk over hot water. Cool. Mix into the whipped cream. Blend in the liqueurs. Pour into pie shell and freeze. Sprinkle grated chocolate over top, if desired, at serving time. 6 to 8 servings

Heavenly Lemon Pie

Jean Kleffman Clauser

Crust:

¼	tsp cream of tartar		4	egg whites
1	cup sugar			
	Coconut or finely chopped nuts			

Heat oven to 275°. Meanwhile, sift sugar and cream of tartar. Beat egg whites until stiff but not dry. While beating, slowly add sugar-tartar. When eggs are stiff and glossy peaks form, spread over bottom and sides of greased 9-inch pie plate. Make bottom ¼-inch and sides 1-inch thick. Bring meringue just to rim of plate. Sprinkle rim of meringue with coconut (finely chopped nuts). Bake 1 hour until light golden brown and crisp. Cool in oven with door open.

Filling:

4	egg yolks		1	pt heavy cream
½	cup sugar			Slivered toasted almonds or chopped Macadamia nuts
1	tsp gelatin			
6	Tb lemon juice			Fresh strawberries in season (if desired)
1	Tb grated lemon peel			
⅛	tsp salt			

Beat egg yolks slightly in thick pan or in top of double boiler. Stir in sugar, gelatin softened in the lemon juice, grated lemon peel, and salt. Cook, stirring constantly 8 to 10 minutes until thick. Cool. Whip 1 cup cream and carefully fold into the cooled custard. Slowly pour into cooled meringue shell, making sure all pockets are filled. Whip remaining cream and spread over top of custard filling. Sprinkle with toasted almonds (Macadamia nuts) or leave plain. Refrigerate 12 to 14 hours to mellow meringue and filling. To assure easy removal of pie wedges and easy cutting, set pie plate on a hot wet towel for a few seconds, slices then come out with no trouble. Serve with fresh strawberries in season if desired. 6 to 8 servings

Lemon Refrigerator Cake

Jean Kleffman Clauser

3	eggs, separated		½	pt heavy cream
½	cup sugar		⅔	cup graham cracker or vanilla wafer crumbs
	Peel and juice of 1 lemon			

Mix egg yolks with sugar, lemon peel and juice. Cook over hot (not boiling) water until thick as heavy cream. Stir constantly. Remove from heat and cool. Beat egg whites until they stand in points. In a separate bowl, beat heavy cream until it holds its shape. Stir the cool lemon mixture into the egg whites gently, then add the whipped cream. Again use a gentle touch. Sprinkle ½ the cracker or wafer crumbs over bottom of an ice tray or other container. Pour in dessert mixture and sprinkle remaining crumbs over the top. Freeze for several hours until firm. 8 servings

Lover's Lemonade Pie

Jean Kleffman Clauser

Crust:

3	Tb butter	1½	cups shredded coconut

Filling:

1	cup evaporated milk	⅔	cup sugar
1	envelope unflavored gelatine	1	6-oz can frozen lemonade concentrate*

Melt butter in skillet. Add coconut and stir over medium heat until golden brown. Press firmly into bottom and sides of 9-inch pie plate. Let stand at room temperature until cool. Chill milk in ice tray until almost frozen around edges. In large bowl, soften gelatine in ¼ cup cold water. Add ½ cup boiling water and stir until gelatine is dissolved. Add sugar and lemonade concentrate. Stir until lemonade thaws. Chill until very thick but not set. Put icy cold milk into a cold 1-quart bowl. Whip at high speed until stiff. Fold into chilled gelatine-lemonade mixture. Spoon filling gently into pie shell. Chill until firm, about 3 hours. 6 to 8 servings
*Try limeade another time. It's equally delicious.

Cool Lime Pie

Sophie Shoemaker

1	4-oz container non-dairy whipped topping	2 to 3	Tb fresh lime juice
1	14-oz can sweetened condensed milk	2 to 3	drops green food coloring
1	6-oz can frozen limeade concentrate, thawed	1	Graham Cracker Pie Crust (see recipe below)

Blend together whipped topping and condensed milk. Mix in the next 3 ingredients. Pour into prepared crust and refrigerate 3 to 4 hours. 6 to 8 servings

Key Lime Pie

Limes are of two varieties: the large, like a lemon is known as Tahiti or Persian. The small, walnut-size Spanish lime is known as Key lime. These are rather pale green in color, thin skinned and most flavorful. Key limes have been in abundance in southern Florida and on the long chain of reefs and sand of Key West. And since Key West couldn't graze cattle and didn't have refrigeration for many years, this recipe is the authentic way that the Conchs (of English and Spanish descent) made their famous pie.

1	Graham Cracker Pie Crust (below) or baked pie shell	½	cup Key lime juice or ¾ cup Persian lime juice
3	eggs, at room temperature, separated	1	tsp grated lime peel
1	14-oz can sweetened condensed milk	¼	tsp cream of tartar
		¼	cup sugar

Beat together egg yolks, condensed milk, lime juice and peel. Pour into prepared crust. Beat egg whites with cream of tartar until foamy. Gradually add sugar, continuing to beat until eggs whites are stiff but not dry. Carefully spread egg white meringue over top of lime mixture, right to the edges of the pie shell. Bake at 350° for 15 minutes. Cool, then chill before serving. 6 to 8 servings

Graham Cracker Pie Crust:

1½ cups crushed graham crackers

½ cup (8 Tb) butter/margarine, softened

¼ cup sugar

Blend all ingredients well with a fork. Press into a 9-inch pie plate. Using an 8-inch pie plate to press crumbs evenly is very effective. Bake at 350° for 8 minutes.

Macadamia Angel Pie

Jean Kleffman Clauser

Just divine!
Crust:

3	egg whites, at room temperature	¼	tsp vanilla extract
½	tsp cider vinegar		Dash salt
		⅔	cup sugar

274

Macadamia Filling:

½ lb marshmallows (32 large)	Dash salt
2 egg yolks	½ cup heavy cream, whipped
1 tsp vanilla extract	1 cup chopped Macadamia
¼ tsp ground nutmeg or ⅛	nuts
tsp grated fresh nutmeg	

Beat egg whites until foamy; add vinegar, vanilla, and salt and beat until stiff. Gradually beat in sugar and continue to beat until very stiff. Spoon meringue into a well-greased 9-inch pie plate and press into shell shape with back of spoon. Bake at 300° for 45 minutes, then cool thoroughly.

Combine ½ cup water and marshmallows in top of double boiler and heat over boiling water until marshmallows are melted. Beat egg yolks, stir in a little of the hot marshmallow mixture, then stir eggs into the hot mixture. Cook over boiling water, stirring now and then, for 2 minutes, or until slightly thickened. Remove from heat and stir in vanilla, nutmeg, and salt. Chill until filling begins to set. Beat until fluffy, then fold in whipped cream and nuts. Spoon into meringue shell and chill thoroughly. 6 to 8 servings

Peach Kuchen

Jean Kleffman Clauser

Crust:

1 pkg white cake mix	½ cup (8 Tb) butter/
½ cup flaked coconut, toasted	margarine, softened

Combine cake mix and coconut; cut in butter/margarine until mixture resembles coarse crumbs. Lightly press into bottom and ½ inch up sides of 13- x 9-inch baking pan. Bake at 350° for 10 to 15 minutes.

Filling:

4 cups drained canned sliced peaches	½ tsp cinnamon
	1 cup sour cream
2 Tb sugar	1 egg, slightly beaten

Arrange peach slices over baked crust. Combine sugar and cinnamon; sprinkle evenly over peaches. Blend sour cream and egg; pour over all. Bake at 350° until sour cream is set, about 10 minutes. 10 to 12 servings

Peanut Butter Pie

Doris Dietrich

1   8-oz pkg cream cheese
2   cups confectioners sugar
½   cup smooth peanut butter
1   envelope whipped topping
    mix *exclusively*

¼   cup crushed peanuts
1   9-inch Graham Cracker Pie
    Crust (see recipe)

Soften cream cheese and gradually beat in sugar with electric mixer until light and fluffy. Beat in peanut butter. Mix topping mix according to package directions and blend into mixture. Pour mixture into prepared crust and top with crushed peanuts (a handful in the mixture itself works beautifully). Refrigerate for several hours before slicing. The pie will keep refrigerated for several days. 6 to 8 servings

Pecan-Chocolate Morsel Pie

Capt. N.A. Helfrich, Ret. U.S.N.

1   cup sugar
½   cup flour
2   eggs, beaten
½   cup (8 Tb) butter/
    margarine, melted

1   cup chopped pecans
1   6-oz pkg chocolate
    semi-sweet morsels
1   tsp vanilla extract
1   9-inch unbaked pie shell

Combine sugar and flour and mix well. Stir in eggs and butter. Add pecans, chocolate morsels, and vanilla. Mix well. Pour into unbaked pie shell. Bake at 350° for 40 to 45 minutes. 6 to 8 servings

Pie Torte

Marsiella Greenfield

3   egg whites
1   cup sugar
1   cup crushed graham
    crackers
1   tsp baking powder

½   tsp salt
½   cup finely chopped dates
½   cup chopped nuts
1   tsp vanilla extract
    Whipped cream

Beat egg whites until stiff; add sugar gradually. Fold in rest of ingredients except whipped cream. Pour into greased pie plate. Bake at 350° for 25 minutes. Cool. Top with whipped cream. 6 to 8 servings

Pineapple Dessert

Marsiella Greenfield

1 cup sugar	2 egg yolks, beaten
¼ cup (4 Tb) butter/ margarine, softened	1 cup chopped nuts
1 Tb light cream	½ lb vanilla wafers, crushed
1 cup well-drained crushed pineapple	Whipped cream

Cream together sugar, butter, and light cream. Stir in the pineapple. Add egg yolks to pineapple mixture. Stir in the nuts. Butter an 8-inch-square pan or an 8-inch pie plate. Spread bottom of it with ⅓ of the wafers, then alternate pineapple mixture with wafers, ending with a layer of wafers. Refrigerate until well set. Top each serving with a dollop of whipped cream. 6 to 8 servings

Raspberry Dessert

Lois Paulucci

20 graham crackers, crushed	½ cup confectioners sugar
½ cup (8 Tb) butter/ margarine, softened	½ pt heavy cream, whipped
⅓ cup sugar	3 pkgs raspberry gelatin
1 8-oz pkg cream cheese	2 pkgs frozen raspberries

Cream together cracker crumbs, butter, and sugar. Pat into a 9- x 12-inch pan. Blend together cream cheese and confectioners sugar; fold in the whipped cream and spread over the first mixture in pan. Pour 3¼ cups hot water over gelatin and add the frozen raspberries. Let congeal slightly. Then pour over first 2 mixtures. Refrigerate. 8 to 10 servings

At an autograph party for Rowena Billeter's book, *Rowena's Recipes With Memories*, Rowena and I reminisced about parties Rowena had catered for us, as far back as 1959, the year of the great Navy Relief Luau in Sanford, Florida.

When she retired, Rowena compiled a book of recipes of foods which were enjoyed by so many guests at her Tea Room in downtown Orlando.

She gave me two of her recipes: Rowena's Chocolate Mint Pie and Rowena's Cola-Fudge Cake, both ever so delightful and which we are including in loving memory of Rowena Billeter.

Rowena's Chocolate Mint Pie

From Rowena's Recipes With Memories.

Rowena Billeter

Crust:

20	graham crackers, rolled fine
½	cup (8 Tb) butter/ margarine, softened

Filling:

¾	cup (12 Tb) butter/ margarine, softened	1	tsp pure mint and peppermint extract
1½	cups confectioners sugar		Vanilla ice cream
3	eggs		
4	sqs unsweetened baking chocolate		

To make crust, blend together both ingredients. Press into an 8- or 9-inch pie plate. Bake at 325° about 8 to 10 minutes. Cool.

For filling, in an electric mixer, cream together butter/margarine and confectioners sugar. Add eggs one at a time, blending after each addition. Melt chocolate over hot water or in Microwave oven and add. Mix in the extract. Pour mixture into pie shell. Chill in refrigerator several hours or freeze and remove to refrigerator an hour or so before serving. Top with vanilla ice cream. 6 to 8 servings

Rowena used no sugar in the graham cracker crust, and Rowena said that *a twist of vanilla ice cream was a must on each serving.*

This pie freezes beautifully and is so delicious that it is worth making three pies at a time. For three pies; you'll need: for the crust—1 box of graham crackers and 2½ sticks of butter or margarine; for the filling—1 lb of butter or margarine, 2 boxes of confectioners sugar, 8 large eggs, 12 squares (2 boxes) of unsweetened baking chocolate, and 3 tsp of the extract.

Rowena's Cola-Fudge Cake

Cake:

2	cups sugar
2	cups flour
½	cup (8 Tb) butter, melted
½	cup vegetable oil
3	rounded Tb cocoa
1	cup cola
½	cup buttermilk
2	eggs
1	tsp baking soda
1	tsp vanilla extract
1½	cups miniature marshmallows

Icing:

1	16-oz box powdered sugar
½	cup (8 Tb) butter/margarine
6	Tb cola
3	rounded Tb cocoa
1	cup chopped nuts

In a large bowl, sift together sugar and flour. In a saucepan, combine butter, oil, cocoa, and cola. Bring to a boil over low heat, then pour over dry mixture. Add remaining ingredients and blend and beat well by hand or electric mixer.

Pour into a well-greased and floured 9- x 13- x 2-inch cake pan. Bake at 350° about 40 minutes, or until toothpick inserted in center comes out dry. This is a very moist cake so do not over bake. Do not remove from pan.

Put powdered sugar in large bowl of an electric mixer. In a saucepan, bring butter/margarine, cola, and cocoa to a boil over low heat. Pour over the powdered sugar and beat well. Add nuts. When cake is slightly cool, cover with icing. 10 to 12 servings

Seven Layer Bars

Lois Paulucci

So delicious and easy to make, fellows with a sweet tooth can whip this up themselves with aplomb!

½	cup (8 Tb) butter, melted
1½	cups graham cracker crumbs
1	6-oz pkg chocolate chips (morsels)
1	6-oz pkg butterscotch chips (morsels)

1	cup shredded coconut
1	cup walnuts, chopped
1	14- or 15-oz can sweetened condensed milk

Melt butter in 13- x 9-inch pan in which bars are to be baked. Then add the other ingredients by layers in the order listed. Pour condensed milk over top. Place pan in unheated oven, turn oven to 350°, and bake 25 to 30 minutes. Cool thoroughly before slicing. 10 to 12 servings

Sanford's Celery Pie

Bertha Mims

When we were packing celery at the Chase & Company Wash House for Chun King here in Sanford, our help introduced us to this pie. It tastes like coconut actually.

2	unbaked pie crusts		Pinch salt
	Celery (to make 4 cups)	¼	tsp lemon juice
1¼	cups sugar	¼	cup (4 Tb) butter/
2	Tb cornstarch		margarine, melted
¼	tsp cinnamon	½	cup raisins or pecans
¼	tsp nutmeg		

Wash celery, pull off all strings. Cut into ½-inch pieces. Fill formed pie shell level to the top with celery pieces. Combine sugar, cornstarch, spices and salt and sprinkle over celery. Lift with fork so it will coat all the celery. Drizzle lemon juice over, then pour butter/margarine over. Sprinkle with raisins (pecans). Cover with top crust, sealing the edges. Slit top crust. Bake at 400° for 55 to 60 minutes. 6 to 8 servings

INDEX — ALPHABETICAL
For index by type of food, see page 285

Ailloli, 119
Almond Chicken Ladeva, 110,
Amazing Coconut Pie, 269
Annie's Cheese Biscuits, 44
Antipasto, 152
Apple Crisp, 77,
Apple Curranty, 46
Apple Pye, 44
Arroz con Pollo (Chicken with Rice), 227
Artichoke Pie, 171
Asparagus with Prosciutto, 171
Aubergine Moussaka Patrice, 211
Austrian Goulash, 201
Avgolemono, 210
Avocado Fruit Squares, 258
Bagels, 219
Baked Squash, 25
Baklava, 214
Baklava Syrup, 214
Banana Split, 267
Bananas Foster d'Agostino, 138
Barbecue Sauce, 258
Barmbrack Cake, 56
Béchamel Sauce, 121
Bee Lee's Grilled Shrimp Sandwiches, 42
Beef Rib Roast, 37
Beer Bread, 65
Befera's Lobster Tail Cantonese, 234
Befera's Teriyaki, 234
Bellini Cocktail, 197
Berlinerkranz, 75
Biscotti, 191
Biscottini, 192
Boeuf Bourgogne, 106
Boliche Hazado Ramirez, 226
Bollen Norsk, 73
Bouillabaisse Lisette, 100
Bouillabaisse Marseillaise, 99
Bouquet Garni, 119
Boston Baked Beans, 249
Brasciòle di Manzo, 178
Brasciòle, 153
Bread Dressing, 120
Broccoli Casserole, 250
Broccoli with Cheese Sauce en Casserole
   André, 128
Bubble and Squeak, 40
Cabbage Salad, 186
Caeser Salad, 123
Caeser Salad Dressing Lisette, 126
Caeser Salad Junia, 186
Cafe Gaelac, 58
Cake Genoise, 136
Candle Salad Norsk, 74
Caneton aux Cerises Lisette, 116
Caneton à la Liqueur de Peches, 116
Caneton Rôti, 115
Cannelloni, 159
Cannoli, 192
Cappelletti in Brodo, 156
Carpaccio, 154
Carrot-Pineapple Bundt Cake, 65
Carottes Raifort, 128,
Castagnoli, 192

Cassata Siciliana, 194
Castleford Toad-in-the-Hole, 31
Celery Dip, 154
Champagne-Glazed Ham, 254
Cheddar, Corkscrew and Son Fondue, 92
Cheese Apples, 31
Cheese Ball Neufchatel, 85
Cheese Balls, 31
Cheese Potatoes en Casserole Georges, 132
Cheese Puffs, 246,
Cheese Soup St. Galloise, 87
Cherry Pie, 47
Chicken en Brochette, 110
Chicken Divine, 256
Chicken Jambalaya Orleans, 111
Chicken Kiev, 204
Chicken Salad, 259
Chili con Carne, 223
Chili con Carne Roberto, 223
Chili con Frijoles, 224
Chilled Gazpacho, 222
Chinese Cucumber Tong, 233
Chipped Beef Spread, 246
Chocolate Balls, 268
Chocolate Chip Bars, 268
Chocolate Honey-Graham Pie, 268
Chocolate Mousse Cordon Bleu, 138
Chopped Liver, 217
Christmas Plum Pudding, 57
Chuck Steak in Onion Gravy, 254
Chutney Balls, 243
Classic Quiche Lorraine, 93
Clam Sauce for Spaghetti, 168
Cocktail Meatballs, 246
Coconut Pie, 269
Coffee Cake, 145
Coffee Royal, 197
Colcannon, 55
Cold Buttered Rum Coffee, 198
Coleslaw, 64
Cool Lime Pie, 273
Coq au Vin Cordon Bleu, 112
Coq au Vin Lisette, 112
Coquille St. Jacques Manfred, 101
Corn on the Cob, 21
Corn Fritters Calumet, 21
Corned Beef and Cabbage, 53
Corned Beef Salad, 259
Cornish Hens aux Gousses d'Ail, 115
Cornish Hens with Wild Rice Dressing, 38
Cornstarch Thickener for Gravies &
   Sauces, 122
Crab Cakes, 253
Crab Meat Pie, 102
Crab Meat au Gratin Pontchartrain, 102
Crab Meat Ravigote Lousiane, 102
Cranberry Putinki, 146
Cream Cheese Pie, 269
Crèma-Zuppa Inglese, 195
Creole Seafood Gumbo with Okra, 104
Creole Fried Chicken, 113
Crêpes à la Crab, 103
Crêpes Italian, 159
Crescia, 189

Crispy Baked Potatoes, 40
Croque Madame Diane, 85
Croque Monsieur Louis, 135
Cucumber Salad Cordon Blue, 124
Curry, 242
Cuisses de Grenouille Provençale, 105
Dandelion, 186
Date and Orange-Slice Bars, 270
Deviled Crab, 34
Dip Delite, 247
Dip for Vegetables, 247
Dolmadkia Stella Maris, 209
Ede's Doughnuts, 270
Egg Brunch Casserole, 33
Egg Cheese Grits, 22
Egg Coffee, 79
Egg Rolls, 231
Eggplant Casserole Parmigiana, 172
Elegant Cheescake, 220
Émincé de Veau Zürichoise, 109
English Breakfast, 34
English Shepherd's Pie, 32
Enrico's Spaghetti Carbonara, 160
Escargots d'Alsace, 86
Excelsior Piano Bar Special, 197
Farmer French Fries, 131
Fegato Romano, 178
Fettucine Alfredo, 160
Finnic Sauce, 144
Finnish Cabbage Rolls, 143
Finnish Coffee. 146
Fish Batter Siegfred, 62
Fish Cakes from Devonshire, England, 35
Fish Fry at the Outpost Camp, 25
Fish Fry Batter at the Outpost Camp, 253
Fish Souvlakia, 212
Fleisch Rolladen, 62
Fondue, 92
Four Season Salad, 124
French Peas Cordon Bleu, 128
Fresh Blueberry Pie Vicotria, 46
Fresh Peach and Brandy Pie, 138
Fresh Spinach Salad Cordon Bleu, 126
Fried Zucchini, 188
Frozen Fruit Salad,259
Frozen Party Salad, 261
Fruit Rocks, 45
Frukt Soppa Svensk, 71
Garlic Broiled Crevettes, 104
Garlic Butter Cordon Bleu, 120
Garlic Fried Scampi, 174
Garlic-Steamed Clams or Mussels, 174
Gefilte Fish, 217
Ghuy Hunan, 235
Girdle Buster Barbizon, 271
"Giving a Party" Burgundy Stew, 256
Glace-Sorbet Flambé, 139
Glazed Corn Beef, 54
Gnocchi, 162
Golden Corn Bread,22
Goose, 117
Grasshopper Pie, 271
Great Grandmother Paulucci's Minestrone

Soup, 158
Great Meat Loaf, 255
Greek Salad Pappas, 213
Green Beans Southern, 264
Green Grapes Delite, 77
Green Pepper Soup, 201
Guacamole Dip, 222
Gyoza, 237
Haluski Capüsta, 202
Ham Glaze, 254
Ham Loaf, 254
Hamburger Pot Pie, 250
Hampurin Pihvi, 144
Heavenly Lemon Pie, 272
Heavenly Rice, 78
Hillopannukakkuja, 145
Hobo Eggs, 252
Hog Howls and Black-Eyed Peas, 250
Hollandaise Sauce, 121
Horseradish Sauce, 38
Husarenkrapferl, 66
Hush Puppies, 265
Indian Corn Pudding, 23
Indian Dessert, 27
Iron Range Lamb Stew, 54
Irish Soda Bread, 56
Italian Broccoli salad, 185
Italian Cheese Bread, 189
Italian Spinach Lisette, 188
Italian Sausage and Peppers, 172
Japanese Fried Rice, 238
Jean's Sauerkraut, 61
Juicy, Crisp Roast Chicken, 111
Kalahia Mojakka, 143
Karen's Old-Fashioned Fudge, 270
Kartoffelsalat, 64
Key Lime Pie, 274
Kiwifruit Cassata, 194
Knishes, 219
Kraut Perogs, 60
Krum Kaka, 75
Kunglig Kött Bollen Svensk, 73
Lamb Kebabs, 212
Lasagne, 162
Lasagne à la Française, 93
Lefse, 74
Leg of Lamb, 179
Légumes Mornay Gratinés, 133
Lemon Butter Cordon Bleu, 121
Lemon Dressing, 39
Lemon Refrigerator Cake, 272
Lentil Soup, 157
Lime Gelatin Treat, 260
Lingonberries, 77
Liz's Fried Chicken Italian, 182
Liz's Spaghetti Sauce with Meatballs, 168
London Broil Rouladen Sophia, 203
Lover's Lemonade Pie, 273
Lutefisk, 72
Macadamia Angel Pie, 274
Macedònia, 195
Manicotti, 163
Marmite de Cultivateur, 88

Matzo Balls, 218
Meat Loaf, 255
Meat Stuffing for Fowl, 184
Meat Stuffing for Turkey, 185
Melon Basket, 244
Melva's Noodle Kugal, 202
Meringue Glacée Cordon Bleu, 140
Middle East Hamburgers, 213
"Mix-in-Pie-Pan" Pie shell, 47
Molasses Bran Brown Bread, 265
Mother's Tuna Loaf, 218
Mozzarella DeLucca, 155
Mrs. Grider's Pie Crust, 47
Munch 'n Crunch Party Mix, 247
Mushroom Sauce Cordon Bleu, 122
Naoe's Teriyaki Chicken, 236
Oatmeal Cake, 78
Oil and Vinegar Salad Dressing, 187
Old Fashioned Boiled Dinner, 60
Olives à la Romana, 155
Omelette Brouillée Lisette, 98
Orange Salvador Salad, 260
Oriental Marinade, 235
Oriental Ribs, 231
Oriental Style Rice, 238
Oysters Rockefeller Lisette, 86
Paistettu Norsia, 144
Paprika Chicken Ladeva, 114
Parsley Potatoes Cordon Bleu, 132
Party Rye, 248
Party Salad, 261
Pasta Bellisiana, 163
Pasties, 32
Peach Kuchen, 275
Peanut Butter Pie, 276
Pecan-Chocolate Morsel Pie, 276
Pepper Kakor, 76
Pesce al Forno, 175
Pesce Piquante, 155
Pesto, 170
Petits Pois François, 129
Pickled Octopus Fotopolus, 209
Pickled Okra-Cauliflower Delite, 248
Pie Crust Mix, 79
Pie Crust for Pasties and Tourtière, 98
Pie Torte, 276
Pineapple Dessert, 277
Pistachio-Pineapple Salad, 261
Pizza, 190
Pizzelle, 193
Poached Fillets Lavinia, 35
Poivrons Français, 130
Polenta, 164
Pollo al Forno, 182
Pollo alla Graticola, 183
Pollo Ragù, 183
Pollo di Roma, 184
Pommes Frites, 131
Porchetta, 179
Pork Roast, 63
Potages de France Bonne Femme, 88
Potato Balls, 72
Potato Casserole, 251

Potato Onion Soup Gaelac, 53
Potato Pancakes, 64
Potatoes al Forno, 188
Potatoes d'Or, 132
Potpourri Soufflé, 94
Potica, 204
Potiza, 206
Poulet Rôti Lisette, 114
Praline Brittle Pumpkin Pie, 137
Préférence de Monsieur, 107
Prosciutto e Melone, 156
Quick Spaghetti Sauce, 170
Raisin Sauce, 258
Raspberry Dessert, 277
Ravioli, 164
Ravioli Fillings, 166
Red Beans and Rice with Hot Sausage, 95
Rhubarb Pie, 79
Risotto Milanese, 167
Roast Goose, 118
Rock Cornish Hens, 38
Rosettes Svensk, 76
Rouille, 101
Rösti Emil, 65
Roux Thickener for Gravies and Sauces, 123
Rowena's Chocolate Mint Pie, 278
Rowena's Cola-Fudge Cake, 279
Saffron Rice, 242
Rumaki, 232
Salad Dressing Lisette, 127
Salade Niçoise, 124
Salade de Poivrons et Pastèque, 125
Salad Provençale, 125
Salmon and Cucumber Sandwiches, 41
Salmon Loaf, 253
Sanford's Celery Pie, 280
Sausage Cheese Balls, 248
Sausage and Escarole Soup, 158
Savoy Cabbage, 188
Schwarzwalder Black Forest Torte, 67
Scobac Gaelac O'Sullivan, 54
Serbian Cheese Cake, 205
Serbian Potica, 206
Serbian Sarma, 202
Seven Layer Bars, 279
Short Bread, 55
Shrimp Curry, 243
Shrimp Gumbo Lisette, 105
Shrimp Tomato Mousse, 262
Simple Bernaise Sauce, 122
Skewered Cookery, 211
Skinka Bollen Svensk, 74
Sodt Suppe Norsk, 71
Soupe du Jour, 88
Soup à l Oignon Le Cordon Bleu, 89
Soupe de Poisson, 90
Sour Cream Dressing Cordon Bleu, 127
Sourdough Rolls, 266
Sourdouugh Starter, 266
Sourdough Starter Feeder, 266
Southern Fried Chicken, 257
Southern Greens, 264
Spanakopitta, 210

Spritz, 77
Squid Sauté, 176
Squid Tempura, 241
Staeck Tartare, 83
Steak Diane, 107
Steak and Kidney Pie, 33
Steak au Poivre, 108
Steamed Fresh Shrimp, 36
Stockpot, 90
Stone Crab Claws; 34
Stovies, 40
Stracciatella Soup, 159
String Beans Italian, 187
Stuffed Green Peppers, 129
Stuffed Peppers Marie, 130
Stuffed Squid, 177
Sukiyaki, 239
Sweet and Sour Rumaki, 233
Swiss Apple Pie, 137
Swiss Onion Soup, 89
Taco Sauce, 225
Taco Sauce Caliente, 226
Taramosalata Stella Maris, 209
Tea Party Sandwich Loaf, 42
Tempura for Chicken, Fish, Seafood, 240
Teriyaki Chicken Wings from Nellie, 233
Teriyaki Imperial, 235
"Those Were the Days" Stew, 256
Three or Four Bean Salad, 262
Toast Round Puffs, 249
Tomato Aspic, 262
Tomatoes Farcies, 132
Torta Pasqualina, 173
Tortoni di Torrone, 196
Tostadas or Tacos, 225
Tournedos Rossini, 108

La Tourte au Roquefort, 96
Tourtière, 97
Trifle, 48
Tuna Casserole, 251
Tuna Fish Sauce for Spaghetti, 171
Tuna Pâté, 87
Turkey Suprême, 118
Twenty-four Hour Salad, 264
Twice Baked Potatoes, 40
Two Pound Cakes, 49
Ursula's Sauerkraut, 61
Veal Cordon Bleu, 109
Veal Fontina Fiorella, 180
Veal Parmigiana, 180
Veal Scaloppine Lisette, 180
Veal Scaloppine Marsala, 181
Vegetable Casserole Provençale, 134
Vegetable Tempura, 240
Velvet Hammer, 228
Vichyssoise (2 recipes), 89, 91
Vinaigrette Marsielle, 127
Vitèllo Saltimbocca, 181
Watercress Salad, 39
Wiener Schnitzel, 63
Wild Rice Casserole, 26
Wild Rice Dish, 252
Wild Rice Dressing Nokomis, 27
Yorkshire Pudding, 37
Zabalone, 196
Zesty Cocktail Sauce, 36
Zucchini Bread Norina, 191
Zucchini French Fries, 135
Zucchini Au Gratin, 252
Zucchini Napolitan, 173
Zucchini and Tomatoes Provençale, 134

INDEX—BY TYPE OF FOOD

INDEX LIST ORDER

Antipasto - Hors d'Oeuvre

Soups

Pasta

Entrées - Side Dishes

Eggs

Fish - Seafood

Meat

Poultry

Condiments

Salads

Salad Dressings

Légumes - Vegetables

Bakery

Sandwiches

Confections

Potables

ANTIPASTO—HORS D'OEUVRE
Antipasto, 152
Brasciòle, 153
Carpaccio, 154
Celery Dip, 154
Cheese Apples, 31
Cheese Ball Neufchâtel, 85
Cheese Balls, 31
Cheese Puffs, 246
Chipped Beef Spread, 246
Chopped Liver, 217
Chutney Balls, 243
Cocktail Meatballs, 246
Croque Madame Diane, 85
Dip Delite, 247
Dip For Vegetables, 247
Dolmadkia Stella Maris, 209
Egg Rolls, 231
Escargots d'Alsace, 86
Gefilte Fish, 217
Guacamole Dip, 222
Mozzarella DeLucca, 155
Munch N Crunch Party Mix, 247
Olives à La Romana, 155
Oriental Ribs, 231
Oysters Rockefeller Lisette, 86
Party Rye, 248
Pesce Piquante, 155
Pickled Octopus Fotopolus, 209
Pickled Okra - Cauliflower Delite, 248
Prosciutto e Melone, 156
Rumaki, 232
Sausage Cheese Balls, 248
Sweet and Sour Rumaki, 233
Teriyaki Chicken Wings from Nellie, 233
Toast Round Puffs, 249

Tuna Pâté, 87

SOUPS
Avgolemono, 210
Cappelletti in Brodo, 156
Cheese Soup St. Galloise, 87
Chinese Cucumber Tong, 233
Frukt Soppa Svensk, 71
Chilled Gazpacho, 222
Gyoza, 237
Lentil Soup, 157
Marmite de Cultivateur, 88
Great Grandmother Paulucci's Minestrone
Soup, 158
Green Pepper Soup, 201
Potatges de France Bonne Femme, 88
Soupe du Jour, 88
Swiss Onion Soup, 89
Vichyssoise, 89
Potato Onion Soup Gaelac, 53
Sausage and Escarole Soup, 158
Sodt Suppe Norsk, 71
Soupe a l'Oignon Le Cordon Bleu, 89
Soupe de Poissons, 90
Stockpot, 90
Beef, 90
Poultry, 91
Pork, 91
Fish, 91
Stracciatella Soup, 159
Vichyssoise, 91

PASTA
Crêpes Italian (Cannelloni, 159
Enrico's Spaghetti Carbonara, 160
Fettucine Alfredo, 160
Gnòcchi, 162
Gyoza, 237
Lasagne, 162
Lasagne a la Française, 93
Manicotti, 163
Pasta Bellisiana, 163
Polenta, 164
Ravioli, 164
Ravioli Fillings, 166
Risotto Milanese, 167

ENTREE—SIDE DISHES
Artichoke, Pie, 171
Asparagus with Prosciutto, 171
Aubergine Moussaka Patrice, 211
Austrian Goulash, 201
Boston Baked Beans, 249
Red Beans and Rice with Hot Sausage, 95
Old Fashioned Boiled Dinner, 60
Broccoli Casserole, 250
Broccoli with Cheese Sauce en
Casserole Andre, 128
Finnish Cabbage Rolls, 143
Castleford Toad-in-the-Hole, 31
Cheddar, Corkscrew and Son Fondue, 92
Cheese Potatoes en Casserole Georges, 132
Chili Con Carne, 223
Chili Con Carne Roberto, 223
Chili Con Frijoles, 224

Corned Beef and Cabbage, 53
Curry, 242
Shrimp Curry, 243
Eggplant Casserole Parmigiana, 172
English Shepherd's Pie, 32
Hamburger Pot Pie, 250
Hog Jowls and Black-eyed Peas, 250
Knishes, 219
Kraut Perogs, 60
Légumes Mornay Gratinés, 133
Matzo Balls, 218
Meat Loaf, 255
Great Meat Loaf, 255
Melva's Noodle Kugal, 202
Pasties, 32
Stuffed Peppers Marie, 130
Stuffed Green Peppers, 129
Potato Balls, 72
Potato Casserole, 251
Potato Pancakes, 64
Potpourri Soufflé, 94
Classic Quiche Lorraine, 93
Japanese Fried Rice, 238
Oriental Fried Rice, 238
Risotto Milanese, 167
Wild Rice Casserole, 26
Wild Rice Dish, 252
Ursula's Sauerkraut, 61
Serbian Sarma, 202
Haluski Capüsta, 202
Italian Sausage and Peppers, 172
Spanakopitta, 210
Steak and Kidney Pie, 33
"Giving a Party" Burgundy Stew, 256
Iron Range Lamb Stew, 54
Scobac Gaelac O'Sullivan, 54
"Those Were The Days" Stew, 256
Sukiyaki, 239
Tempura for Chicken, Fish, Seafood, 240
Vegetable Tempura, 240
Squid Tempura, 241
Tomatoes Farcies, 132
Torta Pasqualina, 173
Tostadas or Tacos, 225
La Tourte au Roquefort, 96
Tourtière, 97
Tuna Casserole, 251
Mother's Tuna Loaf, 218
Vegetable Casserole Provençale, 134
Zucchini Au Gratin, 252
Zucchini Napolitan, 173
Zucchini and Tomatoes Provençale, 154

EGGS
Egg Brunch Casserole, 33
Egg Cheese Grits, 22
Hobo Eggs, 252
English Breakfast, 34
Omelette Brouillée Lisette, 98

FISH-SEAFOOD
Bouillabaisse Lisette, 100
Bouillabaisse Marseillaise, 99

Garlic Steamed Clams or Mussels, 174
Coquille St. Jacques Manfred, 101
Crab Cakes, 253
Deviled Crab, 34
Stone Crab Claws, 34
Crabmeat au Gratin Pontchartrain, 102
Crab Meat Pie, 102
Crabmeat Ravigote Louisiane, 102
Crêpes à La Crab, 103
Creole Seafood Gumbo with Okra, 104
Garlic Broiled Crevettes, 104
Cuisses de Grenouille Provençale, 105
Poached Fillets Lavinia, 35
Fish Cakes from Devonshire,
    England, 35
Fish Fry at the Outpost Camp, 25
Fish Souvlakia, 212
Kalahia Mojakka, 143
Befera's Lobster Tail Cantonese, 234
Lutefisk, 72
Paistettu Norsia, 144
Pesce al Forno, 175
Salmon Loaf, 253
Garlic Fried Scampi, 174
Steamed Fresh Shrimp, 36
Shrimp Gumbo Lisette, 105
Squid Sauté, 176
Stuffed Squid, 177

MEAT
Beef Rib Roast, 37
Glazed Corned Beef, 54
Boeuf Bourgogne, 106
Boliche Hazado Ramirez, 226
Brasciòle di Manzo, 178
Middle East Hamburgers, 213
Hampurin Pihvi, 144
Préférence de Monsieur, 107
Steak Diane, 107
Staeck Tartare, 83
Steak au Poivre, 108
Chuck Steak in Onion Gravy, 254
Tournedos Rossini, 108
Fleisch Rouladen, 62
London Broil Rouladen Sophia, 235
Teriyaki Imperial, 235
Befera's Teriyaki, 234
Lamb Kebabs, 212
Leg of Lamb, 179
Fegato Romano, 178
Champagne Glazed Ham, 254
Ham Loaf, 254
Porchetta, 179
Pork Roast, 63
Veal Cordon Bleu, 109
Veal Fontina Fiorella, 180
Veal Parmigiana, 180
Veal Scaloppine Lisette, 180
Veal Scaloppine Marsala, 181
Émincé de Veau Zürichoise, 109
Vitello Saltimbocca, 181
Wiener Schnitzel, 63
Meatballs
Bollen Norsk, 73

Kunglig Kött BollenSvensk, 73
Skinka Bollen Svensk, 74
Poultry
Almond Chicken Ladeva, 110
Chicken en Brochette, 110
Chicken Divine, 256
Creole Fried Chicken, 113
Liz's Fried Chicken Italian, 182
Southern Fried Chicken, 257
Chicken Jambalaya Orleans, 111
Chicken Kiev, 204
Arroz con Pollo (Chicken with Rice), 227
Juicy Crisp Roast Chicken, 111
Naoe's Teriyaki Chicken, 236
Paprika Chicken Ladeva, 114
Coq au Vin Cordon Bleu, 112
Coq au Vin Lisette, 112
Ghuy Hunan, 236
Pollo al Forno, 182
Pollo alla Graticola, 183
Pollo Ragù, 183
Pollo di Roma, 184
Poulet Rôti Lisette, 114
Caneton a la Liqueur de Pêches, 116
Caneton aux Cerises Lisette, 116
Caneton Rôti, 115
Roast Goose, 118
Cornish Hens aux Gousses d'Ail, 115
Cornish Hens with Wild Rice Dressing, 38
Rock Cornish Hens, 38
Turkey Suprême, 118

CONDIMENTS
Ailloli, 119
Barbecue Sauce, 258
Simple Bearnaise Sauce, 122
Béchamel Sauce, 121
Brandy Hard Sauce, 58
Zesty Cocktail Sauce, 36
Finnic Sauce, 144
Hollandaise Sauce, 121
Horseradish Sauce, 38
Mushroom Sauce, 122
Raisin Sauce, 258
Rouille La Calangue, 101
Taco Sauce, 225
Taco Sauce Caliente, 226
Taramosalata Stella Maris, 209
Bread Dressing, 120
Wild Rice Dressing Nokomis, 27
Meat Stuffing for Fowl, 184
Meat Stuffing for Turkey, 185
Bouquet Garni, 119
Garlic Butter Cordon Bleu, 120
Lemon Butter Cordon Bleu, 121
Cornstarch Thickener for Gravies
    and Sauces, 122
Roux Thickener for Gravies and Sauces, 123
Clam Sauce for Spaghetti, 168
Liz's Spaghetti Sauce With Meatballs, 168
Pesto, 170
Quick Spaghetti Sauce, 170
Tuna Fish Sauce for Spaghetti, 171
Fish Batter Siegfred, 62
Fish Fry Batter at the Outpost Camp, 253

Baklava Syrup, 214
Ham Glaze, 254
Oriental Marinade, 235

SALADS
Avocado Fruit Squares, 258
Cabbage Salad, 186
Caesar Salad, 123
Caesar Salad Junia, 186
Candle Salad Norsk, 74
Chicken Salad, 259
Cole Slaw, 64
Corned Beef Salad, 259
Cucumber Salad Cordon Bleu, 124
Dandelion, 186
Four Season Salad, 124
Fresh Spinach Salad, 126
Frozen Fruit Salad, 259
Frozen Party Salad, 261
Greek Salad Pappas, 213
Kartoffelsalat, 64
Lime Gelatin Salad, 260
Orange Salvador Salad, 260
Party Salad, 261
Pistacchio-Pineapple Salad, 261
Salad Nicoise, 124
Salade de Poivrons et Pasteque, 125
Salade Provençale, 125
Shrimp Tomato Mousse, 262
Three or Four Bean Salad, 262
Tomato Aspic, 262
Twenty-Four Hour Salad, 264
Watercress Salad, 39

SALAD DRESSING
Oil and Vinegar Salad Dressing 187
Salad Dressing Lisette, 127
Caesar Salad Dressing Lisette, 126
Lemon Dressing, 39
Sour Cream Dressing Cordon Bleu, 127
Vinaigrette Marsielle, 127

LEGUMES-VEGETABLES
Green Beans Southern, 264
String Beans Italiano, 187
Bubble and Squeak, 40
Colcannon (Potatoes and Cabbage), 55
Savoy Cabbage, 188
Carottes Raifort, 128
Corn on the Cob, 21
Corn Fritters Calumet, 21
Southern Greens, 264
French Peas Cordon Bleu, 128
Poivrons Français, 130
Potatoes
Crispy Baked Potatoes, 40
Farmer French Fries, 131
Parsley Potatoes Cordon Bleu, 132
Pommes Frites, 131
Potatoes al Forno, 188
Potatoes d'Or, 132
Rosti Emil, 65
Stovies, 40
Twice Baked Potatoes, 40

Jean's Sauerkraut, 61
Italian Spinach Lisette, 188
Baked Squash, 25
Zucchini French Fries, 135
Fried Zucchini, 188

BAKERY
Bagels, 219
Beer Bread, 65
Golden Corn Bread, 22
Italian Cheese Bread, 189
Irish Soda Bread, 56
Molasses Bran Brown Bread, 265
Short Bread, 55
Zucchini Bread Norina, 191
Sourdough Rolls, 266
Sourdough Starter, 266
Sourdough Starter Feeder. 266
Annie's Cheese Biscuits, 44
Apple Crisp, 77
Apple Curranty, 47
Baklava, 214
Biscotti, 191
Biscottini, 192
Castagnoli, 192
Coffee Cake, 145
Crescia, 189
Ede's Doughnuts, 270
Hillopannukakkuja, 145
Husarenkrapferl, 66
Hush Puppies, 265
Lefse, 74
Pizzelle, 193
Potica, 204
Serbian Potica, 206
Potiza, 206
Yorkshire Pudding, 37

Cakes
Barmbrack Cake, 56
Cake Genoise, 136
Carrot-Pineapple Bundt Cake, 65
Elegant Cheese Cake, 220
Serbian Cheese Cake, 205
Lemon Refrigerator Cake, 272
Oatmeal Cake, 78
Peach Kuchen, 275
Rowena's Cola-Fudge Cake, 279
Schwarzwalder Black Forest Torte, 67
Two Pound Cakes, 49
Chocolate Chip Bars, 268
Date and Orange Bars, 270
Seven Layer Bars, 279

Cookies
Berlinerkranz, 75
Fruit Rocks, 45
Krum Kaka, 75
Peppar Kakor, 76
Spritz, 77
Rosettes Svensk, 76

Pie Crust
Graham Cracker Crust, 274
Mrs. Grider's Pie Crust, 47
Pie Crust Mix, 79
Pie Crust for Pasties and Tourtieres, 98
"Mix-in-Pie-Pan" Pie Shell, 47

Pies
Apple Pye, 44
Swiss Apple Pie, 137
Fresh Bluebery Pie Victoria, 46
Cherry Pie, 47
Sanford's Celery Pie, 280
Chocolate Honey-Graham Pie, 268
Rowena's Chocolate Mint Pie, 278
Coconut Pie, 269
Amazing Coconut Pie, 269
Cream Cheese Pie, 269
Girdle Buster Barbizon, 271
Grasshopper Pie, 271
Heavenly Lemon Pie, 272
Lover's Lemonade Pie, 273
Cool Lime Pie, 273
Key Lime Pie, 274
Macadamia Angel Pie, 274
Fresh Peach and Brandy Pie, 138
Peanut Butter Pie, 276
Pecan-Chocolate Morsel Pie, 276
Pie Torte, 276
Praline Brittle Pumpkin Pie, 137
Rhubarb Pie, 79

Sandwiches
Croque Monsieur Louis, 135
Salmon and Cucumber Sandwiches, 41
Bee Lee's Grilled Shrimp Sandwiches, 42
Tea Party Sandwich Loaf, 42

CONFECTIONS
Bananas Foster d'Agostino, 138
Banana Split, 267
Cannoli, 192
Cassata Siciliana, 194
Kiwifruit Cassata, 194
Chocolate Balls, 268
Chocolate Mousse Cordon Bleu, 138
Christmas Plum Pudding, 57
Cranberry Putinki, 146
Crèma-Zuppa Inglese, 195
Karen's Old-Fashioned Fudge, 270
Glace-Sorbet Flambé, 139
Green Grapes Delite, 77
Heavenly Rice, 78
Indian Corn Pudding, 23
Indian Dessert, 27
Lingonberries, 77
Macedònia, 195
Melon Basket, 244
Meringue Glacée Cordon Bleu, 140
Pineapple Dessert, 277
Raspberry Dessert, 277
Tortoni di Torrone, 196
Trifle, 48
Zabalone, 196

POTABLES
Cafe Gaelac, 58
Egg Coffee, 79
Finnish Coffee, 146
Coffee Royal, 197
Cold Buttered Rum Coffee, 198
Bellini Cocktail, 197
Excelsior Piano Bar Special, 197
Velvet Hammer, 228